Praise for *The Sexual Politics of Meat* and Carol J. Adams

"A clearheaded scholar joins the ideas of two movements—vegetarianism and feminism—and turns them into a single coherent and moral theory. Her argument is rational and persuasive. . . . New ground—whole acres of it—is broken by Adams."

—Colman McCarthy, *Washington Post Book World*

"*The Sexual Politics of Meat* examines the historical, gender, race, and class implications of meat culture, and makes the links between the practice of butchering/eating animals and the maintenance of male dominance. Read this powerful new book and you may well become a vegetarian."

—*Ms.*

"Adams's work will almost surely become a 'bible' for feminist and progressive animal rights activists. . . . Depiction of animal exploitation as one manifestation of a brutal patriarchal culture has been explored in two [of her] books, *The Sexual Politics of Meat* and *Neither Man nor Beast: Feminism and the Defense of Animals.* Adams argues that factory farming is part of a whole culture of oppression and institutionalized violence. The treatment of animals as objects is parallel to and associated with patriarchal society's objectification of women, blacks, and other minorities in order to routinely exploit them. Adams excels in constructing unexpected juxtapositions by using the language of one kind of relationship to illuminate another. Employing poetic rather than rhetorical techniques, Adams makes powerful connections that encourage readers to draw their own conclusions."

—*Choice*

"A dynamic contribution toward creating a feminist/animal rights theory."

—*Animals' Agenda*

"A cohesive, passionate case linking meat-eating to the oppression of animals and women. . . . [It is] a well-researched, provocative, and stimulating argument."

—*The [Australian] Age*

"*The Sexual Politics of Meat* is an excellent book. Combining a knowledge of recent work in language studies . . . with a clearly defined moral line, Adams argue that the cruelty and doublethink involved in meat eating is closely linked to the attitudes that have supported the oppression of women."

—*Oxford Times*

"With this bold and provocative book, a powerful champion of animal rights has entered the lists, challenging the patriarchal domination of the Western world's eating habits."

—*National Women's Studies Association Journal*

"*The Sexual Politics of Meat* couldn't be more timely, or more disturbing."

—*Environmental Ethics*

"*The Sexual Politics of Meat* is a book from which those opposed to all forms of tyranny can draw sustenance."

—*San Antonio Light*

"I found this book to be loaded with ideas and connections that I never before read or heard. Drawing on historical and literary parallels between feminist and vegetarian movements, Adams details the interrelationships between meat eating and male dominance. To talk about vegetarianism, she says, is to threaten one of the pillars of patriarchy. Adams also makes a strong case for animal rights."

—*Vegetarian Times*

The Sexual Politics of Meat

A Feminist-Vegetarian Critical Theory

Carol J. Adams

TENTH ANNIVERSARY EDITION

continuum
NEW YORK • LONDON

2006

The Continuum Internataional Publishing Group Inc
80 Maiden Lane, New York, NY 10038

The Continuum International Publishing Group Ltd
The Tower Building, 11 York Road, London SE1 7NX

Printed in the United States of America

Library of Congress Cataloging-in-Publication Data

Adams, Carol J.
The sexual politics of meat : a feminist-vegetarian critical theory / Carol J. Adams. — 10th-anniversary ed.
p. cm.
Includes bibliographical references and index.
ISBN 0-8264-1184-3 (pbk. : alk. paper)
1. Animal welfare. 2. Vegetarianism—Social aspects. 3. Patriarchy. 4. Feminist theory. I. Title.
HV4708.A25 2000
179′.3—dc21 99-31195
CIP

Copyright Acknowledgments will be found on page 261, which constitutes an extension of this page.

In memory of

31.1 billion each year,
85.2 million each day,
3.5 million each hour,
59,170 each minute

It is not possible now, and never will be, to say I renounce. Nor would it be a good thing for literature were it possible. This generation must break its neck in order that the next may have smooth going. For I agree with you that nothing is going to be achieved by us. Fragments—paragraphs—a page perhaps: but no more. . . . The human soul, it seems to me, orientates itself afresh every now and then. It is doing so now. No one can see it whole, therefore. The best of us catch a glimpse of a nose, a shoulder, something turning away, always in movement. Still it seems better to me to catch this glimpse.

—Virginia Woolf to Gerald Brenan
Christmas Day, 1922

We have learned to use anger as we have learned to use the dead flesh of animals, and bruised, battered and changing, we have survived and grown and, in Angela Wilson's words, we *are* moving on.

—Audre Lorde
"The Uses of Anger: Women Responding to Racism"

Say Stella, when you copy next,
Will you keep strictly to the text?

—Jonathan Swift
"To Stella, Who Collected and Transcribed His Poems"

Contents

Illustrations

Preface to the Tenth Anniversary Edition

"My vegetarianism had little to do with my feminism, or so I thought." These words begin the preface to the first edition of *The Sexual Politics of Meat*. I wrote them in 1975 as the opening sentence for a paper in a feminist ethics class taught by Mary Daly. I used these words again in 1990 to honor the strivings of the individual I was when I began my quest for a feminist-vegetarian theory and in quiet homage to Mary Daly's early support of my work as well as her ongoing biophilic vision. What occurred in those intervening years? That poses in an oblique way the most frequently asked question of me in the past decade: "How did you come to write *The Sexual Politics of Meat?*" The answer spans seventeen years of my life, and describes a long process that was both painful and exhilarating.

Feminism addresses relations between men and women. But it is also an analytic tool that helps expose the social construction of relationships between humans and the other animals. In chapter 9, I quote feminist philosopher Sandra Bartky, who observes that feminists are not aware of different things from other people; "they are aware of the same things differently. Feminist consciousness, it might be ventured, turns a 'fact' into a 'contradiction.' " I was a feminist and a lifelong meat eater when I bit into a hamburger in 1973. Before that, consciousness raising about the political meaning of ostensibly personal acts had already been a part of my life. Inevitably the practice of consciousness raising extended to my eating habits. What prompted me to see the same thing—meat eating—differently? What changed a fact into a contradiction?

At the end of my first year of Yale Divinity School, I returned home to Forestville, New York, the small town where I had grown up. As I was unpacking I heard a furious knocking at the door. An agitated neighbor greeted me as I opened the door. "Someone has just shot your horse!" he exclaimed. Thus began my political and spiritual journey toward a feminist-vegetarian critical theory. It did not require that I travel outside this small village of my childhood—though I have; it involved running up to the back pasture behind our barn, and encountering the dead body of a pony I had loved. Those barefoot steps through the thorns and manure of an old apple orchard took me face to face with death. That evening, still distraught about my pony's death, I bit into a hamburger and stopped in midbite. I was thinking about one dead animal yet eating another dead animal. What was the difference between this dead cow and the dead pony whom I would be burying the next day? I could summon no ethical defense for a favoritism that would exclude the cow from my concern because I had not known her. I now saw meat differently.

Yet change was not immediate. I know how overpowering the meat-eating culture is; I continued to be a part of it for another year. I lived in a communal household in Philadelphia, and issues about food and money, and not knowing how to cook, combined to keep me a passive, and conflicted, meat eater. But I vowed that when I moved I would pick a vegetarian household. That opportunity came the following year. In moving to the Boston area, I checked the housing bulletin board at the Cambridge Women's Center and linked up with two feminist-vegetarian apartment mates.

It was the fall of 1974. My life was filled with feminism: a coveted class with Mary Daly, a history of women and American religion, a class on the theory of women's history at Harvard Divinity School. For Mary Daly's feminist ethics class I was reading Elizabeth Gould Davis's book, *The First Sex*. Scholars discredit it now, but as mythopoesis, as a book that invited the rethinking of the givens of a patriarchal world, it was revelatory. I was also reading Marge Piercy's *Small Changes*. I remember walking down the street toward Harvard Square thinking about Piercy's hero, who had come to live in the Boston area too. She seemed so real that I imagined I could run into her on the street. I mused on the predicament she had been caught in—a controlling husband seeking to force her to be pregnant. Her escape, discussed in chapter 7, linked to a dead animal, brought about her abstinence from eating warm-blooded animals. My mind started thinking of vegetarianism within a feminist context: Gould Davis's claim that a vegetarian matriarchy was overthrown by an animal-eating patriarchy; numerous nineteenth-century feminists who were vegetarian; other novels like Charlotte Perkins Gilman's *Herland*. My own intuitive sense of connection hummed deep within, not yet articulated. Like the three cherries that click into place in a slot machine, these vegetarian-feminist references suddenly did the same. There was a connection! I quickened my pace, and began to see all the scattered references I had been encountering as part of a larger whole.

I was fortunate to be in Cambridge. Mary Daly allowed me to pursue the issue as a paper for her class and the women at New Words, a feminist bookstore, suggested other books that contained pertinent references. In the Schlesinger Library at Radcliffe College, I encountered the manuscripts of Agnes Ryan, an early twentieth-century feminist-vegetarian. The women in the Harvard metahistory class listened to my presentation and offered other associations. References spiraled into connections; connections curved toward a theory. I interviewed over 40 feminists in the Boston-Cambridge community who were vegetarian. The women at *Amazon Quarterly,* an early lesbian-feminist journal, accepted for publication my paper for Mary Daly's class and it appeared in 1975 in the anthology *The Lesbian Reader.*

By 1976, I knew there was a connection; many feminists were responding with energy (both positive and negative) to my ideas. A small press had offered to publish my ideas as a book if I expanded my paper. *The Oedible Complex* was coming into being as a book. (Indeed the Boston Women's Health Collective carried a reference to that book through several editions of *Our Bodies, Ourselves.*) But something bothered me. I felt that I would have only one chance to claim a connection between feminism and vegetarianism, and my 1976 book did not feel ready. It wasn't "cooked." How exactly did I explain the connections? What was my theory? The intellectual quandary was not the only brake being applied to my early efforts at writing this book. I had also experienced some negative repercussions for my work, and I felt exposed and vulnerable. My book was not ready, nor was I. I left the Boston area and put my book aside. Friends warned me. "But someone else might do the book. Someone might beat you to it if you abandon this."

"I'll have to take that chance," I replied. "It's not ready."

Despite other exciting alternatives, including the offer of a fellowship to study in Australia and travel around the world, I returned to upstate New York and became involved with social activism. With my partner I started a Hotline for Battered Women, which we housed at nights in our home. I became immersed in a fair-housing battle that was raw, cruel, enervating, and heartbreaking. We started a soup kitchen and a second-hand clothing store. I wrote grant applications for the purchase and renovation of an old building to become a service center and apartments. I was appointed to Governor Cuomo's Commission on Domestic Violence and chaired the housing committee, trying to innovate connections between housing advocates and battered women advocates. My life was filled with activism.

Though I was busy from morning to night with meetings, phone calls, deadlines, organizing, I also harbored the desire to create this book. The desire was painful and deep; its depth provoked the pain and the ache to write. My day was filled with responding to immediate needs, marshaling resources, agitating, and educating. When was the time to write? I felt a sense of incompleteness, of failing to achieve coherence to something inchoate but vibrant. I was confused because I also felt shame; the shame of wanting to be a writer but not succeeding.

I continued to collect citations and references. Everything I read, from mysteries to herstories, from practical books about ending battering to feminist literary criticism, contained nuggets of meaning. Yet everywhere I went I encountered disconnections—battered women's advocates eating hamburgers while talking about peace in the home; biographies of feminists that failed to consider the vegetarianism of their subject; peace-activist potlucks with dead animals. What I harbored was a terrible burden. I felt I would implode with the blocked energy of making the connection internally and yet not finishing the book I had envisioned years earlier. I felt anger, alienation, and determination.

So I tried to write this book. Not once, or twice, but with many false starts and numerous drafts. All through the Reagan years, I kept at it. Time off from work brought time to research and write. I had drawers full of connections—historical, literary, social. But still the theoretical that would hold it altogether eluded me.

In 1987, I moved with my partner to the Dallas area so that he could pursue a ministry with the homeless and I could devote myself full time to writing what became *The Sexual Politics of Meat* and rearing our young child. On our second night on the road, we stayed in Arkansas. Reading Margaret Homans's *Bearing the Word*, I discovered the concept of the absent referent in the first few pages of the book. I stopped reading; I lowered the book and held it as I contemplated this idea. The absent referent: that was what animals eaten for meat were! The next day, I realized that the absent referent was what enabled the interweaving of the oppression of women *and* animals.

Behind every meal of meat is an absence: the death of the animal whose place the meat takes. The "absent referent" is that which separates the meat eater from the animal and the animal from the end product. The function of the absent referent is to keep our "meat" separated from any idea that she or he was once an animal, to keep the "moo" or "cluck" or "baa" away from the meat, to keep some*thing* from being seen as having been some*one*. Once the existence of meat is disconnected from the existence of an animal who was killed to become that "meat," meat becomes unanchored by its original referent (the animal), becoming instead a free-floating image, used often to reflect women's status as well as animals'. Animals are the absent referent in the act of meat eating; they also become the absent referent in images of women butchered, fragmented, or consumable.

When we arrived in Dallas, I not only had the time to write but a theory that explained the connections. Earlier drafts that meandered were torn through; I uprooted material; and two years later I finished the book.

Nearly fifteen years after withdrawing my initial efforts at this book from a publisher, *The Sexual Politics of Meat* appeared. I was amazed at the immediate responses to it. People who read it and felt confirmed by it began to send me evidence of the connections. I have a veritable museum of matchbox covers, menus, advertisements, photographs of billboards, and other items that confirm the connection between the oppression of women and the oppression of animals. From these I have created a slide show on the sexual politics of meat and have traveled around the country with it.

On the other hand, reporters and commentators who were seeking for the ultimate example of "political correctness" landed upon *The Sexual Politics of Meat* and trumpeted it as the academic excess of the year. I am not an academic; I am a cultural worker. Once in a while I teach one course at Perkins Theological School, but this does not an academic make. I am grateful that with this tenth anniversary edition I can establish that this book evolved from an activist. I am an activist immersed in theory, to be sure. But I am still an *activist*, with all the war wounds of having our house picketed by anti-abortionists; of hearing racists talk about my partner and me on the radio; of having harbored abused women, as well as the hotline itself, in our home.

In chapter 7, I quote philosopher Mary Midgley who observes that "the symbolism of meat-eating is never neutral." Meat eaters see themselves as "eating life." Vegetarians see meat eaters as "eating death." Midgley says that "there is a kind of gestalt-shift between the two positions which makes it hard to change, and hard to raise questions on the matter at all without becoming embattled." Reaction to *The Sexual Politics of Meat* is influenced by which side of the gestalt shift one is on. For many who have enthusiastically embraced its thesis, it has become a touchstone for an empowering worldview and for activism. This is what has given the book that paradoxical status some have termed "an underground classic." For others, it is the book that goes too far. The most enjoyable example of this was a long review by the British essayist and critic Auberon Waugh in the *Sunday Telegraph* in which he speculated that the entire book, the author, and her family, were conceived by a male academic émigré from Eastern Europe, who poses as a madwoman (me!). And I had a good laugh when critics complained that *The Sexual*

Politics of Meat proved that the left still did not have a sense of humor. What they meant is that I did not have *their* kind of humor.

In the years since 1976, I became not only the person who could write this book, but also the person who could handle the responses to this book. By the time Rush Limbaugh began talking about *The Sexual Politics of Meat* on his radio and television shows, I was inured to my work being an object of speculation. And when people buttonhole me demanding "What about the homeless, what about battered women?" and insist that we have to help suffering humans first, I am not thrown off by such assertive narrowing of the field of compassionate activism. I know that vegetarianism and animal activism in general can accompany social activism on behalf of disenfranchised people. I also know that this question is actually a defensive response, an attempt to deflect from an issue with which the interrogator feels uncomfortable. It is an attempt to have a moral upper hand. Only meat eaters raise this issue. No homeless advocate who is a vegetarian, no battered-women's advocate who is a vegetarian, would ever doubt that these issues can be approached in tandem. In addition, the point of *The Sexual Politics of Meat* is that we have to stop fragmenting activism; we cannot polarize human and animal suffering since they are interrelated.

It is a truism that you cannot argue with a people's mythology. Yet, this is what consciousness raising does. It argues with the mythologies we are taught to live by until suddenly we are able to see the same thing differently. At that moment a fact becomes a contradiction. *The Sexual Politics of Meat* represents one attempt at turning a fact into a contradiction.

The process of viewing another as consumable, as *something*, is usually invisible to us. Its invisibility occurs because it corresponds to the view of the dominant culture. The process is also invisible to us because the end product of the process—the object of consumption—is available everywhere.

The Sexual Politics of Meat means that what, or more precisely *who*, we eat is determined by the patriarchal politics of our culture, and that the meanings attached to meat eating include meanings clustered around virility. We live in a racist, patriarchal world in which men still have considerable power over women, both in the public sphere (employment and politics) and in the private sphere (at home, where in this country woman-battering results in the death of four women a day). What *The Sexual Politics of Meat* argues is that the way gender politics is structured into our world is related to how we view animals, especially animals who are consumed. Patriarchy is a gender system that is implicit in human/animal relationships. Moreover, gender construction includes instruction about appropriate foods. Being a man in our culture is tied to identities that they either claim or disown—what "real" men do and don't do. "Real" men don't eat quiche. It's not only an issue of privilege, it's an issue of symbolism. Manhood is constructed in our culture, in part, by access to meat eating and control of other bodies.

Everyone is affected by the sexual politics of meat. We may dine at a restaurant in Chicago and encounter this menu item: "Double D Cup Breast of Turkey. This sandwich is so BIG." Or, we may dine at the restaurant chain Hooters, which has a logo ostensibly of owl's eyes. In its menu, the restaurant explains how it came up with the name "Hooters" which is a slang for "breasts": "Now the dilemma . . . what to name the place. Simple . . . what else brings a gleam to men's eyes everywhere besides beer and chicken wings and an occasional winning football season. Hence, the name—Hooters—it is supposed that they were into owls." Or look at the image of "Ursula Hamdress" on page 52, from a publication called *Playboar: The Pig Farmer's "Playboy"* that continues to be sold in upscale bookstores. In each of these cases, animals are ostensibly the topic, but women are the absent referents.

Through the sexual politics of meat, consuming images such as these provide a way for our culture to talk openly about and joke about the objectification of women without having to acknowledge that this is what they are doing. It is a way that men can bond publicly around misogyny whether they know it or not. It makes the degradation of women appear playful and harmless: "just" a joke. No one has to be accountable because women are not being depicted. Thus everyone can enjoy the degradation of women without being honest about it. "We're *just* looking at a pig." "It's *only* a sandwich." "We're *just* eating at Hooters."

These issues are "in our face" all the time. We do not perceive them as problematic because we are so used to having our dominant culture mirror these attitudes. We become shaped by and participants in the structure of the absent referent. The sexual politics of meat also works at another level: the ongoing superstition that meat gives strength and that men need meat. Just as a proliferation of images in which women and animals are absent referents appeared in the past ten years, so there has been a resurgence of "beef madness" in which meat is associated with masculinity. As an article in the *New York Times* announced shortly after the appearance of *The Sexual Politics of Meat:* "Scotch and beef are served in a new shrine to trousers." The article observes "in keeping with the masculine spirit of the evening, the hors d'oeurves were beefy—roast beef on toast, chunked chicken in pastry shell. None of that asparagus and cucumber fluff here." A "man-pleasing" brunch recipe in *Cosmopol-*

itan called for "4 cups beef." *New Woman* explored the issue of "Love, Sex, and Flank steak" in 1996, querying "What do men want?" The answer, from a writer and *New York Times* reporter:

> In my experience the answer is great sex and a great steak—and not necessarily in that order. Sure, they want money and power, but only because of what those can win them—sex and steak. Both are closely related, as muscular, full-bodied pleasures of the flesh, and each ignites desire for the other. A hot, juicy, blood-red steak or a succulently thick hamburger induces an overall sense of well-being and a surge of self-assurance that is sure to make him feel good about himself and by association, you. That is especially true in this country, where beef is the quintessential macho fare.

Let's face it, the assumptions about men in this article are as insulting as the assumptions about women. The sexual politics of meat traps everyone—"him," "you," and the animals who are supposed to be consumed.

When a book features an idea originally conceived twenty-five years ago, the question appropriately arises: "Are these insights still timely?" Sadly, the answer is yes, even more so. During the past decade, the sexual politics of meat has experienced much cultural expression. The argument in chapter 1 that meat is part of the cultural mythology of maleness, can be found in diverse aspects of popular culture: From a *Seinfeld* episode that features the comedian desperately trying to hide the fact that he is not eating meat so his date will not mistake him for a "wimp," to the examples from *Cosmopolitan* and *New Woman,* the message continues to be that men are supposed to eat meat and that meat is associated with virility. In the ads and menus and match covers and billboards that have appeared in the past ten years, the aspects of the sexual politics of meat proposed in chapter 2—the overlapping, interconnected oppression of women and nonhuman animals—are evident. (See page 32 for example.)

Things feel worse not only in terms of the cultural depiction but also in terms of the staggering numbers. Anyone familiar with the first edition of this book knows that the dedication was to six billion animals slaughtered for food in the United States. Now the number is almost at nine and a half billion, and rising. Added to this number is the conservative estimate of 21.7 billion sea animals killed every year in the United States.

Over the past decade, an immense amount of documentation has appeared confirming the healthful nature of a complete vegetarian diet—one that does not rely on any animal products. Why, given the proven health benefits of a low-fat, low-cholesterol, high-fiber diet, and the associations of meat eating with deaths or illness from "mad cow disease,"

E. coli contamination, listeria, campylobacter, and salmonella poisoning, does meat eating remain such an important part of our culture's diet? Why is it that now, here in Dallas, the waiting time for popular "steakhouses" on a weekend can be two to three hours?

Clearly, meat eating is habitual; inertia militates against change. But that is not the only reason. People are able to change. Contributing to the inertia is the mythology of meat eating. Our culture accepts all the aspects of the sexual politics of meat, including the basic one that people need meat to stay healthy (read: strong). Moreover, government support of meat eating is clear as the politicians launch sexist attacks on "welfare queens" but not on the "cowboy welfare kings" whose cattle raising is subsidized by the federal government.

In the past ten years, our awareness increased about the immense environmental consequences of factory farming and the impact of this dehumanizing treatment on animals and their human tenders. Yet, meat eaters continue to believe they are eating a humane diet. Meat eaters like to believe that they are doing what complete vegetarians do—eating humanely—without actually doing what complete vegetarians do—not eating animal products. And so, images of animals living in freedom on a family farm abound when in fact the animals' lives are nothing like the depictions. We believe both that we are being kind to the animals and that they like how we are treating them. Or we like to believe that the animals have no consciousness of suffering and that their plight should not affect us. To paraphrase Rousseau, everywhere animals are in chains, but we image them as free. This denial is very strong. To convey this sense of the animals' freedom, patriarchal-cultural images draw upon cues about another supposed freedom: the consumption of women's sexuality. Thus animals and women are not only depicted as free, though they are not, but as sexually free. The result is the sexual politics of meat.

Ironically, when I finally finished my book after fifteen years of working on it, a few reviewers accused me of trying to take advantage of the faddishness of vegetarianism in the late 1980s. *The Sexual Politics of Meat* appeared to be "trendy" because of what it was actually doing, offering a synthesis that made sense of two seemingly divergent impulses—justice for women and concern about animals. It is not that this book was the first feminist book to treat vegetarianism seriously as a political act of resistance, though it does do that. And it is not that I challenged animal advocates and vegetarians to become aware of sexual politics, though I do that as well. It was that the book heralds an exciting movement in scholarship that honors connections, recognizes overlapping oppressions, and works to challenge the fragmentation of activism.

Since the publication of *The Sexual Politics of Meat*, I have become immersed in these exciting movements of scholars and activists alike who are challenging a violent and violating worldview. In the 1980s, ecofeminists began to identify the interrelated oppression of women and animals, and in the last decade they have continued these efforts. I have been honored to meet many of these fine women, including Marti Kheel, Lori Gruen, Greta Gaard, Josephine Donovan, Ynestra King, Barbara Noske, and Karen Warren. In addition, there has been important activism and scholarship identifying the relationship between violence against humans and violence against animals, including the direct relationship between child and animal abuse, and woman-battering and animal abuse. The activism of women associated with Feminists for Animal Rights, Marti Kheel, Batya Bauman, Lisa Finlay, and Michelle Taylor, has empowered feminists and animal activists around the world to continue to make connections. In addition, Feminists for Animal Rights provides information on domestic violence and harm to animals, and offers model programs for working with battered women's shelters in providing housing for companion animals of battered women.

I have appreciated the editorial role of Merle Hoffman of *On the Issues*, Robin Morgan at *Ms.*, Kim Stallwood at *Animals' Agenda,* and Martin Rowe at *Satya,* who have published writings that continue to make connections. Campus activism on the issue is increasing. When I travel to campuses, I meet energized students working to educate the campus community. The Bloodroot Collective continues to serve delicious meals in their feminist-vegetarian restaurant at 85 Ferris Street, Bridgeport, Connecticut. Artist Sue Coe's *Dead Meat*, filmmaker Jennifer Abbott's *A Cow at My Table*, Ruth Ozeki's *My Year of Meats*, and Consolidated's compact disk *Friendly Fascism* offer different artistic ways of representing the interconnections of violence.

The discussion about animals and religion is beginning to catch up with the philosophical debate about animals. There is now a working group on animals and religions that is part of the American Academy of Religion. Literary analysis concerning animals outpaces religious studies. Marian Scholtmeijer's important work *Animal Victims in Modern Fiction* has been joined by others who refuse to view animals merely as means to an end, whether it be academic or gustatory. A Society for Animal Advocacy through Literature (SAAL) has emerged, made up of individuals who are researching and teaching on animals in literature from a strong advocacy position.

A concern voiced to me after the appearance of *The Sexual Politics of Meat* was that animal advocacy deflects women from dealing with our own oppression. I understand that concern. Approximately eighty percent of the animal advocacy movement is women. I have met and corresponded with animal advocates around the world who are immersed in forwarding both issues since they recognize how intertwined they are. In two anthologies, Josephine Donovan and I collect the important work of Karen Davis, Brian Luke, Susanne Kappeler, and others to indicate the exciting scholarship that arises from the recognition of the interconnections.

This book does not provide a history of feminism and vegetarianism. It cannot—at least not yet. Even after ten years, there remains so much primary research work that must occur first. Instead, the book challenges traditional vegetarian and women's histories. Vegan-cookbook author and social historian Leah Lenneman's fine article on vegetarianism and the British women's suffrage movement is a model for the kind of work needed to pinpoint exactly how feminist activism and vegetarianism interacted in the past.

What of veganism—the abstaining from all animal products? The vegetarianism envisioned in this book is dairy- and egg-free. *The Sexual Politics of Meat* proposes a specific conceptual term to recognize the exploitation of the reproductive processes of female animals: milk and eggs should be called *feminized protein*, that is, protein that was produced by a female body. The majority of animals eaten are adult females and children. Female animals are doubly exploited: both when they are alive and then when they are dead. They are the literal female pieces of meat. Female animals become oppressed by their femaleness, becoming surrogate wetnurses. Then when their (re)productiveness ends, they are butchered and become animalized protein, or protein in the form of flesh. In the past ten years, an explosion of innovative vegan recipe books has occurred and many vegetarian cookbooks offer vegan alternatives.

This book does not propose an essentialist view of the body. I do not believe definitively in the human vegetarian body; I know that people have survived as omnivores. But many of my sources did believe people were physiologically constructed as vegetarians. All of the health benefits of a complete vegetarian diet affirm their intuitions, if not their science. And presently, our diets have evolved faster than our bodies. I use the term "vegetarian body" metaphorically, trying to evoke these earlier claims, and gesturing to the preventive benefits that scientific studies have now confirmed for vegetarianism. The phrase "vegetarian body" also conveys the transformational nature of becoming a vegetarian. In the act of becoming vegetarians our relationship with our bodies often changes, and even if we humans as a species have not evolved vegetarian bodies, we vegetarians and vegans seem to evolve a vegetarian body—one whose optimum health and happiness is achieved through being vegetarians.

I do not propose an essentialist view of women, either. I do not believe women are innately more caring than men, or have an essential pacifist quality. But many of my feminist-vegetarian sources did believe this. I do believe that when one lacks power in the dominant culture, such disempowerment may make one more alert to other forms of disempowerment. Privilege resists self-examination, but exclusion does not. I do not believe that women essentially "care," but I *do* believe that it is essential for all of us to care and acknowledge relationships.

Over the twenty-five years of working on this issue, I have heard one recurring response, "I'd be a vegetarian but my husband needs to eat meat." If I had a dollar for every time that I have heard this response since 1974, I could endow the Feminists for Animal Rights organization for years to come. By believing they must feed their husbands meat, these women perpetuate the sexual politics of meat that says men need meat to be strong and that men should determine the contents of the dinner plate. Meat eating becomes another vehicle for self-denial, for placing the partner's needs first. Women see themselves as more responsible for taking care of their partner's needs than for taking care of their own needs. Many women appear fearful of what the absence of meat says to their husbands about themselves. Their thinking goes something like this: "It is my responsibility to meet his needs. He wants meat. If I do not prepare meat, I will not be meeting his needs. Since I am supposed to meet his needs, I am failing at a basic level of my responsibilities. This causes me to neglect him." She does not want to be seen as failing in the role expectations that she has assumed are legitimate.

The question may arise: Even if there is a connection between meat eating and a patriarchal worldview, does this necessarily prove the reverse, a connection between feminism and vegetarianism? Feminism should not embrace vegetarianism simply because it is a negation of the dominant world. It should embrace it because of what it is and represents. Vegetarianism is in fact deeply proactive and transformative. It is also delicious. Justice should not be so fragile a commodity that it cannot be extended beyond the species barrier of *Homo sapiens*. I have faith that those humans who have been exploited can empathize with and help nonhumans who have been exploited. The words of poet Fran Winant, "Eat rice have faith in women," remain a credo and a vision.

Preface

My becoming a vegetarian had seemingly little relationship to my feminism—or so I thought. Now I understand how and why they are intimately connected, how being a vegetarian reverberates with feminist meaning. I discovered that what appeared to me as isolated concerns about health and ethics were interrelated and illumined by feminist insights. This book details these interrelationships and examines the connections between male dominance and meat eating. It argues that to talk about eliminating meat is to talk about displacing one aspect of male control and demonstrates the ways in which animals' oppression and women's oppression are linked together.

In some respects we all acknowledge the sexual politics of meat. When we think that men, especially male athletes, need meat, or when wives report that they could give up meat but they fix it for their husbands, the overt association between meat eating and virile maleness is enacted. It is the covert associations that are more elusive to pinpoint as they are so deeply embedded within our culture.

My endeavor in this book is to make the covert associations overt by explaining how our patriarchal culture authorizes the eating of animals and in this to identify the cross-mapping between feminism and vegetarianism.

Besides contributing to feminist theory, this book forms a part of the emerging corpus of works on animal advocacy. Close examination of meat eating is an essential aspect of animal defense theory because meat eating is the most extensive destruction of animals. Where this book deviates from other pro-animal texts is in establishing the relationship between patriarchal culture and this form of animal oppression. Vegetarianism seeks meaning in a patriarchal culture that silences it; it is continually butting up against the sexual politics of meat. Cato cautioned, "It is a difficult task, O citizens, to make speeches to the belly which has no ears."[1] This expresses the dilemma of those who raise their voices against eating animals: it is a difficult task to argue against the dominant beliefs about meat when they have been reinforced by a personal enjoyment of meat eating and are heavily freighted with symbolism.

Consequently, any comprehensive study of vegetarianism and feminism must consider how vegetarianism is received as well as what vegetarianism itself claims. Why has vegetarianism been considered a fad when, like feminist insights, it is a reform and idea that has recurred throughout history? Why is the vegetarian aspect to a writer or her work often ignored by literary critics? I struck upon the idea of the *texts of meat* to answer these questions.

By speaking of the *texts of meat* we situate the production of meat's meaning within a political-cultural context. None of us chooses the meanings that constitute the texts of meat, we adhere to them. Because of the personal meaning meat has for those who consume it, we generally fail to see the social meanings that have actually predetermined the personal meaning. Recognizing the texts of meat is the first step in identifying the sexual politics of meat.

In defining the patriarchal texts of meat, part 1 relies on an expanded notion of what constitutes a text. These include: a recognizable message; an unchangeability of the text's meaning so that through repetition the same meaning recurs; and a system of relations that reveal coherence.[2] So with meat: it carries a recognizable message—meat is seen as an item of food, for most meat is an essential and nutritious item of food; its meaning recurs continuously at mealtimes, in advertisement, in conversations; and it is comprised of a system of relations having to do with food production, attitudes toward animals, and, by extension, acceptable violence toward them.

The *texts of meat* which we assimilate into our lives include the expectation that people should eat animals and that meat is good for you. As a result the rendering of animals as consumable bodies is one of those presumptions that undergirds our attitudes. Rarely is this cultural text that determines the prevailing positive attitudes about consuming animals closely examined. The major reason for this is the patriarchal nature of our meat-advocating cultural discourse. Meat's recognizable message includes association with the male role; its meaning recurs within a fixed gender system; the coherence it achieves as a meaningful item of food arises from patriarchal attitudes including the idea that the end justifies the means, that the objectification of other beings is a necessary part of life, and that violence can and should be masked. These are all a part of the sexual politics of meat.

We will see in the following chapter that sex-role assignments determine the distribution of meat. When the meat supply is limited, men will receive it. Assuming meat to be food for men and consequently vegetables to be food for women carries significant political consequences. In essence, because meat eating is a measure of a virile culture and individual, our society equates vegetarianism with emasculation or femininity.

Another aspect of the sexual politics of meat becomes visible as we examine the myth of Zeus's consumption of Metis. He, patriarch of patriarchs, desires Metis, chases her, coaxes her to a couch with "honeyed words," subdues her, rapes her, and then swallows her. But he claims that he receives her counsel from his belly, where she remains. In this myth, sexual violence and meat eating are collapsed, a point considered in chapter 2, "The Rape of Animals, the Butchering of Women." It is also a myth about masculine consumption of female language. In discussing meat we must direct our attention to issues of patriarchal language about consumption; such a discussion is found in chapter 3.

People do not often closely scrutinize their own meat eating. This is an example of the prerogative of those in the dominant order to determine what is worthy of conversation and critique. Resultingly, earnest vegetarians become trapped by this worldview, and while they think that all that is necessary to make converts to vegetarianism is to point out the numerous problems meat eating causes—ill health, death of animals, ecological spoilage—they do not perceive that in a meat-eating culture none of this really matters. This dilemma is explored in chapter 4, "The Word Made Flesh."

Part 2, "From the Belly of Zeus," provides the beginnings of a feminist history of vegetarianism by focusing on the time period of 1790 to the present in Great Britain and the United States. It attempts to free Metis's voice from the belly of Zeus by freeing vegetarian meaning from the sexual politics of meat and by freeing women's voices from patriarchal interpretation. Rather than analyzing contemporary culture, the focus of this middle section is literary texts and their vegetarian influences. However, the literary-historical analysis found here makes use of the ideas introduced in part 1. It explores answers to the question "what characterizes texts that challenge the sexual politics of meat?" The idea of "bearing the vegetarian word" is examined in chapter 5 as one answer to this question. This idea facilitates the interpretation of the relationship between women's texts and vegetarian history.

In chapter 6, I explore the meaning of vegetarianism in *Frankenstein,* a feminist text that bears the vegetarian word. I am not attempting to compress *Frankenstein* into a didactic vegetarian tract. It is, of course, not that. But vegetarian nuances are of importance in the shaping of the story.

Part 2 also examines representative texts by women writers since World War I that posit a connection between meat eating, male dominance and war. Like *The Great War and Modern Memory* after which the title of chapter 7 is patterned, I trace ideas that crystallized at the time of the Great War and follow their development during this century, including the idea of a Golden Age of feminism, vegetarianism, and pacifism.

Women, of course, have not been the only ones to criticize meat eating. In fact, to read standard vegetarian texts one would conclude that few women have been involved in this task. Conversely, to read many feminist writings, one might think that there is nothing controversial about meat eating. And to read standard histories, vegetarianism is faddish and nothing more. But vegetarian theory is neither unfounded nor unfocused; like feminist theory it must be seen as "comprehensive and cumulative, with each stage retaining some of the values and limitations of its predecessors."[3] Among our vegetarian predecessors were numerous feminists.

The basic vegetarian arguments we hear today were in place by the 1790s, except, of course, for the analysis of late twentieth-century developments in meat production. Vegetarian writings occur within a self-conscious protest tradition that contains recognizable recurring themes and images. Yet, they have not been seen either as comprehensive or cumulative, nor as a form of protest literature. But this failure of comprehension reflects the stasis of our cultural discourse on meat rather than the inadequacies of vegetarianism.

This book is extensively documented to demonstrate precisely the comprehensive and cumulative nature that has gone unrecognized. I am not creating claims for vegetarianism in literature and history. The records are there, but the tendency to trivialize vegetarianism has meant that those records are ignored. In a sense, vegetarians are no more biased than meat eaters are about their choice of food; vegetarians, however, do not benefit as do meat eaters from having their biases actually approved of by the dominant culture.

Because I see the oppression of women and the other animals as interdependent, I am dismayed by the failure of feminists to recognize the gender issues embedded in the eating of animals. Yet this failure is instructive as well. Where I identify feminism's participation in the sexual politics of meat, I am simultaneously identifying the mental tanglehold upon all of us of the texts of meat. Feminist discourse, thus, ironically, reproduces patriarchal thought in this area; part 3, "Eat Rice Have Faith in Women," challenges both by arguing that vegetarianism acts as a sign of autonomous female being and signals a rejection of male control and violence.

Just as feminist theory needs to be informed by vegetarian insights, animal rights theory requires an incorporation of feminist principles.

Meat is a symbol for what is not seen but is always there—patriarchal control of animals.

Ultimately women, who often find themselves in muted dialogue with the dominant culture, become the source for insights into the oppression of animals. Major figures in the feminist canon—writers such as Aphra Behn, Mary Shelley, Charlotte Perkins Gilman, Alice Walker, Marge Piercy, Audre Lorde—have contributed works that challenge the sexual politics of meat.

In establishing the association between vegetarianism and women I do not want to imply that vegetarianism is only for women. On the contrary, as we will see, many individual men who endorsed women's rights adopted vegetarianism as well. To claim that women alone should stop eating animals reinforces the sexual politics of meat. I am more concerned with the fact that feminist theory logically contains a vegetarian critique that has gone unperceived, just as vegetarianism covertly challenges a patriarchal society. However, the sexism of some vegetarians, vegetarian groups, and vegetarian cultures demonstrates the necessity of adopting an overt feminist perspective.

Bronson Alcott, father of Louisa May Alcott, is a telling example of how vegetarianism without feminism is incomplete. It, too, reproduces patriarchal attitudes. Alcott moved his family to a communal farm, Fruitlands, with hopes of living off of the fruit of the earth and not enslaving any animals—either to eat or use for labor. He, however, was not inclined toward performing manual labor himself and had the habit of disappearing from Fruitlands to discuss his ideas in abstract rather than live them in the flesh. At harvest time, his wife and daughters were left to perform the heavy work; thus the only "beasts of burdens" at this utopia were the women themselves. Honoring animals but not women is like separating theory from practice, the word from the flesh.

We could claim that the hidden majority of this world has been primarily vegetarian. But this vegetarianism was not a result of a viewpoint seeking just human relationships with animals. Even so, it is a very important fact that the hidden majority of the world has been primarily vegetarian. If a diet of beans and grains has been the basis for sustenance for the majority of the world until recently, then meat is not essential.[4] While knowledge of the variety of cultures that depended, by and large, on vegetarianism helps to dislodge our Western focus on meat, what is most threatening to our cultural discourse is self-determined vegetarianism in cultures where meat is plentiful.

My concern in this book is with the self-conscious omission of meat because of ethical vegetarianism, that is, vegetarianism arising from an ethical decision that regards meat eating as an unjustifiable exploitation of the other animals. This motivation for vegetarianism is not the one popularized in our culture; instead attraction to the benefits to one's health has brought about many new converts to vegetarianism. Their vegetarianism does not incorporate concern for animals; indeed, many see no problem with organic meat. I rejoice that an ethical decision resonates with improved personal health, that by becoming a vegetarian for ethical reasons one thereby reduces one's risk of heart disease and cancer, among other diseases—a point examined in "The Distortion of the Vegetarian Body." In the concluding chapter, I describe a pattern of adopting ethical vegetarianism that I define as the vegetarian quest. The vegetarian quest consists of: the revelation of the nothingness of meat, naming the relationships one sees with animals, and finally, rebuking a meat eating *and* patriarchal world.

This book would not be the book it is if I had not become a vegetarian, participating in my own vegetarian quest. Holding a minority opinion in a dominant culture is very illuminating. Patterns in the responses of meat eaters to vegetarianism became quite instructive as I sought to define the intellectual resistance to discussing the eating of animals. Approaching a cultural consensus from the underside demonstrated how securely entrenched the attitudes about meat are. But this book would not be the book it is if I had not been involved in the domestic violence, antiwhite racism and antipoverty movements during those same years. To learn of and speak from the reality of women's lives deepened my understanding that we need to discuss the *texts* of meat and not one monolithic text. Meat eating is a construct, a force, an economic reality, and also a very real personal issue.

Yet being involved in the daily struggles against the oppressive forces I encountered made me minimize the importance of the task I set for myself in writing on this subject. How could I spend my time writing when so many people were illiterate? How could I discuss food choices when so many people needed any food whatsoever? How could I discuss violence against animals when women victimized by male violence needed shelter? In silencing myself I adhered to that foundational text of meat, the relative unimportance of vegetarianism. By my own silencing, I endorsed the dominant discourse that I was seeking to deconstruct.

It is past time for us to consider the sexual politics of meat for they are not separate from other pressing issues of our time.

Acknowledgments

In the years during which this book took shape, many people encouraged my ideas and helped me to examine the nature of the sexual politics of meat.

Thanks to Catherine Avril and Mary Sue Henifin who, in 1974, advertised at the Cambridge Women's Center for a feminist-vegetarian roommate—and selected me. Thus it all began. Mary Ann Burr who taught me about vegetarianism in exchange for information on feminism; Mary Daly for whom my first paper on the subject was prepared; and Carroll Smith-Rosenberg who encouraged my early historical excavations.

Originally a book on feminism and vegetarianism by me was to appear in 1976 but though it identified the overt connections I sensed it was incomplete and I withheld it from publication. Thanks to the *Vegetarian Times,* Laurel and Gina of *Amazon Quarterly,* Jean and Ruth Mountaingrove of *WomanSpirit,* and the women's collective of *the second wave: a magazine of the new feminism* for publishing my early work, and to the Boston Women's Health Book Collective for mentioning the book that never was in *Our Bodies, Ourselves.* And to Jane Adams who lived with the dramas of that time.

I owe much gratitude to Carol Barash of *Critical Matrix: Princeton Working Papers in Women's Studies* who energized and catalyzed my thoughts; from this catalyst and energy, my feminist-vegetarian theory took shape. I appreciate the ongoing faith that Susan Squier, Helen Cooper, and Adrienne Munich, the editors of *Arms and the Woman* had in me, and their challenges that helped me refine my ideas. Avis Lang of the *Heresies* Collective helped me frame arguments fundamental to this book. Theresa Corrigan and Stephanie Hoppe asked me if I had written anything on the history of animal rights; "The Distortion of the Vegetarian Body" evolved in response to this question. A different version of this chapter, which incorporates as well themes in "For a Feminist-Vegetarian Critical Theory," appears in their anthology, *And a Deer's Ear, Eagle's Song and Bear's Grace: Relationships between Animals and Women (A Second Collection),* from Cleis Press, and I thank them for asking the question and for supporting my work.

For affirming my voice, giving me guidance and other forms of moral support over the years, thanks to my parents and my many friends, both those named above and Marie Fortune, Nancy and Merv Fry, Chellis Glendinning, Susi Parks Grissom, Mary Hunt, Diane Miller, Ken Reichley, Bina and Dave Robinson, Nancy Tuana, Melinda Vadas, Ann Valliant, Cathy Weller, and the women of the Bloodroot Collective—who enact feminist-vegetarian theory at their restaurant in Bridgeport.

For reading and making valuable comments on parts of the book, I thank Maureen Fries, Diana Hume George, Dudley Giehl, Susanne Kappeler, Liz Kelly, Jim Mason, Rose Sebouhian, and Doug Shepard. My gratitude to Geri Pomerantz for her devoted research on the subject. Thanks, too, to David Erdman for assistance with information on John Oswald; Jim Hala, Paula Sue Hayes, Jane Lilienfeld, Karen Lindsey, CeCe Quinlan, Susan Schweik, Marjorie Procter-Smith, and the women of New Words Bookstore in Cambridge for directing me to valuable references; Alex Hershaft of Farm Animal Reform Movement for statistics on animals who are butchered; the late Henry Bailey Stevens for encouraging my research on Agnes Ryan; Connie Salamone for her pioneering work; Josephine Donovan for information on the Crossroad/Continuum Women's Studies Award; Carol Hurd Green and Elizabeth Rechtschaffen of the Award Advisory Committee; Bruce Cassiday, for entering into the spirit of my challenge to conventional language about animals; and my editor, Evander Lomke, for suggestions that helped to shape my manuscript into a book.

Over the years I have benefited from my association with the women's communities of Cambridge, Massachusetts, Dunkirk and Fredonia, New York, and Dallas, Texas. Without access to good libraries in these cities and elsewhere, I would have been bereft of much historical material that enriches feminist-vegetarian theory. Specifically, the staff of the Arthur and Elizabeth Schlesinger Library on the History of Women of Radcliffe College, the British Library, the New York Public Library, the Harry Ransom Humanities Research Center of the University of Texas at Austin, and the Dallas Public Library provided much assistance. The interlibrary loan staff of the State University College at Fredonia and the Dallas and Richardson Public Libraries worked diligently on my behalf, miraculously obtaining for me obscure books from the eighteenth century as well as more recent writings. I am very grateful to them for this.

Financial support from two sources helped to galvanize my work during the past year and I am deeply indebted to them for their faith in me. My thanks to The Culture and Animals Foundation for funds to complete the book, and Tom and Nancy Regan of the CAF for their support, as well as to the Durfee Foundation which through a Durfee Award provided me with the funds to purchase a computer to expedite writing.

During the flurry of revision, Arthur and Virginia Buchanan and Nancy Hayes were immeasurably helpful by providing child care; Melinda Vadas and Cathy Weller attempted to track down the image reproduced on the cover, and Dorothy Teer discovered it in her slide archives. Thanks to each of them for their time. I am grateful as well to the anti-pornography feminist network and specifically Pornography Awareness, Inc. (PO Box 2728 Chapel Hill, North Carolina, 27515-2728), Women Against Pornography, Women Against Violence in the Media, and Women Against Violence Against Women, for recognizing the implications of a beach towel called "Cattle Queen" that encouraged "Break the Dull Beef Habit," and made accessible an image that had permeated popular culture yet was not easily available.

With a topic such as the one this book addresses the research possibilities were endless. I have had to limit my focus to identify the initial issues that arise when engaging in feminist-vegetarian discourse. Otherwise, like Casaubon's work in George Eliot's *Middlemarch,* my key to the patriarchal meaning of meat eating would have remained only a growing pile of uninterpreted notes. Though in one sense this book is a final product, I see it more as part of a process of analysis that challenges the dominant culture. The issues it has neglected or only partially and perhaps inadequately developed offer future opportunities.

Finally my work owes much to Bruce Buchanan who provided me with the time and space to think and write about this subject and Douglas Buchanan, now nearly five, who enlivens my hope that the next generation can reject the Sexual Politics of Meat.

Ten years later . . . and still we struggle to make the connections and be change-agents. For those who have supported me in my writing and my life, I am immensely grateful. I appreciate all those who have written to me over the past decade with stories and examples. I am thankful for those who have worked to bring me to their campuses, and to engage in dialogue with students about the sexual politics of meat. I am pleased to be a part of an ever-expanding network of activists and thinkers who are working for a more compassionate society; they are truly inspiring! For the help I received in preparing this edition of *The Sexual Politics of Meat,* I would like to thank: Marie Fortune, Mary Hunt, Pat Davis, Batya Bauman, Martin Rowe, Kim Stallwood, Debbie Tanzer, Trisha Lamb Feuerstein, and Evander Lomke. For the statistics on the number of land animals killed yearly, I thank the Farm Animal Reform Movement (P.O. Box 30654, Bethesda, MD 20824). For the statistics on the number of sea animals killed yearly, I thank Dawn Carr and the researchers at People for the Ethical Treatment of Animals (501 Front St., Norfolk, VA 23510). I remember with gratitude the life of Kenneth Reichley; faithful friend. Bruce, who weathers it all in stride, continues to provide me with time, space, and attentiveness. For Douglas, now fifteen, and Benjamin, ten, my hopes continue.

Figure 1

THE HAPPY HOOKER
LIVE BAIT
970-7675
MAKIN' BACON
HOT
970-PORK
7675
Hottest Sex
HARPER'S
COUNTRY HAMS
HAMTASTIC
I ATE A "PIG" AT
DOMINICK'S BAR-B-Q
Spring '79
TASTY CHICK
CHICKEN CLUB
I'M NOT TALKIN' CHICKEN HERE! I'M TALKIN' CHICKS!
"DOUBLE D CUP" BREAST OF TURKEY
This sandwich is so BIG... Just checking to see if you really read the menu!
Freshly cut whole breast of turkey on toasted millet bread with
walnut cream cheese, cranberries, lettuce & sprouts... Gobble, Gobble!
$6.25
Nothing Beats A Great Set of Legs!
Add a half-pound of hot Dungeness Crab Legs to any meal for
$4.95
CHEEP DATE.

part one

The Patriarchal Texts of Meat

The selling should always be specific and mention a definite item.

Wrong: "Anything else?"
Weak: "What about something for breakfast?"
Better: "We have some wonderful ham slices, Mrs. Smith—just the thing for breakfast. They're right in the case."

Watch her face and if she doesn't show interest then say:

"Or perhaps you'd rather have fresh pork sausage tomorrow for breakfast."

This method centers her interest and attention on one item at a time and plainly implies that some meat item is necessary for breakfast.

—Hinman and Harris, *The Story of Meat*

The abbess has just put the kipehook on all other purveyors of the French flesh market. She does not keep her meat too long on the hooks, though she will have her price; but nothing to get stale here. You may have your meat dressed to your own liking, and there is no need of cutting twice from one joint; and if it suits your taste, you may kill your own lamb or mutton for her flock is in prime condition, and always ready for sticking. When any of them are *fried* they are turned out to grass, and sent to the hammer, or disposed of by private contract, but never brought in again; consequently, the rot, bots, glanders, and other diseases incidental to cattle, are not generally known here.

—From a nineteenth-century guidebook to brothels

chapter 1

The Sexual Politics of Meat

Myth from the Bushman:

In the early times men and women lived apart, the former hunting animals exclusively, the latter pursuing a gathering existence. Five of the men, who were out hunting, being careless creatures, let their fire go out. The women, who were careful and orderly, always kept their fire going. The men, having killed a springbok, became desperate for means to cook it, so one of their number set out to get fire, crossed the river and met one of the women gathering seeds. When he asked her for some fire, she invited him to the feminine camp. While he was there she said, "You are very hungry. Just wait until I pound up these seeds and I will boil them and give you some." She made him some porridge. After he had eaten it, he said, "Well, it's nice food so I shall just stay with you." The men who were left waited and wondered. They still had the springbok and they still had no fire. The second man set out, only to be tempted by female cooking, and to take up residence in the camp of the women. The same thing happened to the third man. The two men left were very frightened. They suspected something terrible had happened to their comrades. They cast the divining bones but the omens were favorable. The fourth man set out timidly, only to end by joining his comrades. The last man became very frightened indeed and besides by now the springbok had rotted. He took his bow and arrows, and ran away.

I left the British Library and my research on some women of the 1890s whose feminist, working-class newspaper advocated meatless diets, and went through the cafeteria line in a restaurant nearby. Vegetarian food in hand, I descended to the basement. A painting of Henry VIII eating a steak and kidney pie greeted my gaze. On either side of the consuming Henry were portraits of his six wives and other women. However, they were not eating steak and kidney pie, nor anything else made of meat. Catherine of Aragon held an apple in her hands. The Countess of Mar had a turnip, Anne Boleyn—red grapes, Anne of Cleaves—a pear, Jane Seymour—blue grapes, Catherine Howard—a carrot, Catherine Parr—a cabbage.

People with power have always eaten meat. The aristocracy of Europe consumed large courses filled with every kind of meat while the laborer consumed the complex carbohydrates. Dietary habits proclaim class distinctions, but they proclaim patriarchal distinctions as well. Women, second-class citizens, are more likely to eat what are considered to be second-class foods in a patriarchal culture: vegetables, fruits, and grains rather than meat. The sexism in meat eating recapitulates the class distinctions with an added twist: a mythology permeates all classes that meat is a masculine food and meat eating a male activity.

Male Identification and Meat Eating

Meat-eating societies gain male identification by their choice of food, and meat textbooks heartily endorse this association. *The Meat We Eat* proclaims meat to be "A Virile and Protective Food," thus "a liberal meat supply has always been associated with a happy and virile people."[1] *Meat Technology* informs us that "the virile Australian race is a typical example of heavy meat-eaters."[2] Leading gourmands refer "to the virile ordeal of spooning the brains directly out of a barbecued calf's head."[3] *Virile: of or having the characteristics of an adult male,* from *vir* meaning *man.* Meat eating measures individual and societal virility.

Meat is a constant for men, intermittent for women, a pattern painfully observed in famine situations today. Women are starving at a rate disproportionate to men. Lisa Leghorn and Mary Roodkowsky surveyed this phenomenon in their book *Who Really Starves? Women and World Hunger.* Women, the conclude, engage in deliberate self-deprivation, offering men the "best" foods at the expense of their own nutritional needs. For instance, they tell us that "Ethiopian women and girls of all classes are obliged to prepare two meals, one for the males and a second, often containing no meat or other substantial protein, for the females."[4]

In fact, men's protein needs are less than those of pregnant and nursing women and the disproportionate distribution of the main protein source occurs when women's need for protein is the greatest. Curiously, we are now being told that one should eat meat (or fish, vegetables, chocolate, and salt) at least six weeks before becoming pregnant if one wants a boy. But if a girl is desired, no meat please, rather milk, cheese, nuts, beans, and cereals.[5]

Fairy tales initiate us at an early age into the dynamics of eating and sex roles. The king in his countinghouse ate four-and-twenty blackbirds in a pie (originally four-and twenty naughty boys) while the Queen ate bread and honey. Cannibalism in fairy tales is generally a male activity, as Jack, after climbing his beanstalk, quickly learned. Folktales of all nations depict giants as male and "fond of eating human flesh."[6] Witches—warped or monstrous women in the eyes of a patriarchal world—become the token female cannibals.

A Biblical example of the male prerogative for meat rankled Elizabeth Cady Stanton, a leading nineteenth-century feminist, as can be seen by her terse comment on Leviticus 6 in *The Woman's Bible:* "The meat so delicately cooked by the priests, with wood and coals in the altar, in clean linen, no woman was permitted to taste, only the males among the children of Aaron."[7]

Most food taboos address meat consumption and they place more restrictions on women than on men. The common foods forbidden to women are chicken, duck, and pork. Forbidding meat to women in nontechnological cultures increases its prestige. Even if the women raise the pigs, as they do in the Solomon Islands, they are rarely allowed to eat the pork. When they do receive some, it is at the dispensation of their husbands. In Indonesia "flesh food is viewed as the property of the men. At feasts, the principal times when meat is available, it is distributed to households according to the men in them. . . . The system of distribution thus reinforces the prestige of the men in society."[8]

Worldwide this patriarchal custom is found. In Asia, some cultures forbid women from consuming fish, seafood, chicken, duck, and eggs. In equatorial Africa, the prohibition of chicken to women is common. For example, the Mbum Kpau women do not eat chicken, goat, partridge, or other game birds. The Kufa of Ethiopia punished women who ate chicken by making them slaves, while the Walamo "put to death anyone who violated the restriction of eating fowl."

Correspondingly, vegetables and other nonmeat foods are viewed as women's food. This makes them undesirable to men. The Nuer men think that eating eggs is effeminate. In other groups men require sauces to disguise the fact that they are eating women's foods. "Men expect to have meat sauces to go with their porridge and will sometimes refuse to eat sauces made of greens or other vegetables, which are said to be women's food."[9]

Meat: for the Man Only

> There is no department in the store where good selling can do so much good or where poor selling can do so much harm as in the meat department. This is because most women do not consider themselves competent judges of meat quality and often buy where they have confidence in the meat salesman.
>
> —Hinman and Harris, *The Story of Meat*[10]

In technological societies, cookbooks reflect the presumption that men eat meat. A random survey of cookbooks reveals that the barbecue sections of most cookbooks are addressed to men and feature meat. The foods recommended for a "Mother's Day Tea" do not include meat, but readers are advised that on Father's Day, dinner should include London Broil because "a steak dinner has unfailing popularity with fathers."[11] In a chapter on "Feminine Hospitality" we are directed to serve vegetables, salads and soups. The New *McCall's* Cookbook suggests that a man's favorite dinner is London Broil. A "Ladies' Luncheon" would consist of cheese dishes and vegetables, but no meat. A section of one cookbook entitled "For Men Only" reinforces the omnipresence of meat in men's lives. What is for men only? London Broil, cubed steak and beef dinner.[12]

Twentieth-century cookbooks only serve to confirm the historical pattern found in the nineteenth century, when British working-class families could not afford sufficient meat to feed the entire family. "For the man only" appears continually in many of the menus of these families when referring to meat. In adhering to the mythologies of a culture (men need meat; meat gives bull-like strength) the male "breadwinner" actually received the meat. Social historians report that the "lion's share" of meat went to the husband.

What then was for women during the nineteenth century? On Sundays they might have a modest but good dinner. On the other days their food was bread with butter or drippings, weak tea, pudding, and vegetables. "The wife, in very poor families, is probably the worst-fed of the household," observed Dr. Edward Smith in the first national food survey of British dietary habits in 1863, which revealed that the major difference in the diet of men and women in the same family was the amount of meat consumed.[13] Later investigators were told that the women and children in one rural county of England, "eat the potatoes and look at the meat."[14]

Where poverty forced a conscious distribution of meat, men received it. Many women emphasized that they had saved the meat for their husbands. They were articulating the prevailing connections between meat eating and the male role: "I keep it for him; he *has* to have it." Sample menus for South London laborers "showed extra meat, extra fish, extra cakes, or a different quality of meat for the man." Women ate meat once a week with their children, while the husband consumed meat and bacon, "almost daily."

Early in the twentieth century, the Fabian Women's group in London launched a four-year study in which they recorded the daily budget of thirty families in a working-class community. These budgets were collected and explained in a compassionate book, *Round about a Pound a Week*. Here is perceived clearly the sexual politics of meat: "In the household which spends 10s or even less on food, only one kind of diet is possible, and that is the man's diet. The children have what is left over. There must be a Sunday joint, or, if that be not possible, at least a Sunday dish of meat, in order to satisfy the father's desire for the kind of food he relishes, and most naturally therefore intends to have." More succinctly, we are told: "Meat is bought for the men" and the leftover meat from the Sunday dinner, "is eaten cold by him the next day."[15] Poverty also determines who carves the meat. As Cicely Hamilton discovered during this same period, women carve when they know there is not enough meat to go around.[16]

In situations of abundance, sex role assumptions about meat are not so blatantly expressed. For this reason, the diets of English upper-class women and men are much more similar than the diets of upper-class women and working-class women. Moreover, with the abundance of meat available in the United States as opposed to the restricted amount available in England, there has been enough for all, except when meat supplies were controlled. For instance, enslaved black men received half a pound of meat per day, while enslaved black women often found that they received little more than a quarter pound a day.[17] Additionally, during the wars of the twentieth century, the pattern of meat consumption recalled that of English nineteenth-century working-class families with one variation: the "worker" of the country's household, the soldier, got the meat; civilians were urged to learn how to cook without meat.

The Racial Politics of Meat

The hearty meat eating that characterizes the diet of Americans and of the Western world is not only a symbol of male power, it is an index of racism. I do not mean racism in the sense that we are treating one class of animals, those that are not human beings, differently than we treat another, those that are, as Isaac Bashevis Singer uses the term in *Enemies: A Love Story:* "As often as Herman had witnessed the slaughter of animals and fish, he always had the same thought: in their behavior toward creatures, all men were Nazis. The smugness with which man could do with other species as he pleased exemplified the most extreme racist theories, the principle that might is right."[18] I mean racism as the requirement that power arrangements and customs that favor white people prevail, and that the acculturation of people of color to this standard includes the imposition of white habits of meat eating.

Two parallel beliefs can be traced in the white Western world's enactment of racism when the issue is meat eating. The first is that if the meat supply is limited, white people should get it; but if meat is plentiful all should eat it. This is a variation on the standard theme of the sexual politics of meat. The hierarchy of meat protein reinforces a hierarchy of race, class, and sex.

Nineteenth-century advocates of white superiority endorsed meat as superior food. "Brain-workers" required lean meat as their main meal, but the "savage" and "lower" classes of society could live exclusively on coarser foods, according to George Beard, a nineteenth-century medical doctor who specialized in the diseases of middle-class people. He recommended that when white, civilized, middle-class men became susceptible to nervous exhaustion, they should eat more meat. To him, and for many others, cereals and fruits were lower than meat on the scale of evolution, and thus appropriate foods for the other races and white women, who appeared to be lower on the scale of evolution as well. Racism and sexism together upheld meat as white man's food.

Influenced by Darwin's theory of evolution, Beard proposed a corollary for foods; animal protein did to vegetable food what our evolution from the lower animals did for humans. Consequently:

> In proportion as man grows sensitive through civilization or through disease, he should diminish the quantity of cereals and fruits, which are far below him on the scale of evolution, and increase the quantity of animal food, which is nearly related to him in the scale of evolution, and therefore more easily assimilated.[19]

In his racist analysis, Beard reconciled the apparent contradiction of this tenet: "Why is it that savages and semi-savages are able to live on forms of food which, according to the theory of evolution, must be far below them in the scale of development?" In other words, how is that people can survive very well without a great deal of animal protein? Because "savages" are

> little removed from the common animal stock from which they are derived. They are much nearer to the forms of life from which they feed than are the highly civilized brain-workers, and can therefore subsist on forms of life which would be most poisonous to us. Secondly, savages who feed on poor food are poor savages, and intellectually far inferior to the beef-eaters of any race.

This explanation—which divided the world into intellectually superior meat eaters and inferior plant eaters—accounted for the conquering of other cultures by the English:

> The rice-eating Hindoo and Chinese and the potato-eating Irish peasant are kept in subjection by the well-fed English. Of the various causes that contributed to the defeat of Napoleon at Waterloo, one of the chief was that for the first time he was brought face to face with the nation of beef-eaters, who stood still until they were killed.

Into the twentieth century the notion was that meat eating contributed to the Western world's preeminence. Publicists for a meat company in the 1940s wrote: "We know meat-eating races have been and are leaders in the progress made by mankind in its upward struggle through the ages."[20] They are referring to the "upward struggle" of the white race. One revealing aspect of this "upward struggle" is the charge of cannibalism that appeared during the years of colonization.

The word "cannibalism" entered our vocabulary after the "discovery" of the "New World." Derived from the Spaniards' mispronunciation of the name of the people of the Caribbean, it linked these people of color with the act. As Europeans explored the continents of North and South America and Africa, the indigenous peoples of those lands became accused of cannibalism—the ultimate savage act. Once labeled as cannibals, their defeat and enslavement at the hands of civilized, Christian whites became justifiable. W. Arens argues that the charge of cannibalism was part and parcel of the European expansion into other continents.[21]

Of the charges of cannibalism against the indigenous peoples, Arens found little independent verification. One well-known source of dubious testimony on cannibalism was then plagiarized by others claiming to be eyewitnesses. The eyewitnesses fail to describe just how they were able to escape the fate of consumption they report witnessing. Nor do they explain how the language barrier was overcome, enabling them to report verbatim conversations with "savages." In addition, their reports fail to maintain internal consistency.

One cause of cannibalism was thought to be lack of animal protein. Yet most Europeans themselves during the centuries of European expansion were not subsisting on animal protein every day. The majority of cultures in the world satisfied their protein needs through vegetables and grains. By charging indigenous peoples with cannibalism (and thus demonstrating their utterly savage ways, for they supposedly did to humans what Europeans only did to animals) one justification for colonization was provided.

Racism is perpetuated each time meat is thought to be the best protein source. The emphasis on the nutritional strengths of animal protein distorts the dietary history of most cultures in which complete protein dishes were made of vegetables and grains. Information about these dishes is overwhelmed by an ongoing cultural and political commitment to meat eating.

Meat Is King

During wartime, government rationing policies reserve the right to meat for the epitome of the masculine man: the soldier. With meat rationing in effect for civilians during World War II, the per capita consumption of meat in the Army and Navy was about two-and-a-half times that of the average civilian. Russell Baker observed that World War II began a "beef madness . . . when richly fatted beef was force-fed into every putative American warrior."[22] In contrast to the recipe books for civilians that praised complex carbohydrates, cookbooks for soldiers contained variation upon variation of meat dishes. One survey conducted of four military training camps reported that the soldier consumed daily 131 grams of protein, 201 grams of fat, and 484 grams of carbohydrates.[23] Hidden costs of warring masculinity are to be found in the provision of male-defined foods to the warriors.

Women are the food preparers; meat has to be cooked to be palatable for people. Thus, in a patriarchal culture, just as our culture accedes to the "needs" of its soldiers, women accede to the dietary demands of their husbands, especially when it comes to meat. The feminist surveyors of women's budgets in the early twentieth century observed:

> It is quite likely that someone who had strength, wisdom, and vitality, who did not live that life in those tiny, crowded rooms, in that lack of light and air, who was not bowed down with worry, but was herself economically independent of the man who earned the money, could lay out his few shillings with a better eye to a scientific food value. It is quite as likely, however, that the man who earned the money would entirely refuse the scientific food, and demand his old tasty kippers and meat.[24]

A discussion of nutrition during wartime contained this aside: it was one thing, they acknowledged, to demonstrate that there were many viable alternatives to meat, "but it is another to convince a man who enjoys his beefsteak."[25] The male prerogative to eat meat is an external, observable activity implicitly reflecting a recurring fact: meat is a symbol of male dominance.

It has traditionally been felt that the working man needs meat for strength. A superstition analogous to homeopathic principles operates in this belief: in eating the muscle of strong animals, we will become strong. According to the mythology of patriarchal culture, meat promotes strength; the attributes of masculinity are achieved through eating these masculine foods. Visions of meat-eating football players, wrestlers, and boxers lumber in our brains in this equation. Though vegetarian weight lifters and athletes in other fields have demonstrated the equation to be fallacious, the myth remains: men are strong, men need to be strong, thus men need meat. The literal evocation of male power is found in the concept of meat.

Irving Fisher took the notion of "strength" from the definition of meat eating as long ago as 1906. Fisher suggested that strength be measured by its lasting power rather than by its association with quick results, and compared meat-eating athletes with vegetarian athletes and sedentary vegetarians. Endurance was measured by having the participants perform in three areas: holding their arms horizontally for as long as possible, doing keep knee bends, and performing leg raises while lying down. He concluded that the vegetarians, whether athletes or not, had greater endurance than meat eaters. "Even the *maximum* record of the flesheaters was barely more than half the *average* for the flesh-abstainers."[26]

Meat is king: this noun describing meat is a noun denoting male power. Vegetables, a generic term meat eaters use for all foods that are not meat, have become as associated with women as meat is with men, recalling on a subconscious level the days of Woman the Gatherer. Since women have been made subsidiary in a male-dominated, meat-eating world, so has our food. The foods associated with second-class citizens are considered to be second-class protein. Just as it is thought a woman cannot make it on her own, so we think that vegetables cannot make a meal on their own, despite the fact that meat is only secondhand vegetables and vegetables provide, on the average, more than twice the vitamins and minerals of meat. Meat is upheld as a powerful, irreplaceable item of food. The message is clear: the vassal vegetable should content itself with its assigned place and not attempt to dethrone king meat. After all, how can one enthrone women's foods when women cannot be kings?

The Male Language of Meat Eating

Men who decide to eschew meat eating are deemed effeminate; failure of men to eat meat announces that they are not masculine. Nutritionist Jean Mayer suggested that "the more men sit at their desks all day, the more they want to be reassured about their maleness in eating those large slabs of bleeding meat which are the last symbol of machismo."[27] The late Marty Feldman observed, "It has to do with the function of the male within our society. Football players drink beer because it's a man's drink, and eat steak because it's a man's meal. The emphasis is on 'man-sized portions,' 'hero' sandwiches; the whole terminology of meat-eating reflects this masculine bias."[28] Meat-and-potatoes men are our stereotypical strong and hearty, rough and ready, able males. Hearty beef stews are named "Manhandlers." Head football coach and celebrity Mike Ditka operated a restaurant that featured "he-man food" such as steaks and chops.

One's maleness is reassured by the food one eats. During the 1973 meat boycott, men were reported to observe the boycott when dining out with their wives or eating at home, but when they dined without their wives, they ate London Broil and other meats.[29] When in 1955 Carolyn Steedman's mother "made a salad of grated vegetables for Christmas dinner," her husband walked out.[30]

Gender Inequality/Species Inequality

> The men . . . were better hunters than the women, but only because the women had found they could live quite well on foods other than meat.
>
> —Alice Walker, *The Temple of My Familiar*[31]

What is it about meat that makes it a symbol and celebration of male dominance? In many ways, gender inequality is built into the species inequality that meat eating proclaims, because for most cultures obtaining meat was performed by men. Meat was a valuable economic commodity; those who controlled this commodity achieved power. If men were the hunters, then the control of this economic resource was in their hands. Women's status is inversely related to the importance of meat in nontechnological societies:

> The equation is simple: the more important meat is in their life, the greater relative dominance will the men command. . . . When meat becomes an important element within a more closely organized economic system so that there exist rules for its distribution, then men already begin to swing the levers of power. . . . Women's social standing is roughly equal to men's only when society itself is not formalized around roles for distributing meat.[32]

Peggy Sanday surveyed information on over a hundred nontechnological cultures and found a correlation between plant-based economies and women's power and animal-based economies and male power. "In societies dependent on animals, women are rarely depicted as the ultimate source of creative power." In addition, "When large animals are hunted, fathers are more distant, that is, they are not in frequent or regular proximity to infants."[33]

Characteristics of economies dependent mainly on the processing of animals for food include:

- sexual segregation in work activities, with women doing more work than men, but work that is less valued
- women responsible for child care
- the worship of male gods
- patrilineality

On the other hand, plant-based economies are more likely to be egalitarian. This is because women are and have been the gatherers of vegetable foods, and these are invaluable resources for a culture that is plant-based. In these cultures, men as well as women were dependent on women's activities. From this, women achieved autonomy and a degree of self-sufficiency. Yet, where women gather vegetable food and the diet is vegetarian, women do not discriminate as a consequence of distributing the staple. By providing a large proportion of the protein food of a society, women gain an essential economic and social role without abusing it.

Sanday summarizes one myth that links male power to control of meat:

> The Mundurucu believe that there was a time when women ruled and the sex roles were reversed, with the exception that women could not hunt. During that time women were the sexual aggressors and men were sexually submissive and did women's work. Women controlled the "sacred trumpets" (the symbols of power) and the men's houses. The trumpets contained the spirits of the ancestors who demanded ritual offerings of meat. Since women did not hunt and could not make these offerings, men were able to take the trumpets from them, thereby establishing male dominance.[34]

We might observe that the male role of hunter and distributer of meat has been transposed to the male role of eater of meat and conclude that this accounts for meat's role as symbol of male dominance. But there is much more to meat's role as symbol than this.

"Vegetable": Symbol of Feminine Passivity?

Both the words "men" and "meat" have undergone lexicographical narrowing. Originally generic terms, they are now closely associated with their specific referents. Meat no longer means all foods; the word *man,* we realize, no longer includes *women.* Meat represents *the essence or principal part of something,* according to the *American Heritage Dictionary.* Thus we have the "meat of the matter," "a meaty question." To "beef up" something is to improve it. Vegetable, on the other hand, represents the least desirable characteristics: *suggesting or like a vegetable, as in passivity or dullness of existence, monotonous, inactive.* Meat is *something one enjoys or excels in,* vegetable becomes representative of someone who does not enjoy anything: a *person who leads a monotonous, passive, or merely physical existence.*

A complete reversal has occurred in the definition of the word vegetable. Whereas its original sense was to *be lively, active,* it is now viewed as dull, monotonous, passive. To vegetate is to lead a passive existence; just as to be feminine is to lead a passive existence. Once vegetables are viewed as women's food, then by association they become viewed as "feminine," passive.

Men's need to disassociate themselves from women's food (as in the myth in which the last Bushman flees in the direction opposite from women and their vegetable food) has been institutionalized in sexist attitudes toward vegetables and the use of the word *vegetable* to express criticism or disdain. Colloquially it is a synonym for a person severely brain-damaged or in a coma. In addition, vegetables are thought to have a tranquilizing, dulling, numbing effect on people who consume them, and so we can not possibly get strength from them. According to this perverse incarnation of Brillat-Savarin's theory that you are what you eat, to eat a vegetable is to become a vegetable, and by extension, to become womanlike.

Examples from the 1988 Presidential Campaign in which each candidate was belittled through equation with being a vegetable illustrates this patriarchal disdain for vegetables. Michael Dukakis was called "the Vegetable Plate Candidate."[35] Northern Sun Merchandising offered T-shirts that asked: "George Bush: Vegetable or Noxious Weed?" One could opt for a shirt that featured a bottle of ketchup and a picture of Ronald Reagan with this slogan: "*Nutrition Quiz:* Which one is the vegetable?"[36] (The 1984 Presidential Campaign concern over "Where's the Beef?" is considered in the following chapter.)

The word vegetable acts as a synonym for women's passivity because women are supposedly like plants. Hegel makes this clear: "The difference between men and women is like that between animals and plants. Men correspond to animals, while women correspond to plants because their development is more placid."[37] From this viewpoint, both women and plants are seen as less developed and less evolved than men and animals. Consequently, women may eat plants, since each is placid; but active men need animal meat.

Meat Is a Symbol of Patriarchy

In her essay, "Deciphering a Meal," the noted anthropologist Mary Douglas suggests that the order in which we serve foods, and the foods we insist on being present at a meal, reflect a taxonomy of classification that mirrors and reinforces our larger culture. A meal is an amalgam of food dishes, each a constituent part of the whole, each with an assigned value. In addition, each dish is introduced in precise order. A meal does not begin with a dessert, nor end with soup. All is seen as leading up to and then coming down from the entrée that is meat. The pattern is evidence of stability. As Douglas explains, "The ordered system which is a meal represents all the ordered systems associated with it. Hence the strong arousal power of a threat to weaken or confuse that category."[38] To remove meat is to threaten the structure of the larger patriarchal culture.

Marabel Morgan, one expert on how women should accede to every male desire, reported in her *Total Woman Cookbook* that one must be careful about introducing foods that are seen as a threat: "I discovered that Charlie seemed threatened by certain foods. He was suspicious of my casseroles, thinking I had sneaked in some wheat germ or 'good-for-you' vegetables that he wouldn't like."[39]

Mary McCarthy's *Birds of America* provides a fictional illustration of the intimidating aspect to a man of a woman's refusal of meat. Miss Scott, a vegetarian, is invited to a NATO general's house for Thanksgiving. Her refusal of turkey angers the general. Not able to take this rejection seriously, as male dominance requires a continual recollection of itself on everyone's plate, the general loads her plate up with turkey and then ladles gravy over the potatoes as well as the meat, "thus contaminating her vegetable foods." McCarthy's description of his actions with the food mirrors the warlike customs associated with military battles. "He had seized the gravy boat like a weapon in hand-to-hand combat. No wonder they had made him a brigadier general—at least that mystery was solved." The general continues to behave in a bellicose fashion and after dinner proposes a toast in honor of an eighteen-year old who has enlisted to fight in Vietnam. During the ensuing argument about war the general defends the bombing of Vietnam with the rhetorical question: "What's so sacred about a civilian?" This upsets the hero, necessitating that the general's wife apologize for her husband's behavior: "Between you and me," she confides to him, "it kind of got under his skin to see that girl refusing to touch her food. I saw that right away."[40]

Male belligerence in this area is not limited to fictional military men. Men who batter women have often used the absence of meat as a pretext for violence against women. Women's failure to serve meat is not the cause of the violence against them. Controlling men use it, like anything else, as an excuse for their violence. Yet because "real" men eat meat, batterers have a cultural icon to draw upon as they deflect attention from their need to control. As one woman battered by her husband reported, "It would start off with him being angry over trivial little things, a trivial little thing like cheese instead of meat on a sandwich."[41] Another woman stated, "A month ago he threw scalding water over me, leaving a scar on my right arm, all because I gave him a pie with potatoes and vegetables for his dinner, instead of fresh meat."[42]

Men who become vegetarians challenge an essential part of the masculine role. They are opting for women's food. How dare they? Refusing meat means a man is effeminate, a "sissy," a "fruit." Indeed, in 1836, the response to the vegetarian regimen of that day, known as Grahamism, charged that "Emasculation is the first fruit of Grahamism."[43]

Men who choose not to eat meat repudiate one of their masculine privileges. The *New York Times* explored this idea in an editorial on the masculine nature of meat eating. Instead of "the John Wayne type," epitome of the masculine meat eater, the new male hero is "Vulnerable" like Alan Alda, Mikhail Baryshnikov, and Phil Donahue. They might eat dead fishes and dead chickens, but not red meat. Alda and Donahue, among other men, have not only repudiated the macho role, but also macho food. According to the *Times,* "Believe me. The end of macho marks the end of the meat-and-potatoes man."[44] We won't miss either.

chapter 2

The Rape of Animals, the Butchering of Women

> The first metaphor was animal.
>
> —John Berger, "Why Look at Animals?"

> He handled my breast as if he were making a meatball.
>
> —Mary Gordon, *Final Payments*

> One could not stand and watch [the slaughtering] very long without becoming philosophical, without beginning to deal in symbols and similes, and to hear the hog-squeal of the universe.
>
> —Upton Sinclair, *The Jungle*

A healthy sexual being poses near her drink: she wears bikini panties only and luxuriates on a large chair with her head rested seductively on an elegant lace doily. Her inviting drink with a twist of lemon awaits on the table. Her eyes are closed; her facial expression beams pleasure, relaxation, enticement. She is touching her crotch in an attentive, masturbatory action. Anatomy of seduction: sex object, drink, inviting room, sexual activity. The formula is complete. But a woman does not beckon. A pig does. "Ursula Hamdress" appeared in *Playboar,* a magazine that calls itself "the pig farmer's *Playboy.*"[1] How does one explain the substitution of a nonhuman animal for a woman in this pornographic representation? Is she inviting someone to rape her or to eat her? (See Figure 2.)

In 1987, I described Ursula Hamdress on a panel titled "Sexual Violence: Representation and Reality" at Princeton's Graduate Women's

Studies Conference, "Feminism and Its Translations." In the same month, less than sixty miles away, three women were found chained in the basement of Gary Heidnik's house in Philadelphia. In the kitchen body parts of a woman were discovered in the oven, in a stewpot on the stove, and in the refrigerator. Her arms and legs had been fed to the other women held captive there. One of the survivors reported that during the time that she was chained, Heidnick repeatedly raped her.[2]

I hold that Ursula Hamdress and the women raped, butchered, and eaten under Heidnik's directions are linked by an overlap of cultural images of sexual violence against women and the fragmentation and dismemberment of nature and the body in Western culture.[3] Of special concern will be the cultural representations of the butchering of animals because meat eating is the most frequent way in which we interact with animals. Butchering is the quintessential enabling act for meat eating. It enacts a literal dismemberment upon animals while proclaiming our intellectual and emotional separation from animals' desire to live. Butchering as a paradigm provides, as well, an entry for understanding exactly why a profusion of overlapping cultural images exists.

The Absent Referent

Through butchering, animals become absent referents. Animals in name and body are made absent *as animals* for meat to exist. Animals' lives precede and enable the existence of meat. If animals are alive they cannot be meat. Thus a dead body replaces the live animal. Without animals there would be no meat eating, yet they are absent from the act of eating meat because they have been transformed into food.

Animals are made absent through language that renames dead bodies before consumers participate in eating them. Our culture further mystifies the term "meat" with gastronomic language, so we do not conjure dead, butchered animals, but cuisine. Language thus contributes even further to animals' absences. While the cultural meanings of meat and meat eating shift historically, one essential part of meat's meaning is static: One does not eat meat without the death of an animal. Live animals are thus the absent referents in the concept of meat. The absent referent permits us to forget about the animal as an independent entity; it also enables us to resist efforts to make animals present.

There are actually three ways by which animals become absent referents. One is literally: as I have just argued, through meat eating they are literally absent because they are dead. Another is definitional: when we eat animals we change the way we talk about them, for instance, we no

Figure 2

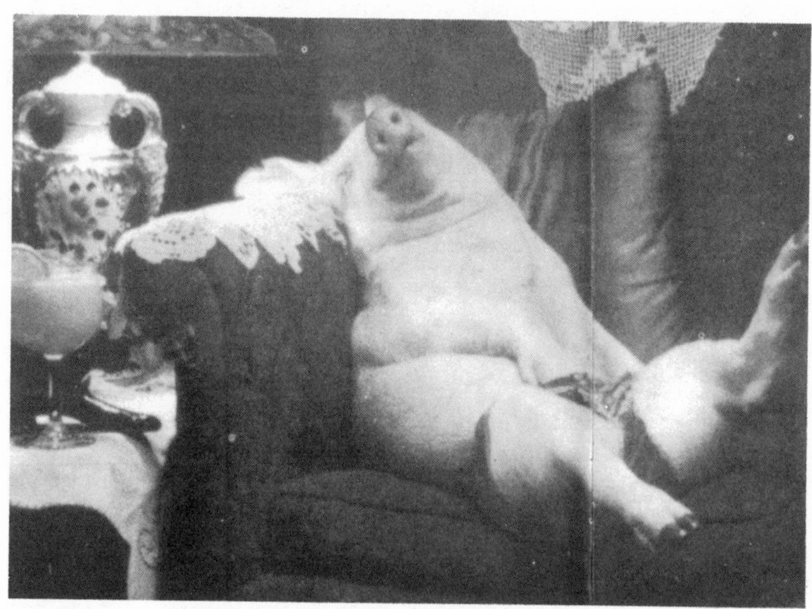

"Ursula Hamdress" from *Playboar.* This copy appeared in *The Beast: The Magazine That Bites Back,* 10 (Summer 1981), pp. 18–19. It was photographed by animal advocate Jim Mason at the Iowa State Fair where it appeared as a "pinup." (More recent issues of *Playboar* have renamed "Ursula" "Taffy Lovely.")

longer talk about baby animals but about veal or lamb. As we will see even more clearly in the next chapter, which examines language about eating animals, the word *meat* has an absent referent, the dead animals. The third way is metaphorical. Animals become metaphors for describing people's experiences. In this metaphorical sense, the meaning of the absent referent derives from its application or reference to something else.

As the absent referent becomes metaphor, its meaning is lifted to a "higher" or more imaginative function than its own existence might merit or reveal. An example of this is when rape victims or battered women say, "I felt like a piece of meat." In this example, meat's meaning does not refer to itself but to how a woman victimized by male violence felt. That meat is functioning as an absent referent is evident when we push the meaning of the metaphor: one cannot truly *feel* like a piece of meat. Teresa de Lauretis comments: "No one can really *see* oneself as an inert object or a sightless body,"[4] and no one can really feel like a piece of meat because meat by definition is something violently deprived of all feeling. The use of the phrase "feeling like a piece of meat" occurs within a metaphoric system of language.

The animals have become absent referents, whose fate is transmuted into a metaphor for someone else's existence or fate. Metaphorically, the absent referent can be anything whose original meaning is undercut as it is absorbed into a different hierarchy of meaning; in this case the original meaning of animals' fates is absorbed into a human-centered hierarchy. Specifically in regard to rape victims and battered women, the death experience of animals acts to illustrate the lived experience of women.

The absent referent is both there and not there. It is there through inference, but its meaningfulness reflects only upon what it refers to because the originating, literal, experience that contributes the meaning is not there.[5] We fail to accord this absent referent its own existence.

Women and Animals: Overlapping but Absent Referents

This chapter posits that a structure of overlapping but absent referents links violence against women and animals. Through the structure of the absent referent, patriarchal values become institutionalized. Just as dead bodies are absent from our language about meat, in descriptions of cultural violence women are also often the absent referent. Rape, in particular, carries such potent imagery that the term is transferred from the literal experience of women and applied metaphorically to other instances of violent devastation, such as the "rape" of the earth in ecological writings of the early 1970s. The experience of women thus becomes a vehicle for describing other oppressions. Women, upon whose bodies actual rape is most often committed, become the absent referent when the language of sexual violence is used metaphorically. These terms recall women's experiences but not women.

When I use the term "the rape of animals," the experience of women becomes a vehicle for explicating another being's oppression. Is this appropriate? Some terms are so powerfully specific to one group's oppression that their appropriation to others is potentially exploitative: for instance, using the "Holocaust" for anything but the genocide of European Jews and others by the Nazis. Rape has a different social context for women than for the other animals. So, too, does butchering for animals. Yet, feminists among others, appropriate the metaphor of butchering without acknowledging the originating oppression of animals that generates the power of the metaphor. Through the function of the absent referent, Western culture constantly renders the material reality of violence into controlled and controllable metaphors.

Sexual violence and meat eating, which appear to be discrete forms of violence, find a point of intersection in the absent referent. Cultural images of sexual violence, and actual sexual violence, often rely on our knowledge of how animals are butchered and eaten. For example, Kathy Barry tells us of "*maisons d'abattage* (literal translation: houses of slaughter)" where six or seven girls each serve 80 to 120 customers a night.[6] In addition, the bondage equipment of pornography—chains, cattle prods, nooses, dog collars, and ropes—suggests the control of animals. Thus, when women are victims of violence, the treatment of animals is recalled.

Similarly, in images of animal slaughter, erotic overtones suggest that women are the absent referent. If animals are the absent referent in the phrase "the butchering of women," women are the absent referent in the phrase "the rape of animals." The impact of a seductive pig relies on an absent but imaginable, seductive, fleshy woman. Ursula Hamdress is both metaphor and joke; her jarring (or jocular) effect is based on the fact that we are all accustomed to seeing women depicted in such a way. Ursula's image refers to something that is absent: the human female body. The structure of the absent referent in patriarchal culture strengthens individual oppressions by always recalling other oppressed groups.

Because the structure of overlapping absent referents is so deeply rooted in Western culture, it inevitably implicates individuals. Our participation evolves as part of our general socialization to cultural patterns and viewpoints, thus we fail to see anything disturbing in the violence and domination that are an inextricable part of this structure. Consequently, women eat meat, work in slaughterhouses, at times treat other women as "meat," and men at times are victims of sexual violence. Moreover, because women as well as men participate in and benefit from the structure of the absent referent by eating meat, neither achieve the personal distance to perceive their implication in the structure, nor the originating oppression of animals that establishes the potency of the metaphor of butchering.

The interaction between physical oppression and the dependence on metaphors that rely on the absent referent indicates that we distance ourselves from whatever is different by equating it with something we have already objectified. For instance, the demarcation between animals and people was invoked during the early modern period to emphasize social distancing. According to Keith Thomas, infants, youth, the poor, blacks, Irish, insane people, and women were considered beastlike: "Once perceived as beasts, people were liable to be treated accordingly. The ethic of human domination removed animals from the sphere of human concern. But it also legitimized the ill-treatment of those humans who were in a supposedly animal condition."[7]

Racism and the Absent Referent

Through the structure of the absent referent, a dialectic of absence and presence of oppressed groups occurs. What is absent refers back to one oppressed group while defining another. This has theoretical implications for class and race as well as violence against women and animals. Whereas I want to focus on the overlapping oppressions of women and animals, further exploration of the function of the absent referent is needed, such as found in Marjorie Spiegel's *The Dreaded Comparison: Human and Animal Slavery*. Spiegel discusses the connection between racial oppression and animal oppression and in doing so demonstrates their overlapping relationship.[8]

The structure of the absent referent requires assistants who achieve the elimination of the animal, a form of alienated labor. Living, whole animals are the absent referents not only in meat eating but also in the fur trade. Of interest then is the connection between the oppression of animals through the fur trade and the oppression of blacks as slaves. Black historians suggest that one of the reasons black people rather than Native Americans were oppressed through the white Americans' institution of slavery is because of the slaughter of fur-bearing animals. As Vincent Harding describes it in *There Is a River: The Black Struggle for Freedom in America:* "One important early source of income for the Europeans in North America was the fur trade with the Indians, which enslavement of the latter would endanger."[9] While the factors that caused the oppression of Native Americans and blacks is not reducible to this example, we do see in it the undergirding of interactive oppressions by the absent referent. We also see that in analyzing the oppression of human beings, the oppression of animals ought not to be ignored. However, the absent referent, because of its absence, prevents our experiencing connections between oppressed groups.

When one becomes alert to the function of the absent referent and refuses to eat animals, the use of metaphors relying on animals' oppression can simultaneously criticize both that which the metaphor points to and that from which it is derived. For instance, when vegetarian and Civil Rights activist Dick Gregory compares the ghetto to the slaughterhouse he does so condemning both and suggesting the functioning of the absent referent in erasing responsibility for the horrors of each:

> Animals and humans suffer and die alike. If you had to kill your own hog before you ate it, most likely you would not be able to do it. To hear the hog scream, to see the blood spill, to see the baby being taken away from its momma, and to see the look of death in the animal's eye would turn your stomach. So you get the man at the packing house to do the killing for you. In like manner, if the wealthy aristocrats who are perpetrating conditions in the ghetto actually heard the screams of ghetto suffering, or saw the slow death of hungry little kids, or witnessed the strangulation of manhood and dignity, they could not continue the killing. But the wealthy are protected from such horror. . . . If you can justify killing to eat meat, you can justify the conditions of the ghetto. I cannot justify either one.[10]

Sexual Violence and Meat Eating

To rejoin the issue of the intertwined oppressions with which this chapter is primarily concerned, sexual violence and meat eating, and their point of intersection in the absent referent, it is instructive to consider incidents of male violence. Batterers, rapists, serial killers, and child sexual abusers have victimized animals.[11] They do so for a variety of reasons: marital rapists may use a companion animal to intimidate, coerce, control, or violate a woman. Serial killers often initiate violence first against animals. The male students who killed their classmates in various communities in the 1990s often were hunters or known to have killed animals. Child sexual abusers often use threats and/or violence against companion animals to achieve compliance from their victims. Batterers harm or kill a companion animal as a warning to their partners that she could be next; as a way of further separating her from meaningful relationships; to demonstrate his power and her powerlessness. The threatened woman or child is the absent referent in pet murders. Within the symbolic order the fragmented referent no longer recalls itself but something else.[12] Though this pattern of killing pets as a warning to an abused woman or child is derived from recent case studies of domestic violence, the story of a man's killing his wife's pet instead of his wife can be found in an early twentieth-century short story. Susan Glaspell's "A Jury of Her Peers" exposes this function of the absent referent and the fact that a woman's peers, i.e., other women, recognize this function.[13]

Generally, however, the absent referent, because of its absence, prevents our experiencing connections between oppressed groups. Cultural images of butchering and sexual violence are so interpenetrated that animals act as the absent referent in radical feminist discourse. In this sense, radical feminist theory participates in the same set of representational structures it seeks to expose. We uphold the patriarchal structure of absent referents, appropriating the experience of animals to interpret our own violation. For instance, we learn of a woman who went to her doctor after being battered. The doctor told her her leg "was like a raw piece of meat hanging up in a butcher's window."[14] Feminists translate this literal description into a metaphor for women's oppression. Andrea Dworkin states that pornography depicts woman as a "female piece of meat" and Gena Corea observes that "women in brothels can be used like animals in cages."[15] Linda Lovelace claims that when presented to Xaviera Hollander for inspection, "Xaviera looked me over like a butcher inspecting a side of beef."[16] When one film actress committed suicide, another described the dilemma she and other actresses encounter: "They treat us like meat." Of this statement Susan Griffin writes: "She means that men who hire them treat them as less than human, as matter without spirit."[17] In each of these examples, feminists have used violence against animals as metaphor, literalizing *and* feminizing the metaphor. When one is matter without spirit, one is the raw material for exploitation and for metaphoric borrowing.[18]

Despite this dependence on the *imagery* of butchering, radical feminist discourse has failed to integrate the *literal* oppression of animals into our analysis of patriarchal culture or to acknowledge the strong historical alliance between feminism and vegetarianism. Whereas women may feel like pieces of meat, and be treated like pieces of meat—emotionally butchered and physically battered—animals actually are made into pieces of meat. In radical feminist theory, the use of these metaphors alternates between a positive figurative activity and a negative activity of occlusion, negation, and ommission in which the literal fate of the animál is elided. Could metaphor itself be the undergarment to the garb of oppression?

The Cycle of Objectification, Fragmentation, and Consumption

What we require is a theory that traces parallel trajectories: the common oppressions of women and animals, and the problems of metaphor and the absent referent. I propose a cycle of objectification, fragmentation, and consumption, which links butchering and sexual violence in our culture. Objectification permits an oppressor to view another being as an object. The oppressor then violates this being by object-like treatment: e.g., the rape of women that denies women freedom to say no, or the butchering of animals that converts animals from living breathing beings into dead objects. This process allows fragmentation, or brutal dismemberment, and finally consumption. While the occasional man may literally eat women, we all consume visual images of women all the time.[19] Consumption is the fulfillment of oppression, the annihilation of will, of separate identity. So too with language: a subject first is viewed, or objectified, through metaphor. Through fragmentation the object is severed from its ontological meaning. Finally, consumed, it exists only through what it represents. The consumption of the referent reiterates its annihilation as a subject of importance in itself.

Since this chapter addresses how patriarchal culture treats animals as well as women, the image of meat is an appropriate one to illustrate this trajectory of objectification, fragmentation, and consumption. The literal process of violently transforming living animals to dead consumable ones is emblematic of the conceptual process by which the referent point of meat eating is changed. Industrialized meat-eating cultures such as the United States and Great Britain exemplify the process by which live animals are removed from the idea of meat. The physical process of butchering an animal is recapitulated on a verbal level through words of objectification and fragmentation.

Animals are rendered being-less not only by technology, but by innocuous phrases such as "food-producing unit," "protein harvester," "converting machine," "crops," and "biomachines." The meat-producing industry views an animal as consisting of "edible" and "inedible" parts, which must be separated so that the latter do not contaminate the former. An animal proceeds down a "disassembly line," losing body parts at every stop. This fragmentation not only dismembers the animal, it changes the way in which we conceptualize animals. Thus, in the first edition of *The American Heritage Dictionary of the English Language,* the definition of "lamb" was illustrated not by an image of Mary's little one but by an edible body divided into ribs, loin, shank, and leg.[20]

After being butchered, fragmented body parts are often renamed to obscure the fact that these were once animals. After death, cows become roast beef, steak, hamburger; pigs become pork, bacon, sausage. Since objects are possessions they cannot have possessions; thus, we say "leg of lamb" not a "lamb's leg," "chicken wings" not a "chicken's wings." We opt for less disquieting referent points not only by changing names from animals to meat, but also by cooking, seasoning, and covering the animals with sauces, disguising their original nature.

Only then can consumption occur: actual consumption of the animal, now dead, and metaphorical consumption of the term "meat," so that it refers to food products alone rather than to the dead animal. In patriarchal culture, meat is without its referent point. This is the way we want it, as William Hazlitt honestly admitted in 1826: "Animals that are made use of as food, should either be so small as to be imperceptible, or else we should . . . not leave the form standing to reproach us with our gluttony and cruelty. I hate to see a rabbit trussed, or a hare brought to the table in the form which it occupied while living."[21] The dead animal is the point beyond the culturally presumed referent of meat.

Consuming Meat Metaphorically

Without its referent point of the slaughtered, bleeding, butchered animal, meat becomes a free-floating image. Meat is seen as a vehicle of meaning and not as inherently meaningful; the referent "animal" has been consumed. "Meat" becomes a term to express women's oppression, used equally by patriarchy and feminists, who say that women are "pieces of meat." Because of the absence of the actual referent, meat as metaphor is easily adaptable. While phrases such as "Where's the Beef?" seem diametrically opposed to the use of "meat" to convey oppression, "Where's the Beef?" confirms the fluidity of the absent referent while reinforcing the extremely specific, assaultive ways in which "meat" is used to refer to women. Part of making "beef" into "meat" is rendering it nonmale. When meat carries resonances of power, the power it evokes is male. Male genitalia and male sexuality are at times inferred when "meat" is discussed (curious locutions since uncastrated adult males are rarely eaten). "Meat" is made nonmale through violent dismemberment. As an image whose original meaning has been consumed and negated, "meat's" meaning is structured by its environment.

Meat has long been used in Western culture as a metaphor for women's oppression. The model for consuming a woman after raping her, as noted in the preface (page 25), is the story of Zeus and Metis: "Zeus lusted after Metis the Titaness, who turned into many shapes to escape him until she was caught at last and got with child." When warned by a sibyl that if Metis conceived a second time Zeus would be deposed by the resulting offspring, Zeus swallowed Metis, who, he claimed, continued to give him counsel from inside his belly. Consumption appears to be the final stage of male sexual desire. Zeus verbally seduces Metis in order to devour her: "Having coaxed Metis to a couch with honeyed words, Zeus suddenly opened his mouth and swallowed her, and that was the end of Metis."[22] An essential component of androcentric culture has been built upon these activities of Zeus: viewing the sexually desired object as consumable. But, we do not hear anything about dismemberment in the myth of Zeus's consumption of Metis. How exactly did Zeus fit her pregnant body, arms, shoulders, chest, womb, thighs, legs, and feet into his mouth in one gulp? The myth does not acknowledge how the absent referent becomes absent.

Eliding Fragmentation

Paralleling the elided relationship between metaphor and referent is the unacknowledged role of fragmentation in eating flesh. Our minds move from objectified being to consumable food. The action of fragmentation, the killing, and the dividing is elided. Indeed, patriarchal culture surrounds actual butchering with silence. Geographically, slaughterhouses are cloistered. We do not see or hear what transpires there.[23] Consequently, consumption appears to follow immediately upon objectification, for consumption itself has been objectified. Discussing the alliance of women and workers during a lively 1907 challenge to vivisection, Coral Lansbury offers this reminder, "It has been said that a visit to an abattoir would make a vegetarian of the most convinced carnivore among us."[24] In "How to Build a Slaughterhouse," Richard Selzer observes that the knowledge that the slaughterhouse offers is knowledge we do not want to know: "Before it is done this field trip to a slaughterhouse will have become for me a descent into Hades, a vision of life that perhaps it would have been better never to know."[25] We don't want to know about fragmentation because that is the process through which the live referent disappears.

Fragment #1: Implemental Violence

Abandon self, all ye who enter here. Become component part, geared, meshed, timed, controlled.

Hell. . . . Hogs dangling, dancing along the convey, 300, 350 an hour; Mary running running along the rickety platform to keep up, stamping, stamping the hides. To the shuddering drum of the skull crush machine, in the spectral vapor clouds, everyone the same motion all the hours through: Kryckszi lifting his cleaver, the one powerful stroke; long continuous arm swirl of the rippers, gut pullers. . . .

Geared, meshed: the kill room: knockers, shacklers, pritcher-uppers, stickers, headers, rippers, leg breakers, breast and aitch sawyers, caul pullers, fell cutters, rumpers, splitters, vat dippers, skinners, gutters, pluckers.

—All through the jumble of buildings . . . of death, dismemberment and vanishing entire for harmless creatures meek and mild, frisky, wild—Hell.

—Tillie Olsen, *Yonnondio*[26]

The institution of butchering is unique to human beings. All carnivorous animals kill and consume their prey themselves. They see and hear their victims before they eat them. There is no absent referent, only a dead one. Plutarch taunts his readers with this fact in his "Essay on Flesh Eating": If you believe yourselves to be meat eaters, "then, to begin with, kill *yourself* what you wish to eat—but do it yourself with your own *natural* weapons, without the use of butcher's knife, or axe, or club." Plutarch points out that people do not have bodies equipped for eating flesh from a carcass, "no curved beak, no sharp talons and claws, no pointed teeth."[27] We have no bodily agency for killing and dismembering the animals we eat; we require implements.

The essence of butchering is to fragment the animal into pieces small enough for consumption. Implements are the simulated teeth that rip and claws that tear. Implements at the same time remove the referent; they bring about "the vanishing entire for harmless creatures."

Hannah Arendt claims that violence always needs implements.[28] Without implemental violence human beings could not eat meat. Violence is central to the act of slaughtering. Sharp knives are essential for rapidly rendering the anesthetized living animal into edible dead flesh. Knives are not so much distancing mechanisms in this case as enabling mechanisms. For farm slaughter some of the implements required include: hog scraper, iron hog and calf gambrel, stunning instrument, large cleaver, small cleaver, skinning knives, boning knives, hog hook, meat saw, steak knife, pickle pump, sticking knife, and meat grinder. Large slaughterhouses use over thirty-five different types of knives. Selzer notes that the men at a slaughterhouse "are synchronous as dancers and for the most part as silent. It is their knives that converse, gossip, press each other along."[29] Implements used against animals are one of the first things destroyed after the overthrow of people in George Orwell's *Animal Farm.*

Fragment #2: The Slaughterhouse

[The slaughterhouse] carries out its business in secret and decides what you will see, hides from you what it chooses.

—Richard Selzer[30]

Generally, if we enter a slaughterhouse we do so through the writings of someone else who entered for us. Early in the century, Upton Sinclair entered the slaughterhouse for his readers. He seized the operations of the slaughterhouse as a metaphor for the fate of the worker in capitalism. Jurgis, the worker whose rising consciousness evolves in *The Jungle,* visits a slaughterhouse in the opening pages. A guide ushers him through the place and he experiences what "was like some horrible crime committed in a dungeon, all unseen and unheeded, buried out of sight and of memory."[31] Hogs with their legs chained to a line that moves them forward hang upside down, squealing, grunting, wailing. The line moves them forward, their throats are slit, and then they vanish "with a splash into a huge vat of boiling water." Despite the businesslike aspect of the place, one "could not help thinking of the hogs; they were so innocent, they came so very trustingly; and they were so very human in their protests—and so perfectly within their rights!"

Then came the dismemberment: the scraping of the skin, beheading, cutting of the breastbone, removal of the entrails. Jurgis marvels at the speed, the automation, the machinelike way in which each man dispatched his job, and he congratulates himself that he is not a hog. The next three hundred pages trace the rising of his consciousness so that he realizes that a hog is exactly what he is—"one of the packer's hogs. What they wanted from a hog was all the profits that could be got out of him; and that was what they wanted from the working man, and also that was what they wanted from the public. What the hog thought of it and what he suffered, were not considered; and no more was it with labor and no more with the purchaser of meat."[32]

In response to Sinclair's novel people could not help thinking of the hogs. The referent—those few initial pages describing butchering in a book of more than three hundred pages—overpowered the metaphor. Horrified by what they learned about meat production, people clamored for new laws, and for a short time, became, as humorist Finley Peter Dunne's "Mr. Dooley" described it, "viggytaryans."[33] As Upton Sinclair bemoaned, "I aimed at the public's heart and by accident hit it in the stomach."[34] Butchering failed as a metaphor for the fate of the worker in *The Jungle* because the novel carried too much information on how the animal was violently killed. To make the absent referent present—that is, describing exactly how an animal dies, kicking, screaming, and is fragmented—disables consumption and disables the power of metaphor.

Fragment #3: The Disassembly Line as Model

> Those who are against Fascism without being against capitalism, who lament over the barbarism that comes out of barbarism, are like people who wish to eat their veal without slaughtering the calf.
>
> —Bertolt Brecht, "Writing the Truth: Five Difficulties"[35]

Using the slaughterhouse as trope for treatment of the worker in a modern capitalist society did not end with Upton Sinclair. Bertolt Brecht's *Saint Joan of the Stockyards* employs butchering imagery throughout the play to depict the inhumanity of large-scale capitalists like the "meat king" Pierpont Mauler. This capitalist does to his employees what he does to the steers; he is a "butcher of men." With the activities of the slaughterhouse as the backdrop, phrases such as "cut-throat prices" and "it's no skin off my back" act as resonant puns invoking the fate of animals to bemoan the fate of the worker.[36] Appropriately, the choice of the trope of the slaughterhouse for the dehumanization of the worker by capitalism rings with historical verity.

The division of labor on the assembly lines owes its inception to Henry Ford's visit to the disassembly line of the Chicago slaughterhouses. Ford credited the idea of the assembly line to the fragmented activities of animal slaughtering: "The idea came in a general way from the overhead trolley that the Chicago packers use in dressing beef."[37] One book on meat production (financed by a meat-packing company) describes the process: "The slaughtered animals, suspended head downward from a moving chain, or conveyor, pass from workman to workman, each of whom performs some particular step in the process." The authors proudly add: "So efficient has this procedure proved to be that it has been adopted by many other industries, as for example in the assembling of automobiles."[38] Although Ford reversed the outcome of the process of slaughtering in that a product is created rather than fragmented on the assembly line, he contributed at the same time to the larger fragmentation of the individual's work and productivity. The dismemberment of the human body is not so much a construct of modern capitalism as modern capitalism is a construct built on dismemberment and fragmentation.[39]

One of the basic things that must happen on the disassembly line of a slaughterhouse is that the animal must be treated as an inert object, not as a living, breathing, being. Similarly the worker on the assembly line becomes treated as an inert, unthinking object, whose creative, bodily, emotional needs are ignored. For those people who work in the disassembly line of slaughterhouses, they, more than anyone, must accept on a grand scale the double annihilation of self: they are not only going to have to deny themselves, but they are going to have to accept the cultural absent referencing of animals as well. They must view the living animal as the meat that everyone outside the slaughterhouse accepts it as, while the animal is still alive. Thus they must be alienated from their own bodies and animals' bodies as well.[40] Which may account for the fact that the "turnover rate among slaughterhouse workers is the highest of any occupation in the country."[41]

The introduction of the assembly line in the auto industry had a quick and unsettling effect on the workers. Standardization of work and separation from the final product became fundamental to the laborers' experience.[42] The result was to increase worker's alienation from the product they produced. Automation severed workers from a sense of accomplishment through the fragmentation of their jobs. In *Labor and Monopoly Capital: The Degradation of Work in the Twentieth Century,* Harry Braverman explains the initial results of the introduction of the assembly line, "Craftsmanship gave way to a repeated detail operation, and wage rates were standardized at uniform levels." Working men left Ford in large numbers after the introduction of the assembly line. Braverman observes: "In this initial reaction to the assembly line we see the natural revulsion of the worker against the new kind of work."[43] Ford dismembered the meaning of work, introducing productivity without the sense of being productive. Fragmentation of the human body in late capitalism allows the dismembered part to represent the whole. Because the slaughterhouse model is not evident to assembly line workers, they do not realize that as whole beings they too have experienced the impact of the structure of the absent referent in a patriarchal culture.

Fragment #4: The Rape of Animals

"Chickens fly in on the table with knife and fork in their thighs," begging to be eaten.

—Nineteenth-century Swedish ballad writer on the plenitude of meat in the United States[44]

"He would tie me up and force me to have intercourse with our family dog. . . . He would get on top of me, holding the dog, and he would like hump the dog, while the dog had its penis inside me."[45] In this description of rape, the dog as well as the woman is being raped. Most rapes do not include animals, yet the phrases used by rape victims when describing their feelings suggest that animals' fate in meat eating is the immediate touchstone for their own experience. When women say that they feel like a piece of meat after being raped, are they saying there is a connection between being entered against one's will and being eaten? One woman reported: "He really made me feel like a piece of meat, like a receptacle. My husband had told me that all a girl was was a servant who could not think, a receptacle, a piece of meat."

In *Portnoy's Complaint,* Philip Roth conveys how meat becomes a receptacle for male sexuality when Portnoy masturbates in it: " 'Come, Big Boy, Come' screamed the maddened piece of liver that, in my own insanity, I bought one afternoon at a butcher shop and, believe it or not, violated behind a billboard."[46] Unless the receptacle is Portnoy's piece of meat, a sexual object is not literally consumed. Why then this doubleness? What connects being a receptacle and being a piece of meat, being entered and being eaten? After all, being raped/violated/entered does not approximate being eaten. So why then does it feel that way? Or rather, why is it so easily described as feeling that way?[47] Because, if you are a piece of meat, you are subject to a knife, to implemental violence.

Rape, too, is implemental violence in which the penis is the implement of violation. You are held down by a male body as the fork holds a piece of meat so that the knife may cut into it. In addition, just as the slaughterhouse treats animals and its workers as inert, unthinking, unfeeling objects, so too in rape are women treated as inert objects, with no attention paid to their feelings or needs. Consequently they feel like pieces of meat. Correspondingly, we learn of "rape racks" that enable the insemination of animals against their will.[48] To feel like a piece of meat is to be treated like an inert object when one is (or was) in fact a living, feeling being.

The meat metaphors rape victims choose to describe their experience and the use of the "rape rack" suggest that rape is parallel and related to consumption, consumption both of images of women and of literal, animal flesh. Rape victims' repeated use of the word "hamburger" to describe the result of penetration, violation, being prepared for market, implies not only how unpleasurable being a piece of meat is, but also that animals can be victims of rape. They have been penetrated, violated, prepared for market against their will. Yet, overlapping cultural metaphors structure these experiences as though they were willed by women and animals.

To justify meat eating, we refer to animals' wanting to die, desiring to become meat. In Samuel Butler's *Erewhon,* meat is forbidden unless it comes from animals who died "a natural death." Resultingly, "it was found that animals were continually dying natural deaths under more or less suspicious circumstances. . . . It was astonishing how some of these unfortunate animals would scent out a butcher's knife if there was one within a mile of them, and run right up against it if the butcher did not get it out of their way in time."[49] One of the mythologies of a rapist culture is that women not only ask for rape, they also enjoy it; that they are continually seeking out the butcher's knife. Similarly, advertisements and popular culture tell us that animals like Charlie the Tuna and Al Capp's Shmoo wish to be eaten. The implication is that women and animals willingly participate in the process that renders them absent.

In *Total Joy,* Marabel Morgan unites women and animals through the use of the metaphor of hamburger. Morgan fosters her own Shmoo syndrome in advising women to consider themselves like hamburger in serving their husbands' needs: "but like hamburger you may have to prepare yourself in a variety of different ways now and then."[50] Her sentence structure—"like hamburger you may"—implies that hamburger prepares itself in a variety of ways, and so must you. But hamburger, long before arriving in the kitchen of the total woman, has been denied all agency and can do no preparing. "You," woman/wife, refers to and stands in for hamburger. Women stand in relationship to the "total woman" as they do to "hamburger," as something that is objectified, without agency, that must be prepared, reshaped, acculturated to be made consumable in a patriarchal world. Though the referent is absent, women cannot escape recognizing themselves in it. And just as animals do not desire to be eaten, Morgan's sentence structure subverts her attempt to convince women that they do.

How does one turn a resistant, kicking, fearful subject into pieces of meat? To be converted from subject into object requires anesthetizing. G. J. Barker-Benfield tells us of a nineteenth-century medical man who came to the assistance of a man who wished to have sex with his wife. The physician arrived at the residence of the couple two or three times a week, "to etherize the poor wife."[51] The anesthetizing of animals as a prelude to butchering reminds us of this doctor's complicity in marital rape.

What cannot easily be done to a fully awake and struggling body *can* be accomplished with an anesthetized one. What is the exceptional case in rape is again typical in butchering: anesthetization is an essential part of mass-producing meat.[52]

A seduced animal results in a more economical operation, safer and better working conditions for the butcher, and, quite simply, produces higher quality meat. Animals' muscular tissue contains sufficient glycogen to produce a preservative, lactic acid, after death. But this glycogen can be used up by physical and nervous tension before death. Thus, a seduction routine to calm the victim, and medical intervention to anesthetize the victim, act as the prelude to butchering. Excited, frightened, and overheated animals will not bleed fully, and their dead flesh will be pink or fiery, making them "unattractive carcasses."[53]

The seduction of "meat-producing animals" begins with tranquilizers, which are either injected into the bodies or inserted into the animals' feed. With a minimum of excitement and discomfort, the animals must then be immobilized. Immobilization may occur by mechanical, chemical, or electrical methods. The goal is not to kill the animals outright—as Arabella informs Jude in Thomas Hardy's *Jude the Obscure*—but to stun them and initiate bleeding while the heart continues to beat, helping to push the blood out.

Curiously, as the animals move closer to the actual act of slaughter, the descriptions of the meat industry use language that implies the animals are willing their own actions. The more immobilized the animals become the more likely the words describing the slaughtering process will refer to them as though they were mobile, so their movements appear entirely their own: "emerging," facing in the same direction, and "sliding."[54] The concept of seduction has prevailed; animals appear to be active and willing agents in the "rape" of their lives.

Fragment #5: Jack the Ripper

I had always been fond of her in the most innocent, asexual way. It was as if her body was always entirely hidden behind her radiant mind, the modesty of her behavior, and her taste in dress. She had never offered me the slightest chink through which to view the glow of her nakedness. And now suddenly the butcher knife of fear had slit her open. She was as open to me as the carcass of a heifer slit down the middle and hanging on a hook. There were . . . and suddenly I felt a violent desire to make love to her. Or to be more exact, a violent desire to rape her.

—Milan Kundera, *The Book of Laughter and Forgetting*[55]

The overlap of categories of violated women and butchered animals is illustrated by the response to Jack the Ripper, who killed eight women in 1888. At the heart of his male violence was not murder alone, but sexual mutilation and possession by the removal of the uterus. He displayed skill in handling his implement of butchering; as the police surgeon concluded, he was "someone very handy with the knife."[56] In addition, he displayed knowledge of women's bodies by his precise butchering of specific body parts. "Indeed the principal objective of the murderer seems to have been evisceration of the body after the victim had been strangled and had her throat cut. When the murderer had enough time, the uterus and other internal organs were removed, and the women's insides were often strewn about."[57] For instance, after Katharine Eddowes was murdered, her left kidney and her uterus were missing.

The image of butchered animals haunted those who investigated the crimes. Women's fate became that traditionally reserved for animals. First, women were disemboweled by Jack the Ripper in such a fashion that it allowed for but one comparison, as the police surgeon reported: "She was ripped open just as you see a dead calf at a butcher's shop."[58] After viewing one victim whose small intestine and parts of the stomach were lying above her right shoulder and part of the stomach over her left shoulder, a young policeman could not eat meat. "My food sickened me. The sight of a butcher shop nauseated me."[59] The absent referent of meat suddenly became present when the objects were butchered women.

Secondly, Jack the Ripper's demonstrated skill with the implement of butchering, the knife, led the authorities to suspect the killer was either a butcher, hunter, slaughterman, or properly qualified surgeon. According to the police report, "seventy-six butchers and slaughterers have been visited and the characters of the men employed enquired into."[60]

Thirdly, one of the motives proposed for Jack the Ripper's interest in the uterus demonstrates that women felt they were being treated like animals in terms of medical experimentation: it was rumored that an American was paying twenty pounds a womb for medical research. Jack the Ripper was thought to be supplying him.[61] Lastly, one London minister, the Reverend S. Barnett, proposed that public slaughterhouses be removed because seeing them tends "to brutalise a thickly crowded population, and to debase the children."[62]

Fragment #6: The Butchering of Women

Now I get coarse when the abstract nouns start flashing.
I go out to the kitchen to talk cabbages and habits.
I try hard to remember to watch what people do.
Yes, keep your eyes on the hands, let the voice go buzzing.

Economy is the bone, politics is the flesh,
watch who they beat and who they eat

—Marge Piercy, "In the men's room(s)"[63]

Animals' fate in butchering is exploited in the oppression of women, and it is invoked by feminists concerned with stopping women's oppression. While animals are the absent objects, their fate is continually summoned through the metaphor of butchering. Butchering is that which creates or causes one's existence as meat; metaphorical "butchering" silently invokes the violent act of animal slaughter while reinforcing raped women's sense of themselves as "pieces of meat." Andrea Dworkin observes that "the favorite conceit of male culture is that experience can be fractured, literally its bones split, and that one can examine the splinters as if they were not part of the bone, or the bone as if it were not part of the body." (We dwell on the T-bone steak or the drumstick as if it were not part of a body.) Dworkin's dissection of the body of culture resounds with meaning when we consider the concept of animals' status as absent referent: "Everything is split apart: intellect from feeling and/or imagination; act from consequence; symbol from reality; mind from body. Some part substitutes for the whole and the whole is sacrificed to the part."[64] Dworkin's metaphorical description of patriarchal culture depends on the reader's knowledge that animals are butchered in this way.

Images of butchering suffuse patriarchal culture. A steakhouse in New Jersey was called "Adam's Rib." Who do they think they were eating? *The Hustler,* prior to its incarnation as a pornographic magazine, was a Cleveland restaurant whose menu presented a woman's buttocks on the cover and proclaimed, "We serve the best meat in town!" Who? A woman is shown being ground up in a meat grinder as *Hustler* magazine proclaims: "Last All Meat Issue." Women's buttocks are stamped as "Choice Cuts" on an album cover entitled "Choice Cuts (Pure Food and Drug Act)." When asked about their sexual fantasies, many men describe "pornographic scenes of disembodied, faceless, impersonal body parts: breasts, legs, vaginas, buttocks."[65] Meat for the average consumer has been reduced to exactly that: faceless body parts, breasts, legs, udders, buttocks. Frank Perdue plays with images of sexual butchering in a poster encouraging chicken consumption: "Are you a breast man or a leg man?"

A popular poster in the butcher shops of the Haymarket section of Boston depicted a woman's body sectioned off as though she were a slaughtered animal, with her separate body parts identified. In response to such an image, dramatists Dario Fo and Franca Rame scripted this narrative:

> There was a drawing of a naked lady all divided up into different sections. You know . . . like those posters in the butcher's shop of a cow? And all the erogenous zones were painted these incredible colours. For instance, the rump was painted shocking pink. (Does a bump and grind and laughs.) Then this part here (Putting her hands on her back just below her neck) . . . butchers call it chuck. It was purple. And the fillet . . . (Briefly diverted) What about the price of fillet nowadays eh? Terrible! Well anyway, it was orange.[66]

Norma Benney in "All of One Flesh: The Rights of Animals" describes the centerfold of a music magazine that "showed a naked woman, spread-eagled and chained on an operating table in a butcher's shop surrounded by hanging animal carcasses and butchers' knives and cleavers while a man in a red, rubber, butcher's apron prepared to divide her with an electric saw."[67] In this context, colloquial expressions such as "piece of ass," "I'm a breast man," and "I'm a thigh man" reveal their assaultive origins. (Although men may be called "stud" and "hunk," these terms only reconfirm the fluidity of the absent referent, and reinforce the extremely specific, assaultive ways in which "meat" is used to refer to women. Men possess themselves as "meat," women are possessed.)

These examples suggest a paradigm of metaphorical sexual butchering of which the essential components are:

- the knife, real or metaphorical, as the chosen implement (in pornography the camera lens takes the place of the knife, committing implemental violence)
- the aggressor seeking to control/consume/defile the body of the victim
- the fetishism of body parts
- meat eating provides the image of butchered animals

Metaphoric sexual butchering recurs in literature and movies extolling images of butchered women. We find the rape and subsequent butchering of a woman in the Hebrew Bible book of Judges. A Levite allows his concubine to be savagely raped by strangers: "They raped her and tortured her all night until the morning."[68] She falls down at the doorway of the house where the Levite is staying. He puts her on his donkey—we do not know if she is dead or alive—and takes her to his house. "He took the knife and he seized his concubine. He cut her, limb by limb, into twelve pieces, and sent her throughout all the territory of Israel."[69] Similarly, in D. H. Lawrence's "The Woman Who Rode Away" a New Woman rides into a situation where she is to be sacrificed to the sun by a group of men in a cave. Lawrence's language evokes both literal and sexual consumption. Kate Millet offers an acute analysis of this tale: "This is a formula for sexual cannibalism: substitute the knife for the penis and penetration, the cave for a womb, and for a bed, a place of execution—and you provide a murder whereby one acquires one's victim's power."[70]

Sexual butchering is a basic component of male pornographic sexuality. The infamous "snuff movies," so-named for the snuffing out of a woman's life in the last few minutes of the movie, celebrate women's butchering as a sexual act:

> A pretty young blond woman who appears to be a production assistant tells the director how sexually aroused she was by the stabbing [of a pregnant woman] finale. The attractive director asks her if she would like to go to bed with him and act out her fantasies. They start fumbling around in bed until she realizes that the crew is still filming. She protests and tries to get up. The director picks up a dagger that is lying on the bed and says, "Bitch, now you're going to get what you want." What happens next goes beyond the realm of language. He butchers her slowly, deeply, and thoroughly. The observer's gut revulsion is overwhelming at the amount of blood, chopped-up fingers, flying arms, sawed-off legs, and yet more blood oozing like a river out of her mouth before she dies. But the climax is still at hand. In a moment of undiluted evil, he cuts open her abdomen and brandishes her very insides high above his head in a scream of orgasmic conquest.[71]

"Snuff" movies are the apotheosis of metaphoric sexual butchering, embodying all the necessary components: the dagger as implement, the female victim, the defiling of the body and the fetishism of female parts. In the absence of an actual victim, snuff exists as a reminder of what happens to animals all the time.

In constructing stories about violence against women, feminists have drawn on the same set of cultural images as their oppressors. Feminist critics perceive the violence inherent in representations that collapse sexuality and consumption and have titled this nexus "carnivorous arrogance" (Simone de Beauvoir), "gynocidal gluttony" (Mary Daly), "sexual cannibalism" (Kate Millet), "psychic cannibalism" (Andrea Dworkin), "metaphysical cannibalism" (Ti-Grace Atkinson); racism as it intersects with sexism has been defined by bell hooks in distinctions based on meat eating: "The truth is—in sexist America, where women are objectified extensions of male ego, black women have been labeled hamburger and white women prime rib."[72] These feminist theorists take us to the intersection of the oppression of women and the oppression of animals and then do an immediate about-face, seizing the function of the absent referent only to forward women's issues, not animals', and so reflecting a patriarchal structure. Dealing in symbols and similes that express humiliation, objectification, and violation is an understandable attempt to impose order on a violently fragmented female sexual reality. When we use meat and butchering as metaphors for women's oppression, we express our own hog-squeal of the universe while silencing the primal hog-squeal of Ursula Hamdress herself.

When radical feminists talk as if cultural exchanges with animals are literally true in relationship to women, they invoke and borrow what is actually done to animals. It could be argued that the use of these metaphors is as exploitative as the posing of Ursula Hamdress: an anonymous pig somewhere was dressed, posed, and photographed. Was she sedated to keep that pose or was she, perhaps, dead? Radical feminist theory participates linguistically in exploiting and denying the absent referent by not including in their vision Ursula Hamdress's fate. They butcher the animal/woman cultural exchanges represented in the operation of the absent referent and then address themselves solely to women, thus capitulating to the absent referent, part of the same construct they wish to change.[73]

What is absent from much feminist theory that relies on metaphors of animals' oppression for illuminating women's experience is the reality behind the metaphor. Feminist theorists' use of language should describe and challenge oppression by recognizing the extent to which these oppressions are culturally analogous and interdependent.

So, too, should animal advocates be wary of language that uses rape metaphorically to describe what happens to animals, without basing their analysis on a recognition of the social context of rape for women in our culture. Metaphoric borrowing that depends on violation yet fails to protest the originating violence does not acknowledge interlocking oppressions. Our goal is to resist the violence that separates matter from spirit, to eliminate the structure that creates absent referents.

It is tempting to think that all that has been discussed in this chapter are words, ideas, "abstract nouns," how images work: that there is no flesh and no kitchen. But there is fragmented flesh and there are kitchens in which it is found. Animals may be an absent referent point in discourse but this need not continue. What if we heeded Marge Piercy's response to abstract nouns; let's go into the kitchen and consider not only "who they beat" but "who [we] eat"? In incorporating the fate of animals we would encounter these issues: the relationship between imperialism and meat eating in imposing a "white" diet of meat eating on the dietary folkways of people of color; the ecological implications of what I consider to be the fourth stage of meat eating—the eating of institutionalized, factory-farmed animals (after stages of (1) practically no meat eating, (2) eating meat of free animals, and (3) eating meat of domesticated animals); the meaning of our dependence on female animals for "feminized protein" such as milk and eggs; issues of racism and classism that arise as we consider the role of the industrialized countries in determining what "first class" protein is—all of which are a part of the sexual politics of meat.

There is a model for us of living, breathing connections awaiting incorporation in our theory; a logical next step in the progression of feminist thought is politicizing the ambiguity and slippage inherent in the metaphors of sexual violence, as well as their social, historical, and animal origins. The next chapter begins this politicizing process by analyzing the role of language in masking violence and defining the conflict between a dominant worldview that accepts meat eating and the muted minority viewpoint of vegetarianism.

chapter 3

Masked Violence, Muted Voices

> Women have had the power of *naming* stolen from us. . . . Inadequate words have been taken as adequate.
>
> —Mary Daly, *Beyond God the Father*

In the previous chapter, we were concerned with the consumption of the referent so that through metaphor it lost all meaning except by its reference to something else. In this chapter our concern is with the *objectification of consumption* through language, so that meat's true meaning is cast out. Behind every meat meal is an absence, the death of the animal whose place the meat takes. With the word "meat" the truth about this death is absent. Thus, in expressing their concern about eating animals, vegetarians cannot ignore the issue of language. In this they are not unlike feminists who find that issues of language imbricate women's oppression.

After using feminist insights to explore how language usage upholds meat eating, this chapter identifies the fusing through language of the oppressions of women and animals. It then considers the muting of vegetarian voices. Vegetarianism exposes meat eating as an effort at subordinating the natural to the human. But since meat eating carries legitimate meaning in the dominant culture that encourages the eating of animals, vegetarian meaning, like nature, is subordinated by meat eating.

Language as Mask

> We have no language that is free of the power dualisms of domination.
>
> —Beverly Harrison
> "Sexism and the Language of Christian Ethics"[1]

So far feminism has accepted the dominant viewpoint regarding the oppression of animals rather than shed the illuminating light of its theory on this oppression. Not only is our language male-centered, it is human-centered as well. When we use the adjective "male," such as in the preceding sentence, we all assume that it is referring solely to human males. Besides the human-oriented notions that accompany our use of words such as male and female, we use the word "animal" as though it did not refer to human beings, as though we too are not animals. All that is implied when the words "animal" and "beast" are used as insults maintains separation between human animals and nonhuman animals. We have structured our language to avoid the acknowledgment of our biological similarity.

Language distances us further from animals by naming them as objects, as "its." Should we call a horse, a cow, dog or cat, or any animal "it"? "It" functions for nonhuman animals as "he" supposedly functions for human beings, as a generic term whose meaning is deduced by context. Patriarchal language insists that the male pronoun is both generic, referring to all human beings, and specific, referring only to males. Similarly, "it" refers either to non-animate things or to animate beings whose gender identity is irrelevant or unknown. But just as the generic "he" erases female presence, the generic "it" erases the living, breathing nature of the animals and reifies their object status. The absence of a non-sexist pronoun allows us to objectify the animal world by considering all animals as "its." I recommend using [sic] when an animal is called "it" just as feminist critics have done when "he" is used generically. Should we even refer to a butchered part of an animal's body as "it"? Is meat an "it"? Isn't the choice of "it" for meat the final capitulation to the dominant reality that renders real animals invisible and masks violence? (Due to the lack of a generic pronoun, I will use "she" in this book to refer to any animal, alive or dead, whose sex is unknown.)

We also distance ourselves from animals through the use of metaphors or similes that distort the reality of other animals' lives. Our representations of animals make them refer to human beings rather than to themselves: one is sly as a fox, hungry as a bear, pretty as a filly. When we talk about the victimization of humans we use animal metaphors derived from animal sacrifice and animal experimentation: someone is a scapegoat or a guinea pig. Violence undergirds some of our most commonly used metaphors that cannibalize the experiences of animals: beating a dead horse, a bird in the hand, I have a bone to pick with you. (See Figure 3: Liberate Your Language.)

From the leather in our shoes, the soap we use to cleanse our face, the down in the comforter, the meat we eat, and the dairy products we rely

Figure 3
Liberate Your Language

Language is a powerful tool. The words we choose do more than name or describe things; they assign status and value. Be careful, then, how you choose words that refer to non-human animals, for you may be using expressions that maintain prejudices against them.

Referring to a non-human animal as an "it" strips *him* or *her* of dignity and perpetuates the view that other animals are objects, inferior things or property.

Referring to people who share their homes and lives with non-human animals as "owners" or "masters" connotes slavery, and we should be uncomfortable with the connotation. *Friends, companions* or *protectors* is preferable.

Avoid calling other animals "living things." They are *living beings.*

Refer to non-domestic animals as *free* or *free-roaming,* not "wild" or "wildlife."

When referring to animal suffering and death caused by human action, use painfully explicit words that reveal the true facts. "Euthanize," "put to sleep," "sacrifice" and "destroy" are favorites of animal researchers (and some animal control people) while "cull," "harvest," "manage" and "thin the herd" are favorites of hunters, trappers, and their ilk. These words mean *kill,* so say *kill.*

Guilty people try to cover up their horrifying cruelties against, and backward exploitation of, non-human animals with deceptive euphemisms like the ones above. Say it like it is, and correct others when they don't, so that people will realize the true nature and full extent of the suffering we inflict on other living beings.

Watch out, too, for expressions that convey contempt for animals. "Son-of-a-bitch," "bird-brain," and "hare-brain" are insults at the expense of animals. Think of alternatives to calling a person a "snake," "turkey," "ass," "weasel," "chicken," "dog" or the like.

Liberate your language, for it's an important step in liberating all animals!

—*By Noreen Mola and*
The Blacker Family
Animals' Agenda, 6, no. 8, October 1986, p. 18

on, our world as we now know it is structured around a dependence on the death of the other animals. For many this is neither disturbing nor surprising. The death of the other animals is an accepted part of life, either envisioned as being granted in Genesis 1:26 by a human-oriented God who instructs us that we may dominate the animals or conceptualized as a right because of our superior rationality. For those who hold to this dominant viewpoint in our culture, the surprise is not that animals are oppressed (though this is not the term they would use to express human beings' relationship to the other animals), the surprise is that anyone would object to this. Our culture generally accepts animals' oppression and finds nothing ethically or politically disturbing about the exploitation of animals for the benefit of people. Hence our language is structured to convey this acceptance.

We live in a culture that has institutionalized the oppression of animals on at least two levels: in formal structures such as slaughterhouses, meat markets, zoos, laboratories, and circuses, and through our language. That we refer to meat eating rather than to corpse eating is a central example of how our language transmits the dominant culture's approval of this activity.

Meat carries many meanings in our culture. However, no matter what else it does, meat eating signals the primary oppression of animals. Peter Singer observes that "for most humans, especially those in modern urban and suburban communities, the most direct form of contact with nonhuman animals is at meal time: we eat them. This simple fact is the key to our attitudes to other animals, and also the key to what each one of us can do about changing these attitudes."[2] Because animals have been made absent referents it is not often while eating meat that one thinks: "I am now interacting with an animal." We do not see our meat eating as contact with animals because it has been renamed as contact with food.

On an emotional level everyone has some discomfort with the eating of animals. This discomfort is seen when people do not want to be reminded of what they are eating while eating, nor to be informed of the slaughterhouse activities that make meat eating possible; it is also revealed by the personal taboo that each person has toward some form of meat: either because of its form, such as organ meats, or because of its source, such as pig or rabbit, insects or rodents. The intellectual framework of language that enshrouds meat eating protects these emotional responses from being examined. This is nothing new; language has always aided us in sidestepping sticky problems of conceptualization by obfuscating the situation.

While self-interest arising from the enjoyment of meat eating is obviously one reason for its entrenchment, and inertia another, a process of language usage engulfs discussions about meat by constructing the discourse in such a way that these issues need never be addressed. Language distances us from the reality of meat eating, thus reinforcing the symbolic meaning of meat eating, a symbolic meaning that is intrinsically patriarchal and male-oriented. Meat becomes a symbol for what is not seen but is always there—patriarchal control of animals and of language.

False Naming

> Undoubtedly our own meanings are partially hidden from us and it is difficult to have access to them. We may use the English language our whole lives without ever noticing the distortions and omissions.
>
> —Dale Spender[3]

> Him: I can't go to Italian restaurants with you anymore because I can't order my favorite meal: veal Parmesan.
>
> Her: Would you order it if it were called pieces of butchered, anemic baby calves?

Dale Spender refers to "the falseness of patriarchal terms."[4] Falseness pervades language about animals whom we eat. Recently, the British *Meat Trades Journal*—concerned about the association between meat and slaughtering—proposed replacing the words "butcher" and "slaughterhouse" with "meat plant" and "meat factory."[5] To this Emarel Freshel, an early twentieth-century vegetarian, would have retorted: "if the *words* which tell the truth about meat as food are unfit for our ears, the *meat* itself is not fit for our mouths."[6]

Through detachment, concealment, misrepresentation, and shifting the blame, the structure of the absent referent prevails: we see ourselves as eating pork chops, hamburger, sirloins, and so on, rather than 43 pigs, 3 lambs, 11 cows, 4 "veal" calves, 2,555 chickens and turkeys, and 861 fishes that the average American eats in a lifetime.[7] By speaking of meat rather than slaughtered, butchered, bleeding pigs, lambs, cows, and calves, we participate in language that masks reality. As an objector to meat eating complained in 1825, "No man says, therefore, of such an ox at pasture, Lo! how he lasheth his beefsteaks with his tail,—or he hath a fly upon his brisket."[8] Many vegetarians protest the use of euphemisms such as speaking of white meat rather than of breasts and of dark meat rather than thighs. Dismembered bodies are called "whole," creating the contradiction of purchasing a "whole bird" whose feathers, feet and head are missing. Can a dead bird really be a 'fresh young chicken" as the plastic wrapping at the meat counters proclaims?

To think comfortably about meat we are told in effect to "Forget the pig [or a cow, a chicken, etc.] is an animal." Instead, call her and view her as "a machine in a factory."[9] She becomes a food-producing unit, a protein harvester, an object, product, computerized unit in a factory environment, egg-producing machine, converting machine, a biomachine, a crop. A recent example of erasure of animals can be found in the United States Department of Agriculture's description of cows, pigs, and chickens as "grain-consuming animal units." As Colman McCarthy observes, this makes meat eaters "animal consuming human units."[10]

Language can make animals absent from a discussion of meat because the acts of slaughtering and butchering have already rendered the animal as absent through death and dismemberment. Through language we apply to animals' names the principles we have already enacted on their bodies. When an animal is called a "meat-bearing animal" we effect a misnomer, as though the meat is not the animal herself, as though the meat can be separated from the animal and the animal would still remain.

The desire to separate the concept of meat from thoughts about animals can be seen in the usage patterns that determine when the word "meat" is appended to the names of animals, such as we find in words like dogmeat or horsemeat. In our culture we generally append the word "meat" to an animal's name *only* when that form of meat is not consumed. As Paul Postal describes it, we form compounds with the word *"meat"* [such as horsemeat, dogmeat] "where the first element is the name of an animal type [such as horse, dog] only if American culture does not sanction the eating of that animal."[11] Thus we have *wombatmeat* but not *sheepmeat, dogmeat* but not *chickenmeat, horsemeat* but not *cowmeat.* Renaming is a constant: *sheepmeat* becomes *mutton, chickenmeat* drops the "meat" reference, and *cowmeat* undergoes numerous changes depending on the location from which the meat was derived (*chuck,* etc.) or the form *(hamburger).* If we retain the name of the animal to describe her as food, we drop the article "a" stripping the animal of any individuality: people eat turkey, not *a* turkey.

Josiah Royce and Mary Daly argue that "it is impossible to consider any term apart from its relations to the whole."[12] Vegetarians who challenge the fragmenting of the whole animal into edible parts wish to reunite the segmented terms with the whole. Joseph Ritson, an eighteenth-century vegetarian planned "A new Dictionary" that would have included these definitions:

> *Carrion.* The flesh of animals, naturally dead, or, at least, not artificially murdered by man.
>
> *Lobster.* A shel-fish [*sic*], which is boiled alive, by people of nice feelings & great humanity.[13]

Elsa Lanchester recalls how her mother, "Biddy" Lanchester—feminist, suffragette, socialist, pacifist, vegetarian—challenged the false naming of meat. When Elsa refers to the word "offal" she explains, "Biddy the vegetarian inspired the use of this word. That's what meat was to her."[14] Vegetarians choose words that parallel the effect of feminist terms such as *manglish* and *herstory,* which Varda One calls "reality-violators and consciousness-raisers."[15] To remind people that they are consuming dead animals, vegetarians create a variety of reality-violators and consciousness-raisers. Rather than call meat "complete protein," "iron-rich food," "life-giving food," "delectable," or "strength-inducing food" they refer to meat as "partly cremated portions of dead animals," or "slaughtered nonhumans," or in Bernard Shaw's words, "scorched corpses of animals." Like Benjamin Franklin, they consider fishing "unprovok'd murder" or refer, like Harriet Shelley to "murdered chicken."[16] (Buttons, T-shirts, posters, and stickers are now available announcing "meat is murder."[17])

Granted, vegetarian naming wrests meat eating from a context of acceptance; this does not invalidate its mission. One thing must be acknowledged about vegetarian naming as exemplified in the above examples: these are true words. The dissonance they produce is not due to their being false, but to their being *too* accurate. These words do not adhere to our common discourse which presumes the edibility of animals.

Just as feminists proclaimed that "rape is violence, not sex," vegetarians wish to name the violence of meat eating. Both groups challenge commonly used terms. Mary Daly calls the phrase "forcible rape" a reversal by redundancy because it implies that all rapes are not forcible.[18] This example highlights the role of language in masking violence, in this case an adjective deflects attention from the violence inherent in the meaning of the noun. The adjective confers a certain benignity on the word "rape." Similarly, the phrase "humane slaughter" confers a certain benignity on the term "slaughter." Daly would call this the process of "simple inversion": "the usage of terms and phrases to label . . . activities as the opposite of what they are."[19] The use of adjectives in the phrases "humane slaughter" and "forcible rape" promotes a conceptual misfocusing that relativizes these acts of violence. Additionally, as we ponder how the end is achieved, "forcibly," "humanely," our attention is continuously framed so that the absent referents—women, animals—do not appear. Just as all rapes are forcible, all slaughter of animals for food is inhumane regardless of what it is called.

To understand ethical vegetarianism, we must define meat eating. Meat eating fulfills Simone Weil's definition of force "—it is that *x* that turns anybody who is subjected to it into a *thing*."[20] Meat eating is to animals what white racism is to people of color, anti-Semitism is to Jewish people, homophobia is to gay men and lesbians, and woman hating is to women. All are oppressed by a culture that does not want to assimilate them fully on their grounds and with rights. Yet, an enormous void separates these forms of oppression of people from the form in which we oppress the other animals. We do not consume people. We do consume the other animals. Meat eating is the most oppressive and extensive institutionalized violence against animals. In addition, meat eating offers the grounds for subjugating animals: if we can kill, butcher, and consume them—in other words, completely annihilate them—we may, as well, experiment upon them, trap and hunt them, exploit them, and raise them in environments that imprison them, such as factory and fur-bearing animal farms.

Consider the reaction to the words of the dominant culture as portrayed in a children's book about a family of pigs.

> "Quick," said William, "Stand in a circle everyone," and he began to count round:
>
> *Ham, bacon, pork chop,*
> *Out you must hop.*
>
> Mrs. Pig held up her trotters in horror and turned away her eyes. "Goodness me, where do they pick up such words? I am sure they have never heard them in this house." (See Figure 4.)[21]

What distinguishes William and his siblings from being ham, bacon, or pork chop is an act of violence. This is what Mrs. Pig knows with horror and what we construct our language to avoid acknowledging.

Fused Oppressions

> Now they are led back to the slaughterhouse. I hear the soothing murmur of the herder making his sweet deceit. "Come along now, ladies. Be polite. No need to crowd. It's all the same in the end."
>
> —Richard Selzer imagining the ideal slaughterhouse[22]

Language fuses women's and animals' inferior status in a patriarchal culture. As we learned in chapter 1, meat-eating cultures are named *virile cultures*. In chapter 2 we saw that when violence against women is talked about, the referent point is slaughtered animals. The pairing of "meat eater" with "virile male" and women with animals suggests another pairing as well: In talking about the fate of animals we are talking about

Figure 4

"Quick," said William. "Stand in a circle everyone," and he began to count round:

Ham, bacon, pork chop,
Out you must hop.

Mrs Pig held up her trotters in horror and turned away her eyes. "Goodness me, where do they pick up such words? I am sure they have never heard them in this house."

Mary Rayner, *Garth Pig and the Ice Cream Lady* (New York: Atheneum, 1977), p. 5.

a traditional female fate. We oppress animals by associating them with women's lesser status.

A discussion of which pronouns one should use in reference to animals—whether one should call animals "it," "she," or "he"—demonstrates how in talking about the fate of animals we invoke femaleness. André Joly observes that the use of the word "it" "signifies basically that the animal is excluded from the human sphere and that no personal relationship of any kind is established with the speaker."[23] The use of the word "it" obviates any need to identify the sex of an animal. Yet, there are times when one uses "he" or "she" for an animal regardless of whether the animal actually is male or female. What grammatical rules decide this? Joly explains it this way: "Now any animal, however small or big, and irrespective of its sex, may be considered as a *major power* (he) or a *minor power* (she)." "He" is used when "whatever its size, the animal is presented as an active power and a possible danger to the speaker." "She" on the other hand signals a *"minor power."* This explains why whales are called "shes" and we hear from the crow's nest the call "There *she* blows!" As Joly points out, "sportsmen will often speak of a *hare* and a *fish* as *she*." He continues:

> In fact, *she* has acquired a very specific function in Modern English: it is expressly used to refer to an *animal regarded as a minor power.* This accounts in particular for the "professional" use of *she.* Sportsmen, whalers, fishermen are in special relation to the animal. Whatever its size or strength, it is regarded as a potential prey, a power that has to be destroyed—for sport or food—, hence a dominated power. (See Figure 5.)

Figure 5

he[1] ← *it*
animate: power — inanimate: no power

he[2] major power — *she* minor power

Adapted from: André Joly, "Toward a Theory of Gender in Modern English" in *Studies in English Grammar,* ed. André Joly and T. Fraser (Paris: Editions Universitaires, 1975), figure 8, p. 273.

"She" represents not only a "minor power," but a vanquished power, a soon-to-be-killed powerless animal. Male animals become symbolically female, representing the violated victim of male violence. In fact, the bloody flesh of the animal recalls the sex who cyclically bleeds. In this case, the symbolic rendering of animals' fate as female resonates with the literal facts about animals used for food. The sexual politics of meat is reinforced in the literal oppression of female animals.

We subsist by and large on female flesh. We eat female chickens because "males don't lay eggs, and the flesh of these strains is of poor quality."[24] (The males are equally victimized although not consumed.) Chickens and cows produce eggs and dairy products for us during their lives before being slaughtered. In this we exploit their femaleness as well. Meat textbooks recognize the female state as requiring special attentiveness. They caution slaughterers: "Animals should not be slaughtered in the advanced stages of pregnancy. The physiological condition of the female is disturbed and the flesh is not normal."[25] Animal bodies can be condemned as unfit for human consumption because of

> *Parturient Paresis.*—This is a condition of paralysis and loss of consciousness occurring usually at the termination of parturition.
>
> *Railroad Sickness.*—This condition, which is similar to parturient paresis in many respects, affects cows which are usually in the advanced stages of pregnancy and occurs during or after a long continued transportation by rail.[26]

The text of the body upon whom we write the fate of being meat is symbolically if not predominantly female.

One animal-rights and feminist writer comments on the English tradition of hunting hares, traditionally female (as in Playboy bunnies): "So important was the hare's femininity that breaking its [*sic*] back, with the foot was (and still is) called 'dancing on the hare', the usual erotic movement of courtship being transferred to death."[27] The language of the hunt implies that it is a variation of rape. For instance, the word *venison* (which originally included in its meaning the dead flesh of any beast or bird of the chase) comes from Latin *venetus:* to hunt; and is akin to the Sanskrit term meaning *he desires, attacks, gains.* According to the *American Heritage Dictionary,* the word *venery* had two definitions (now both archaic): *Indulgence in or the pursuit of sexual activity,* (from *venus,* love) and also *the act, art, or sport of hunting, the chase* (from *vener,* to hunt). Paul Shepard suggests that "there is a danger in all carnivores [including humans] of confusing the two kinds of veneral aggression, loving and hunting."[28] Kate Millet demonstrated in *Sexual Politics* that the word "fuck" was synonymous with "kill, hurt, or destroy."[28]

The fused oppression of women and animals through the power of naming can be traced to the story of the Fall in Genesis in which women and an animal, the serpent, are blamed for the Fall; Adam is entitled to name both Eve (after the Fall) and the other animals (before the Fall).

Since Adam's initial naming of woman and animals, patriarchal culture has presumed to continue naming those it oppresses. Stereotyping through dualism occurs with both women and animals: they are either good or evil, emblems of divine perfection or diabolical incarnations, Mary or Eve, pet or beast, sweet beasts *(bestes doulces)* or stenchy beasts *(bestes puantes)*.[30] We learn of the parallel legal categories of *femme covert* and *beste covert*—married woman, domesticated animal—and ponder the relationship between these legal categories and husbands and husbandmen, battered women and battery chicks.

Thinking Literally

> "coffin:" the *mould of paste for a pie; the crust of a pie.* Obsolete. "Season your lamb with pepper, salt . . . So put it into your coffin." (The 1750 *Complete Housewife*)
>
> —Definition and use of coffin, *The Oxford English Dictionary*

The issue of false naming is hidden behind the dichotomy of thinking literally or symbolically. The statement "meat is fragments of dead, butchered animals," or more baldly "meat is murder," speaks the literal truth and calls one away from symbolic thinking. Part of the battle of being heard as a vegetarian is being heard about literal matters in a society that favors symbolic thinking. By laying claim to speaking literally both the message and the method of vegetarianism are at odds with the dominant viewpoint.

An example from popular culture may help in discerning the way we fail to focus on the literal fate of animals. In *The Birds,* the shock of the violent attacks on people by the birds is acutely felt because there is no explanation as to why these birds have suddenly turned on humans. Yet at least two literal representations of the oppression of birds are offered in the movie. In the first, we find Alfred Hitchcock's signature—his appearance in the film—when he enters a pet shop full of caged birds. In the second, the local ornithologist, Mrs. Bundy, argues against the notion that birds would ever turn against humankind. This opinion is voiced in a restaurant as orders for "Three southern fried chicken" sound in the background. We are reminded of the fate of the birds (they are dead and fried), that they are victims of multiple violations (three chickens rather than one are ordered, each was first incarcerated and then murdered), though language obscures this fact, since the word chicken implies the singular. The literal chickenmeat about to be eaten appears to challenge Mrs. Bundy's opinion that birds have no reason for attacking humans. She acknowledges in general that human beings are a violent species, but her concern does not encompass the activities within that restaurant. The restaurant setting and the food consumed confirm her claim that humans are violent—that is, if one takes the setting and its activities literally. Both shoppers in a bird store and eaters of fried chickenmeat enact the acceptance of the structure of the absent referent, a structure that the birds through their massed presence appear insistently to avenge.

In examining the reactions of children to the literal truth about meat eating, we can see how our language is a distancing device from these literal facts. Children, fresh observers of the dominant culture, raise issues about meat eating using a literal viewpoint. One part of the socialization process to the dominant culture is the encouragement of children to view the death of animals for food as acceptable; to do so they must think symbolically rather than literally. "Vladimir Estragon" (the *Village Voice's* Geoffrey Stokes) sardonically observes, "Remind a kid that chicken was alive and there's a nasty scene, but let him think they make it in factories and everything is fine."[31]

Children often try to restore the absent referent. Dr. Alan Long reports of his becoming a vegetarian at eight: "I began to ask about the fate of the animals, and I began to inquire about the sources of my food, and I discovered to my horror that the lamb, the mutton on my plate, was obtained from the lambs I had seen in the fields. I said, in effect, that I liked lambs and I didn't like lamb, and that was the start of it all."[32] Harvard philosophy professor Robert Nozick credits his two-year-old daughter with bringing about his vegetarianism. During a Thanksgiving dinner, she queried: "That turkey wanted to live. Why was it [*sic*] killed?"[33] One three-year-old vegetarian demanded that he and his mother confront the local marketpersons with the literal truth that they were selling "poor dead mommie and baby animals."[34]

Most children, however, are inculcated into a basic aspect of patriarchal language by experiencing simultaneously the masks of language and the relativizing of the death of animals. The failure to consider meat literally becalms vegetarianism as an issue.

Muted Voices

> Difficulty arises when one group holds a monopoly on naming and is able to enforce its own particular bias on everyone,

> including those who do not share its view of the world. . . . The dominant reality remains the reference point even for those of us who seek to transform it.
>
> —Dale Spender, *Man Made Language*[35]

Vegetarians face the problem of making their meanings understood within a dominant culture that accepts the legitimacy of meat eating. As the feminist detective in Lynn Meyer's *Paperback Thriller* remarks early in the novel, "I could tell you now that I'm a vegetarian, but let's just leave it at that. I won't go into the reasons. If you don't understand them, there's not much I can say; and if you do, there's no need for me to say anything." But she does go on to explain, and traces her vegetarianism to learning the literal truth about meat eating as a child: "It all goes back to a duckling I had when I was a kid. It grew up to be a duck, and then we killed it and cooked it. And I wouldn't eat it. Couldn't. From that, it was all obvious and logical."[36]

The difficulty of introducing meaning for which there is no conceptual space has been theorized by anthropologist Edwin Ardener as a problem of dominance and mutedness. The theory of dominance-mutedness explains why vegetarians are not heard by the dominant culture. The term "muted" connotes issues of language and power. As Elaine Showalter explains it, "muted groups must mediate their beliefs through the allowable forms of dominant structures."[37] Vegetarians are frustrated in their attempts to unmask violence by the muting of their voices.

When vegetarians protest meat eating, they are silenced in a patriarchal world because the dominant viewpoint holds that thinking about animals "ain't no everyday thought." These are the words of Janie, the hero of Zora Neale Hurston's *Their Eyes Were Watching God,* to her husband after he purchases an old and overworked mule to protect her from further abuse. Janie had been outraged by the mistreatment of this tired and misused mule. Though "a little war of defense for helpless things was going on inside her," she speaks only to herself about the disgraceful activities. Her husband, upon overhearing her, acts in the mule's defense. Janie places his action within the historic tradition of liberators: "Freein' dat mule makes uh mighty big man outa you. Something like George Washington and Lincoln." Here she creates her own mythopoesis, enlarging the meaning of an individual's actions so that it carries political importance; actions that are usually muted within a dominant culture that decides what is appropriately political. Janie concludes, "You have tuh have power tuh free things."[38]

Mary Helen Washington sees Hurston's novel as representing "women's exclusion from power, particularly the power of oral speech."[39] The mule episode reflects this issue: Janie mutes her voice, at first talking only to herself, yet she is empowered to speak on behalf of another being. This empowerment may arise from recognizing the fused oppression of women and mules—silenced and overworked. As her grandmother told here: "De nigger woman is de mule uh de world so fur as Ah can see."[40] Lorraine Bethel, interpreting this passage's meaning, explains: "Throughout the remainder of the novel we observe Janie's struggle against conforming to this definition of the Black woman."[41] When Janie is concerned about the fate of a real mule, she herself could be seen as the absent referent in an oppressive structure. To Janie, challenging the fate of domesticated, objectified beings follows upon her grandmother's insights; Janie is defying "her status as mule of the world" simultaneously with challenging the mule's status.[42]

Janie's muted voice is heard and responded to; when she proclaims Jody a liberator her public speaking is applauded: " 'Yo' wife is uh born orator, Starks. Us never knowed dat befo'. She put jus' de right words tuh our thoughts.' "[43] But the applause is indirect; it is her husband who is complimented, and Janie is only the indirect recipient of recognition for raising a muted voice against dominant beliefs. She remains still an object who reflects glory upon her husband.[44] "It ain't no everyday thought" to think about those beings who become our absent referents; these thoughts are muted. Janie's is a female voice muted in a male world; this is how we need to consider vegetarian protests.

When vegetarians attempt to disarm the dominant control of language, they are seen as picky, particular, embittered, self-righteous, confrontative, and especially sentimental, rather than political liberators like Washington and Lincoln. The objection to the killing of animals is equated with sentimentality, childish emotions, or "Bambi-morality." By extension, this objection is seen as "womanish." Spinoza's oft-quoted opinion was that "The objection to killing animals was 'based upon an empty superstition and womanish tenderness, rather than upon sound reason.' "[45] Consequently it is no wonder that vegetarianism has been seen as a woman's project and equated with women's status.

The attack on vegetarians for being emotional demonstrates how the dominant culture attempts to deflect critical discourse. As Brigid Brophy comments, "To assert that someone other than oneself has rights is not sentimental. Not that it would be the gravest of sins if it were. 'Sentimentalist' is the abuse with which people counter the accusation that they are cruel."[46] The characterization of the objection to animals killed for food as feminine or "womanish" because of its perceived "emotional" tone contributes to its muting through its association with women who are also muted in a patriarchal culture.

New Naming

> What are the words you do not have? What do you need to say? What are the tyrannies you swallow day by day and attempt to make your own, until you will sicken and die of them, still in silence?
>
> —Audre Lorde, "The Transformation of Silence into Language and Action"[47]

Vegetarians reform inadequate language by coining new words. Through new naming, vegetarians apply principles that demand that the existing relationship between human beings and the other animals be changed.

Let us consider some examples of the new naming engendered by vegetarianism:

New Naming: Vegetarian

Until 1847 and the self-conscious coining of the word "vegetarian," the most common appellation to describe those who did not eat animals was the term "Pythagorean." As with many other reform movements, self-naming through the coining of the word "vegetarian" was an important milestone. The word vegetarian can be described in words similar to those Nancy Cott uses to explain the appearance of the word feminism: "Feminism burst into clear view a few years later because it answered a need to represent in language a series of intentions and a constituency just cohering, a new moment in the long history of struggles for women's rights and freedoms."[48] The word "vegetarian" represents the intersection of a historic moment with centuries of protest against the killing of animals.

Yet the coining of this word has caused a conflict in interpretation about its etymology. *The Oxford English Dictionary* states that the name is derived irregularly from "veget-able" plus "arian". Vegetarians hold to a different etymology. They argue that it is "from the Latin word *vegetus,* meaning 'whole, sound, fresh or lively,' as in the ancient Latin term *homo vegetus*—a mentally and physically vigorous person. Thus, the English vegetarians were trying to make a point about the philosophical and moral tone of the lives they sought to lead. They were not simply promoting the use of vegetables in the diet."[49] (Later in the nineteenth century when the Vegetarian Society debated a name change, Francis Newman proposed "anti-creophagist" but got little support for this new name.[50])

From this self-naming arises a constant battle for meaning, which consigns vegetarians to appearing even more literal minded (or petty or narrow-minded), for inevitably the word has been corrupted. The battle for meaning occurs over who, precisely, is a vegetarian. Vegetarianism as a word defining a certain set of "restrictions" has been appropriated by meat eaters who dilute it by the inclusion of chickenmeat and fishmeat in their definition. Can one eat dead fishes or chickens and be a vegetarian?

What is literally transpiring in the widening of the *meaning* of vegetarianism is the weakening of the *concept* of vegetarianism by including within it some living creatures who were killed to become food. Ethical vegetarians complain of this because they know it signifies that the structure of the absent referent is prevailing; once the concept is tolerated—i.e., some beings may be consumed—then their radical protest is being eviscerated. People who eat fishmeat and chickenmeat are not vegetarians; they are omnivores who do not eat red meat. Allowing those who are not vegetarians to call themselves vegetarians dismembers the word from its meaning and its history. It also, on a very practical level, redounds on vegetarians who appear at restaurants or parties where nonvegetarians have prepared "vegetarian food" only to find that this means dead fishes or a dead chicken.

Vegetarians are muted when made to feel that they are the insensitive, picky ones by complaining when people call themselves vegetarians even though they eat dead chickens and fishes. The process of neutralization/generalizing of the word vegetarian so that it only means objection to red meat—which even meat eaters see as having merit because of cholesterol concerns—is one of the consequences of seeking to establish new naming within a dominant culture resistant to it.

New Naming: Animalized and Feminized Protein

Animalized protein is a historical term deserving current use. This term was used in the nineteenth century to refer to food from animals' bodies. A letter from Ellen G. White in 1896 represents the way vegetarians used this term:

> The diet of the animals is vegetables and grains. Must the vegetables be animalized, must they be incorporated into the system of animals, before we get them? Must we obtain our vegetable diet by eating the flesh of dead creatures?[51]

The animalizing of protein is the main agent in the structure of the absent referent. The term "animalized" in describing meat achieves the goal of reinserting the absent referent into the discussion, acting as a reminder of what process is used to produce meat—the feeding and fattening of animals. Through the animalizing of protein animals are reduced to being means to our ends, converted from being some*one* to some*thing*. They are seen as bodies to be manipulated as incubators of protein. As a concept, the animalizing of protein posits that this is the proper way for humans to get their protein, and that the proper role for animals is to produce this protein. But as a phrase, animalized protein insists that animals cannot be left out of the definition of meat eating.

A corollary and prelude to animalized protein is *feminized protein:* milk and eggs. Again, animals are means to our ends, this time as producers of dairy products. Besides the bee's production of honey, the only beings who produce food from their own body *while living* are females of child-bearing age who produce milk and eggs.[52] Female animals become oppressed by their femaleness, and become essentially surrogate wet-nurses. These other animals are oppressed as *Mother* animals. When their productiveness ends, then they are butchered and become animalized protein. Vegans boycott feminized *and* animalized protein.

New Naming: The Fourth Stage

New naming is required to identify the recent developments in the way animals animalize protein. Since World War II, a new way of treating animals has evolved that is named in euphemistic terms, "factory farming." I suggest we consider the development that incarcerates animals into these misnamed factory farms as the fourth stage of meat eating. The first stage in the development of people's meat eating was that of relying predominantly on vegetarian foods, and what little meat (from small animals or bugs) consumed was acquired with one's hands or sticks. The first stage of meat eating met Plutarch's "do-it-yourself" standards for eating animals described in the previous chapter.

Hunting is the second stage of meat eating. When meat is obtained through killing animals who are not domesticated, there is little reliance on feminized protein. With the second stage, implemental violence is introduced, as well as the selection of some members of a community to be hunters. Distance from the animal is achieved through the implements used to kill the animal as well as from the division of a culture into hunters and nonhunters.

The third stage of meat eating is the domestication of animals, providing them with the trappings of care and security while planning their execution. With the third stage, meat consumption increases because meat is now from domesticated, easily available, animals. Domestication of animals provides another food resource: feminized protein.

The fourth stage of meat eating involves the imprisoning of animals. In the fourth stage we find the highest per capita consumption of animalized and feminized protein: 60 percent of the food Americans now eat is provided by the meat, dairy, and egg industries. Animals are separated from most people's everyday experience, except in their final fate as food. With the fourth stage, we have started thinking in terms of how much meat or dairy products we need, rather than how much protein we need. This is because animalized protein and feminized protein made up two out of the four basic food groups. Seventy percent of protein for Americans is derived from these two food groups; in contrast, 80 percent of the protein in the Far East is from vegetable proteins.

The changes in the stages of meat eating signal the increasing dependence of a culture on the structure of the absent referent. In addition, the changes in the stages of meat eating signal the increasing interpolation of white racism—because of failure to understand alternative protein sources—into the structure of the absent referent. If androcentrism through white racism eliminates competing models for relationships between men and women, white racism upholds a model of consumption that fixates on animalized protein and obscures the use of alternative protein sources that characterize the majority of second stage cultures. White racism distorts cultures that were or are gynocentric and not completely dependent on animalized protein.[53]

New Namers: Charlotte and Vegetarian Protest Literature

A model for alternative naming can be found in one of the most famous writers and weavers of webs: Charlotte in E. B. White's *Charlotte's Web*. Charlotte weaves words into her web to prevent the butchering of Wilbur the pig. Rather than accede to the false naming of Wilbur the pig as pork, bacon, and ham, Charlotte effects new naming: Wilbur is "some pig," not a meat-bearing animal but rather "terrific."[54] Charlotte's words are a form of vegetarian protest literature. The alternative naming of this protest literature attempts to keep all Wilburs alive and whole, rather than dead, fragmented, and renamed.

Once we stop thinking of meat eating as a set of nutritional or evolutionary givens, we are free instead to examine language about meat eating as historical justificatory strategies. Language about eating animals creates cultural meaning in support of oppressing animals. Protest literature that challenges this cultural meaning has most frequently appeared in the form of the essay, which can be traced from Plutarch to contemporary nonfiction works. These attempts to untangle the web of violence against animals and weave new words. This protest literature is characterized by a self-conscious tradition with certain recurring themes and images. An essential aspect of this protest literature is the rephrasing of questions meat eaters pose. Plutarch says in response to the question of why it was that Pythagoras abstained from eating flesh: "You ought rather, in my opinion, to have enquired who first began this practice, than who of late times left it off."[55] Or Bernard Shaw who retorted when asked why he was a vegetarian, why do you call me to account for eating decently?

The following chapter explores the dynamics that occur when meat eaters call vegetarians to account for eating decently. This analysis pinpoints that which prevents the vegetarian word from being made flesh. The subtle barriers which prevent the hearing of vegetarian words represent the final elements in the patriarchal texts of meat.

chapter 4

The Word Made Flesh

The Teachings of Pythagoras

There was a man here. . . .
. . . .
He was first
To say that animal food should not be eaten,
And learned as he was, men did not always
Believe him when he preached, "Forbear, O mortals,
To spoil your bodies with such impious food!"

—Ovid, *Metamorphoses*

A Word made Flesh is seldom
And tremblingly partook.

—Emily Dickinson

This chapter considers the dialectic between those who hear vegetarian words and become vegetarians and the majority who do not. While there are many who follow in Pythagoras's steps and say "Forbear, O mortals, / To spoil your bodies with such impious food!" most people respond as did Pythagoras's listeners: they do not believe the words they hear. The proselytizing vegetarian, no matter how learned, encounters subtle barriers which prevent hearing the protests being articulated. Most vegetarians do not perceive these subtle barriers. One reason is that their own conversion to vegetarianism leads them to believe that others can also be converted. Another factor in the failure to perceive these barriers is the absence of a feminist perspective on the issue of eating animals that would emphasize the primacy of political and cultural forces. A major factor in weakening the vegetarian argument is the time and place during which vegetarian ideas are discussed: frequently at dinnertime over a meal, a time when a vegetarian often finds her/himself in the minority. This creates a political climate in which the idea of vegetarianism is defeated both by the presence of meat and the idea of meat eating. A cultural perspective determines this defeat as well; I will argue that it is connected to our ideas about stories and their proper endings.

After considering the reforming impulse of vegetarians, the fact that vegetarian conversion does take place and is related to reading vegetarian protest literature this chapter offers an analysis of those subtle political and cultural forces that prevail over vegetarian words.

Various meanings to the idea of the word made flesh exist. The first meaning is perhaps the most obvious: converting from meat eating to vegetarianism as a result of hearing or reading someone's vegetarian arguments; this embodies in the flesh the vegetarian word. At dinnertime, conversations about meat eating involve an alternative word made flesh: meat eaters' arguments are reinforced by the literal presence of animal flesh. Their words endorse this flesh; the flesh reinforces the words. Lastly, in the subtle ways that meat eating adheres to traditional narrative structure, the words of stories and the flesh of meals become interchangeable.

Vegetarian Protest Literature

> For what is finally at stake is not so much how "to make visible the invisible" as how to produce the conditions of visibility for a different social subject.
>
> —Teresa de Lauretis[1]

A body of literature that proclaims vegetarianism's legitimacy stretches from Plutarch's two essays against meat eating to contemporary books such as *Vegetarianism: a Way of Life, The Vegetarian Alternative,* and *A Vegetarian Sourcebook.*[2] They argue for the reasonableness of vegetarianism and the necessity to adopt it. Historical examples of this genre can be found in numerous vegetarian writings of the eighteenth, nineteenth, and early twentieth centuries. My three-and-a-half-year-old son determined to add his own voice to his body as a way of convincing his father to stop eating dead chickens. Frustrated that conversations over dinnertime were not succeeding, he created a "Don't Eat Meat" book. As he wrote in it, he reported on what he was writing:

Don't eat fish.
Don't each chicken.
Don't eat crabs.
Don't eat whales.
Don't eat roosters.
Don't eat octopus.
Don't eat chicken.
Don't eat fish.
Don't eat lobsters.

Unable to spell, what he inscribed were signs meaningful only to him. These are emblematic of the way a meat-eating culture greets vegetarian writings: they may be well written but ultimately they are without meaning. Vegetarians, despite the variety of ways in which to argue their perspective, always appear to be saying, "Don't eat meat." Meat eaters cannot make sense of this because a part of their definition of what makes sense is eating meat. Yet, vegetarians believe that they will be heard by a meat-eating culture. Literal faith in the word made flesh through books was not lost on my son. Once he had written down his important injunctions he announced to his father, "Sorry, Daddy, but you can't eat meat anymore. I wrote it."

The Vegetarian Word Made Flesh

As my son may have intuited, vegetarians' relationships to earlier vegetarian writings demonstrates that vegetarianism is often parented to a large degree by books. Their own vegetarianism becomes a way of making the vegetarian word flesh. Historian Keith Thomas describes this influence: "Their inspiration was often literary, many claiming to have been converted by reading the arguments of Pythagoras or Plutarch."[3] In a culture where the majority eat meat, reading texts is often the only way by which vegetarianism is presented in a positive light. In essence, the authority of previous vegetarian texts authors new vegetarians who take vegetarian words literally.

It is thought that Percy Shelley's vegetarianism arose from reading Plutarch's two essays on flesh eating. By patterning the title of his first vegetarian essay—*A Vindication of Natural Diet*—after Mary Wollstonecraft's infamous *A Vindication of the Rights of Woman* he intimates that he may be bearing a feminist word as well.

Aphra Behn celebrates seventeenth-century vegetarian Thomas Tryon's methods for healthy living and explains that his writings have influenced her to try his methods.[4] After reading Tryon, Benjamin Franklin tried vegetarianism for a while as well.[5]

Joseph Ritson, author of the 1802 *An Essay on Abstinence from Animal Food as a Moral Duty,* became a vegetarian by taking literally the words of an earlier text. Ritson reports—in introducing himself as the author of his vegetarian book—that he was

> induc'd to serious reflection, by the perusal of Mandevilles *Fable of the bees,* in the year 1772, being the 19th year of his age, has ever since, to the reviseal of this sheet, firmly adhere'd to a milk and vegetable diet, haveing, at least, never tasteëd, dureing the whole course of those thirty years, a morsel of flesh, fish, or fowl.[6]

The passage from Mandeville that prompted this change of diet reads:

> I have often thought, if it was not for this Tyranny which Custom usurps over us, that Men of any tolerable Good-nature could never be reconcil'd to the killing of so many Animals for their daily Food, as long as the bountiful Earth so plentifully provides them with Varieties of vegetable Dainties.[7]

Historian James Turner implies that Ritson took Mandeville's words literally when they were meant ironically. Mandeville's book, Turner writes, "belittled the supposed differences between men and animals and wondered (tongue in cheek?) whether people would continue to eat animals if they stopped to ponder what they were doing."[8] One of Ritson's biographers acknowledges that the influence of Mandeville on Ritson "notably reveals the vital way in which his reading affected him."[9] Near the end of his *Essay,* Ritson refers to the similar effect the speech of Pythagoras in Ovid's *Metamorphoses* had upon Lord Chesterfield, who reported that "it was some time before I could bring myself to our college-mutton again, with some inward doubt, whether I was not making myself an accomplice to a murder."[10]

As a teenager, Robert Browning read Percy Shelley's writings and became a practicing vegetarian for two years.[11] When he arrived in London, Gandhi's discovery of the writings of his British contemporary, Henry Salt, specifically his *A Plea for Vegetarianism,* provided the ethical grounding he needed to continue his vegetarianism. Gandhi reported,

"From the date of reading this book, I may claim to have become a vegetarian by choice."[12] Bernard Shaw attributes his vegetarianism to the influence of Percy Shelley: " 'It was Shelley,' he recorded in one of his *Sixteen Self Sketches,* 'who first opened my eyes to the savagery of my diet,' though 'it was not until 1880 or thereabouts that the establishment of vegetarian restaurants in London made a change practicable for me.' " Feminist, vegetarian, and pacifist Charlotte Despard was greatly influenced by Shelley's *Queen Mab.*

Today many people encounter the idea of vegetarianism not through reading vegetarian words but by discussing vegetarianism with a vegetarian. This often occurs over a meal. What transpires is the opposite of the vegetarian word made flesh. At dinnertime, vegetarians can become unwittingly embattled when the texts of meat are simultaneously broached conversationally and incarnated on the dinner plate.

Embattled Conversations

> An individual woman who appears as the spokeswoman for the freedom of all women is a pathetic and isolated creature. . . . She presents no threat. An individual "emancipated" woman is an amusing incongruity, a titillating commodity, easily consumed.
>
> —Sheila Rowbotham[14]

> Remark upon learning of the death of Dr. Lambe, early nineteenth-century vegetarian author:
>
> "If he wished, rather rashly, to deprive us of flesh diet, nevertheless he must be forgiven. For whom then did he harm? So far as I know none, unless it were himself, for no-one else paid attention to it."[15]

Vegetarianism provokes conversation, but vegetarianism faces the problem of making its meanings understood within a dominant discourse that approves of meat eating. A sempiternal concern of vegetarians is the fate of their beliefs when talking with meat eaters. The most likely place to experience a conflict in meaning between vegetarians and meat eaters is during dinnertime. That vegetarians discuss their vegetarianism is inevitable. For if vegetarians do not volunteer opinions, like Sir Richard Phillips "who once rang a peal" in William Cobbett's ears "against shooting and hunting," they are continually called upon to defend their diet.[16]

Harriot Kezia Hunt, nineteenth-century American feminist health reformer and friend of vegetarian and feminist Mary Gove Nichols, demonstrates this in reporting that "I always quarreled with her Grahamism."[17] John Oswald opens his 1791 vegetarian book by stating that he is "fatigued with answering the enquiries, and replying to the objections of his friends, with respect to the singularity of his mode of life." With the publication of his *The Cry of Nature; or, an Appeal to Mercy and to Justice on Behalf of the Persecuted Animals,* he expresses the hope that he can pursue his diet "without molestation" as he now has set forth his thoughts about meat eating.[18]

Thomas Holcroft seems proud of himself as he confides to his journal the gist of his dinner conversation with a vegetarian:

> June 24th, 1798
> —Dined, Godwin and Reece present. . . . Spoke to Mr. Reece on the morality of eating animal food: he said we had no right to kill animals, and diminish the quantity of sensation. I answered that the quantity of sensation was greatly increased; for that the number of living animals was increased, perhaps ten, perhaps a hundred fold, by the care which man bestowed on them; and that as I saw no reason to suppose they meditated on, or had any fore-knowledge of death, the pain of dying to them is scarcely worth mentioning. . . . Ritson joined our party in the evening.[19]

In a situation where flesh is consumed, vegetarians inevitably call attention to themselves. They have made something absent on their plates; perhaps a verbal demurral has been required as well. They then are drawn into a discussion regarding their vegetarianism. Frequently, there will be someone present who actually feels hostile to vegetarianism and regards it as a personal challenge. If this is the case, all sorts of outrageous issues are thrown out to see how the vegetarian will handle them. The vegetarian, enthusiastic reformer, sees the opportunity as one of education; but it is not. Instead it is a teasing game of manipulation. At times, ludicrous questions are raised; they imply that the entire discussion is ludicrous.

George Borrow, reporting on a dinnertime conversation with Sir Richard Phillips, Romantic radical and publisher, demonstrates this phenomenon:

> "You eat no animal food, sir?" said I.
>
> "I do not, sir," said he; "I have forsworn it upwards of twenty years. In one respect, sir, I am a Brahmin. I abhor taking away life—the brutes have as much right to live as ourselves."

"But," said I, "if the brutes were not killed, there would be such a superabundance of them, that the land would be overrun with them."

"I do not think so, sir; few are killed in India, and yet there is plenty of room."

"But," said I, "Nature intended that they should be destroyed, and the brutes themselves prey upon one another, and it is well for themselves and the world that they do so. What would be the state of things if every insect, bird and worm were left to perish of old age?"

"We will change the subject," said the publisher; "I have never been a friend to unprofitable discussions."[20]

The situation is established not only to provoke defensiveness but to sidetrack the reformer into answering the wrong questions, as Phillips implies by changing the conversation. In this, the pattern of discourse resembles that of dinnertime conversations about feminism in the early 1970s. Questions of definition often predominate. Whereas feminists were parlaying questions which trivialized feminism such as "Are you one of those bra burners?" vegetarians must define themselves against the trivializations of "Are you one of those health nuts?" or "Are you one of those animal lovers?" While feminists encountered the response that "men need liberation too," vegetarians are greeted by the postulate that "plants have life too." Or to make the issue appear more ridiculous, the position is forwarded this way: "But what of the lettuce and tomato you are eating; they have feelings too!"

The attempt to create defensiveness through trivialization is the first conversational gambit which greets threatening reforms. This pre-establishes the perimeters of discourse. One must explain that no bras were burned at the Miss America pageant, or the symbolic nature of the action of that time, or that this question fails to regard with seriousness questions such as equal pay for equal work. Similarly, a vegetarian, thinking that answering these questions will provide enlightenment, may patiently explain that if plants have life, then why not be responsible solely for the plants one eats at the table rather than for the larger quantities of plants consumed by the herbivorous animals before they become meat? In each case a more radical answer could be forwarded: "Men need first to acknowledge how they benefit from male dominance," "Can anyone really argue that the suffering of this lettuce equals that of a sentient cow who must be bled out before being butchered?" But if the feminist or vegetarian responds this way they will be put back on the defensive by the accusation that they are being aggressive. What to a vegetarian or a feminist is of political, personal, existential, and ethical importance, becomes for others only an entertainment during dinnertime.

After trivialization, the discourse challenges the legitimacy of the issues. A feminist would encounter an earnest couple, with either the man or the woman asserting that they are a very happy couple: "Does my wife (Do I) look oppressed?" There really was no interest in a complex feminist analysis of oppression. Similarly, vegetarians encounter this: "Would you make carnivorous animals become vegetarian too? What about your (our) dog, cat?" In each case, the reformer is made to appear that she or he would take analysis or reform too far, disrupting the sacred nature of established relationships (a marriage, a carnivorous animal).

The rules regarding politeness at dinnertime favor the status quo and limit the range of the conversation. By the mid seventies when the issues of rape, domestic violence, and pornography were quickly gaining prominence as feminist issues, were feminists to anatomize the problem of violence against women during pleasant hours of conversing and eating? Correspondingly, vegetarians who are asked why they are vegetarians while everyone else eats meat must consider: do they really want to know that I object to the way animals are butchered, and how much detail can I supply when everyone else is eating meat? What are my duties to the hostess?

What one faces at this time are efforts at disempowerment. That which is threatening, such as feminism and vegetarianism, must be redefined, delimited, disempowered. Often one individual holds the position of redefining, delimiting, disempowering the vegetarian. A feminist's emphasis on sexual violence is judged as hysterical; a vegetarian's emphasis on the death of animals as emotional. Both feminists and vegetarians are accused of negativity because they appear to require that something be given up (the most obvious trappings of femininity; the meat on the plate) as opposed to their own perspective in which they are emphasizing the positive choice (aspiring to emancipation and liberation; choosing vegetables, grains, and fruits). Who is a feminist or a vegetarian becomes a vexed question and the principles behind feminism and vegetarianism are transformed into "being moralistic."[21]

As though a text of meat must be recapitulated on the level of discourse—the flesh made word—you become the rabbit, the other person the hunter who must vindicate the sport. You will be teased, you will be baited. You are the quarry, not your beliefs. The other attacks, backs off. This activity may be neither as blatant nor aggressive as the following anecdote reveals, but the issue of control over the conversation is similar:

> Well knowing Ritson's holy horror of all animal food, Leyden complained that the joint on the table was overdone. "Indeed, for that

> matter," cried he, "meat can never be too little done, and raw is best of all." He sent to the kitchen accordingly for a plate of literally raw beef, and manfully ate it up, with no sauce but the exquisite ruefulness of the Pythagorean's glances.[22]

Though you are kept under control by this control of conversation, you appear to be the manipulator, the one who is redefining, delimiting, disempowering meat eating, and the other is the protector of the meaning of meat eating:

> On their return to the cottage, [Sir Walter] Scott inquired for the *learned cabbage-eater,* meaning Ritson, who had been expected to dinner. "Indeed," answered his wife, "you may be happy he is not here, he is so very disagreeable. Mr. Leyden, I believe, frightened him away." It turned out that it was even so. When Ritson appeared, a round of cold beef was on the luncheon-table, and Mrs. Scott, forgetting his peculiar creed, offered him a slice. The antiquary, in his indignation, expressed himself in such outrageous terms to the lady, that Leyden first tried to correct him by ridicule.

At a dinner where meat is eaten, the vegetarian must lose control of the conversation. The function of the absent referent must be kept absent especially when incarnated on the platter at the table. The flesh and words about it must be kept separate. Meat eaters cannot capitulate to vegetarianism at this point; they would have to re-vision their menus while in the midst of adhering to the texts of meat.

The meaning of meat is reproduced each time it is served and eaten. Food in general and meat in specific, like the female body, is a "site of visual pleasure, or lure of the gaze."[23] Vegetarianism announces that it will destroy the pleasure of meals as they are now experienced. Thus it is a given that vegetarians will be unable to determine the shape of the discourse when eating with meat eaters. But, it is inevitable that vegetarians will eat with meat eaters; and it is also inevitable that the absence of meat on their table will touch off a discussion. In this situation, the *issue of vegetarianism is a form of meat to meat eaters:* it is something to be trapped and dismembered, it is a "dead issue." Vegetarian words are treated like animal flesh.

While the codes of the texts of meat must be broken down, they cannot be broken down when meat is present because it reifies the old codes. And while the vegetarian is faulted for a failure to maintain objectivity, none at the dinner table is actually objective. Complicating the lack of objectivity is the fact that vegetarianism as it is experienced by meat eaters is ambiguous: just what does one replace meat with? The final complication is the existence of the "story of meat," which influences the perspective of meat eaters. When I say the story of meat I refer to the worldview that determines that meat is acceptable food. This viewpoint consists of various parts similar to the sequence a story follows.

The Story of Meat

> These pheasants of course, if one wanted to be legalistic about it, wouldn't be here at all if we hadn't put them here, got the eggs, hatched them out, reared the chicks—you might say we gave them life and then after a bit we take it away again—arrogating to ourselves somewhat God-like powers I must admit. But let's not bother with all that.
>
> —The host of a shooting party
> in Isabel Colegate's *The Shooting Party*[24]

The story of meat follows the narrative structure of story telling. Alice B. Toklas implies this in her cookbook when, in a chapter entitled "Murder in the Kitchen," she uses the style of a detective story to describe killing and cooking animals.[25] Through recipes she provides the appropriate conclusion to the animals' death according to the texts of meat; the animal becomes delectable, edible.

There are some incontrovertible assumptions that determine our approach to life: Stories have endings, meals have meat. Let us explore whether these statements are interchangeable—stories have meat, that is, meaning, and meals have endings. When vegetarians take meat out of the meal, they take the ending out of the story of meat. Vegetarians become caught within a structure they attempt to eliminate. Our experience of meat eating cannot be separated from our feelings about stories.

We are a species who tell stories. Through narrative we confer meaning upon life. Our histories are structured as stories that postulate beginnings, crises, resolutions; dramas and fictions animate our imagination with stories that obviously have a beginning and an end. Narrative, by definition, moves forward toward resolution. By the time the story is concluded we have achieved some resolution, whether comic or tragic, and we are given access to the meaning of the story as a whole. Often meaning can only be apprehended once the story is complete. Detective stories demonstrate the closure of narrative, because the act of discovering at the end of the story who really "done it" often causes a reordering of all that transpired before the end of the story. Closure accomplishes the revelation of meaning and reinscribes the idea that meaning is achieved through closure.

Meat eating is story applied to animals, it gives meaning to animals' existence. To say this is to take Roland Barthes's statement literally: "Narrative is first and foremost a prodigious variety of genres, themselves distributed amongst different substances—as though any material were fit to receive human's stories."[26] Animals' lives and bodies become material fit to receive human's stories: the word becomes flesh.

We can isolate determining points in which the creation of meat recalls the movement of narration. There is a beginning, a postulating of origins that positions the beginning of the story: we give animals life. There is the drama of conflict, in this case of death. And there is the closure, the final summing up, which provides resolution to the drama: the consumption of the animal.

The story of meat follows a sacred typology: the birth of a god, the dismemberment of the god's body, and the god's resurrection. This sacred story paves the way for a mundane enaction of the meaning of dismemberment and resurrection—achieved through consumption of meat.

The story begins with the birth of the animal, who would not have existed if meat eating did not require the animal's body. As we saw, Holcroft confides to his journal that his argument against vegetarianism is that meat eating has given innumerable animals life and thus increased "the quantity of sensation." His is one of the most frequently reiterated defenses of meat eating in which benignity is conferred with the beginning of the story because life has been conferred upon an animal. Here we have the reassurance that accompanies the doubling of origins: the birth of an animal and the beginning of the story lock the story in a traditional movement of narrativity and a cultural one of reciprocity. We give them life and later we can take it, precisely because in the beginning we gave it. Based on our knowledge of how the story is going to end we interpret its beginning. The way in which the story of meat is conceptualized is with constant references to humans' will; we allow animals their existence and we begin to believe that animals cannot exist without us.

The subterfuge in the story of meat occurs in the absence of agency and the emphasis on personal choice. The phrase humane slaughter and the eliding of fragmentation contribute to an elaborate artifice in which the person consuming meat is not implicated, because no agency, that is, no responsibility, no complicity, is inscribed in the story. A person can proudly proclaim his or her meat-eating habits. Though inculcated through social processes, meat eating is unambiguously experienced as personal.

Meat eaters must assume the role of literary critic, attempting to impose a positive interpretation on what they know to be a tragedy (the tragedy of killing animals), but which they see as a necessary tragedy. They do so by manipulating language and meaning creating a story that subjugates animals' lives to human needs. The story of meat involves re-naming, repositioning the object, and re-birth. As we saw in chapter 3, re-naming occurs continuously. We re-position the animal from subject to object by making ourselves the subjects in meat eating. The story ends not with death but re-birth and assimilation into our lives. Thus meat gives life. We accept meat eating as consumers because this role is continuous with our role of consumers of completed stories. Only through closure is the story resolved; only through meat eating does meat achieve its meaning and provide the justification for the entire meat production process. The meat herself represents the closure that occurs at the end of any story.

The threat to this story arises from two sources: vegetarianism and feminism. The vegetarian perspective seeks to establish agency and implicate the consumer. It challenges the notion that animals' deaths can be redeemed by applying human meaning to it; thus it stops the story of meat. The feminist theorist has concluded that traditional narrative is determined by patriarchal culture. According to feminist theory, patriarchal narrative depicts male quests and female passivity. Teresa de Lauretis comments, "For there would be no myth without a princess to be wedded."[27] It suggests that it is in the gaps and silences of traditional narrative that feminist meaning can be found. Thus it questions the structure of stories. With the lens of feminist interpretation we can see that the animal's position in the story of meat is that of the woman's in traditional patriarchal narrative; she is the object to be possessed. The story ends when the Prince finds his Princess. Our story ends when the male-defined consumer eats the female-defined body. The animals' role in meat eating is parallel to the women's role in narrative: we would have neither meat nor story without them. They are objects to others who act as subjects.

Vegetarians see themselves as providing an alternative ending, veggie burgers instead of hamburgers, but they are actually eviscerating the entire narrative. From the dominant perspective, vegetarianism is not only about something that is inconsequential, which lacks "meat," and which fails to find closure through meat, but it is a story about the acceptance of passivity, of that which has no meaning, of endorsing a "vegetable" way of living. In this it appears to be a feminist story that goes nowhere and accepts nothingness.

If, through the story of meat, the word and the flesh are united, we might further argue that the body equals a text, a text is a body.

From this perspective, changing an animal from her original state into food parallels changing a text from its original state into something more palatable. The result is dismembered texts and dismembered animals. Freeing Metis's voice from the sexual politics of meat involves re-membering both.

part two

From the Belly of Zeus

Zeus lusted after Metis the Titaness, who turned into many shapes to escape him until she was caught at last and got with child. An oracle of Mother Earth then declared that this would be a girl-child and that if Metis conceived again, she would bear a son who was fated to depose Zeus, just as Zeus had deposed Cronus, and Cronus had deposed Uranus. Therefore, having coaxed Metis to a couch with honeyed words, Zeus suddenly opened his mouth and swallowed her, and that was the end of Metis, though he claimed afterward that she gave him counsel from inside his belly.

chapter 5

Dismembered Texts, Dismembered Animals

> Documents originate among the powerful ones, the conquerors. History, therefore, is nothing but a compilation of the depositions made by assassins with respect to their victims and themselves.
>
> —Simone Weil, *The Need for Roots*

> This I have consider'd: but tigers eat men; and the opinion of the world is hard to be defeated.—Heetopades
>
> —Closing words of Joseph Ritson's *An Essay on Abstinence from Animal Food as a Moral Duty*

Feminism and vegetarianism often appear together in novels but the meaning of this is left unexplored. The use of vegetarian characters by women writers is a tradition that illustrates how to remember vegetarian words.

A double meaning to dismemberment pervades this chapter: that which fragments animals and that which distorts texts. Dismemberment of vegetarianism in literary criticism follows the objectification/fragmentation/consumption model discussed in chapter 2. First, the text is objectified, held open to scrutiny, reduced to some essential aspects of itself. Then the text is fragmented from itself and its context; this is dismemberment. Once dismembered, the text can be consumed as though it is saying nothing new, nothing that undercuts the patriarchal model of consumption that has obliterated alternative meaning.

Defining Dismemberment

> A book is a dead man, a sort of mummy, embowelled and embalmed, but that once had flesh, and motion, and a boundless variety of determinations and actions.
>
> —William Godwin, *Fleetwood*[1]

> the outside anti-vegetarian world
>
> —Bernard Shaw[2]

It is obvious what is meant by dismembered animals; that is how we obtain food from them. Dismemberment of texts occurs in many ways in regard to vegetarianism: by ignoring vegetarianism in texts; by failing to provide context or meaning to vegetarianism when it is mentioned; by deeming it inconsequential; and by forcing its meaning to adhere to the dominant discourse of meat.

Critical dismemberment is a major issue for feminists. We learn that literary history dismembers by excluding women's writings from the established canon.[3] In addition, acts of dismemberment of a text occur when it is slit from its cultural context, such as the "mishandling of Black women writers by whites."[4] Similarly, if the existence of vegetarianism is not ignored, texts that include vegetarianism are often interpreted without any reference to vegetarian tradition or the positive climate of vegetarianism that might have served as a backdrop to the author's treatment of the issue of vegetarianism.

Feminist critics convey the idea that textual violation has occurred through the use of violent imagery. Elizabeth Robins complains that critic Max Beerbohm proceeds "to dismember . . . the lady's literary remains."[5] Lorraine Bethel comments that Zora Neale "Hurston, like many Black women writers, has suffered 'intellectual lynching' at the hands of white and Black men and white women."[6] Just as a black writer refers to the treatment of a black writer by conjuring one of the quintessential forms of white racist violence against black people—rape of black women by white men would offer another metaphor of violation—so a vegetarian writer may express feelings about textual violation by referring to images of butchered animals and raising the issue of dismemberment.

Caren Greenburg adds to this discussion of dismembered texts by exploring the meaning of the "specific relationships among reader, text, and author" in the light of "an Oedipal form of reading." The Oedipus myth "implies that the roles at both ends of the creative process are essentially male and that the mediating text is female—and dead."[7] Acts of criticism on this representative dead female body, the text, are acts in which "the critic reduces the text to a repetition of *himself*." She turns to the myth of Echo to develop more fully this insight:

> Echo's mythic body *dismembered* is the myth disseminated and become versions, the Word disseminated and become words. . . . Why must the text be eliminated? Why must Echo be picked to shreds or ignored? The underlying threat posed by the text and exposed in this reading is that without textual violation, the mark or body which remains may be a locus from which language may seem to emanate.

Greenburg's analysis of the fate of the (female) text provides a basis for understanding the projects of vegetarians who are concerned with the literal, the animals' (symbolically female) bodies and the fate of texts in general.

What feminists see in the fate of women's texts, vegetarians see in the fate of animals. If the fate of the literal text parallels the fate of the literal animal—both becoming dismembered and consumed—then there is a parallel in wanting to preserve the integrity of an original text and being a vegetarian. In their parallel concerns, feminists and vegetarians seek to establish definitions against patriarchal authority. Inevitably they write against the texts of meat.

The interrelated sensibilities involved in respecting the integrity of a text and the integrity of animals' bodies become evident in a brief review of the writings of Joseph Ritson (1761–1803). Ritson is of interest because of his attempts to defend texts from the imposition of (male) editors and because of his avid vegetarianism.

Joseph Ritson: Vegetarian-at-Arms

> The particularity which governed Ritson in the higher criticism made him a fussy stickler in the humble walks of life. What appears in one sphere as critical scrupulousness seems in the other like finical foolishness. The editorial care for an accurate text becomes a personal anxiety about the teeth and the diet.
>
> —H. S. V. Jones, "Joseph Ritson: A Romantic Antiquarian"[8]

Joseph Ritson's life exemplifies the interweaving of literal concerns. Ritson was concerned with mangled and massacred animals, words, phrases, and texts. Besides refusing to view dead animals as meat he was devoted to issues of the proper spelling, definition, and etymology of words and the overzealous critical treatment of texts. Just as the text was not editorial property that could be changed and altered according to the whims and tastes of the editor so animals were not human's property to be altered, castrated, or killed according to the whims and tastes of meat eaters. He became enraged at dismembered texts and dismembered animals.

Ritson, called by one of his biographers "Scholar-at-Arms," was also a *vegetarian-at-arms,* ready and willing to battle with the larger meat-eating culture to forward vegetarian meaning. When one studies the caricature of Ritson by James Sayer that appeared in 1803 (See Figure 6), the year Ritson died, his concerns and that of his detractors are evident. In the background, nature is omnipresent: large rats are eating carrots, a cow sticking her head in a window is munching lettuce from a large bowl. Parsnips, beets, and other root vegetables stand among the books on the bookshelves, juxtaposing this vegetarian food with written texts. Joseph Ritson's own *An Essay on Abstinence from Animal Food as a Moral Duty* lies opened to the title page. In front of it a chained (carnivorous) cat is straining at her restraints, trying to reach the rats. (We infer that Ritson would deny even cats their right to eat meat.) The only other identifiable book on the bookshelves is the Bible, and it is also the only one that is tilted, askew, not allowed to stand upright. In Ritson's left pocket sits *The Atheist Pocket Companion.* A frog, atop some books and next to the root vegetables, watches as Ritson dips his quill into an inkstand labeled "Gall." A "Bill of Fare" reads: "Nettle Soup, Sour Crout, Horse Beans, Onions Leeks."

The caricature implies that Ritson really consumes other eighteenth-century scholars and their books, as he was an avid critic of others' works. He is writing a manuscript called "Common Place." Among the notable comments are "Warburton a fool and Percy a Liar/Warton an infamous Liar/ a piper [?] better than a Parson" referring to three of his fellow antiquarians. Two knives stab a picture of Thomas Warton as depicted in the frontispiece of his book *History of English Poetry,* a book with which Ritson had numerous quarrels. This caricature of Ritson is entitled, "Fierce meagre male no commentator's friend." This is Ritson as his contemporaries saw him.

Ritson devoted his adult life to re-membering texts and protecting animals. In describing what editors have done to their texts, such as Shakespeare's plays, he uses explicit references to violation, alteration, corruption, injuring. This inflamed manner of speaking appears when he

Figure 6

RITSON AS HIS CONTEMPORARIES SAW HIM

From the caricature by Sayer, published by Humphrey on March 22, 1803

Frontispiece to vol. 2, Bertrand H. Bronson *Joseph Ritson: Scholar-at-Arms* (Berkeley: University of California Press, 1938, 1966).

writes about meat eating. Ritson called meat eating "the horrid, unnatural crime of devouring your fellow creatures."[9]

Ritson believed in the integrity of any surviving text and its right to be unabused by editors who laid their hands on it. One biographer calls this a "devoted attachment to the very form and body of these ancient productions."[10] He spent years gathering ballads, folk songs, nursery rhymes; in a sense, an attempt to protect "anonymous"—that "prolific female author"[11]—from having her works disappear as well. He challenged overzealous editors who continually imposed their egos on the text; protecting the (female) text from (male) violation.

Applying Ritson's formula for respecting the integrity of the literal texts to basic vegetarian precepts reveals the following vegetarian standards. First, the proper role of the editor who respects the text would become the proper role of humans who control animals. Rather than dismembering them, s/he permits them wholeness. No editorial egocentricity will impose a (male) will on the (female) body. Encumbering a text with superfluity parallels what is done to an animal to make her, once dead, palatable: cooking her, seasoning her.

In *An Essay on Abstinence from Animal Food as a Moral Duty,* Ritson forwards two arguments simultaneously—consider these facts about vegetarianism, he argues in the main text, and in the footnotes he suggests, consider these ideas about texts in general. In attempting to assemble arguments against meat eating, Ritson must ponder the nature of humanity and the nature of texts. He creates antiphonal voices; the first discusses the Golden Age of vegetarianism, the other is concerned with a similar "Golden Age" of writers—Hesiod, Homer, and others.

Chapter 1, entitled "Of Man," demonstrates the basic unity in this antiphonal dialogue. What we encounter is a doubling of genesis, a focus on beginnings. Not only can one say that "in the beginning was the word" but in the beginning were the words of orators and writers about the beginning, a beginning that was vegetarian. Succinctly stated, his formula appears to be: to talk of vegetarianism is to talk of beginnings; to talk of beginnings is to talk of authors and their texts. By returning to beginnings we talk against succeeding texts of meat.

In arguing that people ought not to eat the other animals Ritson tries to erase the boundaries that distinguish humans from animals. He points out that human beings are similar to vegetarian animals such as monkeys and "oran-outangs." Evidence of human quadrupeds who lived like or with animals, such as a wolf boy, in his view further erode differences between human beings and the other animals. Finally, he argues that language itself might come from the other animals. Ritson, assuming that meat eating arises because of differences between human and nonhuman animals, seeks to establish their similarities.

Many of the topics in his book appear in subsequent vegetarian writings: one does not need meat to survive; animal food is not necessary for strength; animal food is unhealthy; a vegetable diet promotes health; humanity and ethics require a fleshless diet. As evidence, Ritson cites example after example of individuals or countries living mainly as vegetarians. It is not surprising that he frequently overstates his case: animal food, he argues, was the cause of human sacrifices, and cannibalism follows from meat eating. At these times, he fell prey to colonialist views and inherited the legacy of racist misunderstanding of Africans and Aztecs.[12]

Ritson's detractors were actually gleeful with the appearance of *An Essay on Abstinence from Animal Food,* for they saw it as discrediting his other works, writings that challenged their editorial decisions. In their eyes, his scholarly arguments were undercut by his exaggerated claims on behalf of vegetarianism. Ritson unfortunately announced "that the use of animal food disposes man to cruel and ferocious actions." How then did he explain his vitriolic writings against other scholars? For, of course, people noticed the contrast between his scathing and venomous writing style when discussing texts and his paean to a pacific vegetarianism. The review of *An Essay on Abstinence from Animal Food as a Moral Duty* in the *Edinburgh Review* refers to "the bloody, murderous, carnivorous *ritson,* a newly discovered animal of anomalous order." Or the *British Critic,* which gibed at Ritson's temper, referring to "his *tranquility of soul,* which has led him to maintain a restless and envenomed warfare with the whole human race, and chiefly with the most respectable part of it, cannot be too strongly pressed on the reader's notice, as one of the happy effects flowing from a total abstinence from animal food."[13] Ritson's ideas were attacked by his critics as ludicrous claims by an irrational man. Later generations were equally critical; the *Dictionary of National Biography* ungenerously believes that his *Essay* shows marks of Ritson's "insipient insanity."[14] (Though the *DNB* exhibits a similar dismissive viewpoint in their biographies of other vegetarians.)

Ritson's last book, left in manuscript at his death, is seen as an early example of modern scholarship; but his penultimate book, *An Essay on Abstinence from Animal Food,* has been viewed as a sign of a degenerative mental illness. In his final manuscript, subsequently published as *The Life of King Arthur: From Ancient Historians and Authentic Documents,* Ritson reached conclusions that are "in an astonishingly large number of cases essentially those of the best recent authorities" according to a twentieth-century reviewer who sees Ritson as "one of the greatest pioneers of modern scholarship."[15] *King Arthur,* similar in style to *An Essay,* relies on assembling translations and citations from other texts; called "the culmination of Ritson's researches into the history and literature of the middle ages, it was the fruit of mature experience."[16] His last work "reveals the author as a scholar of no ordinary attainments," as one who exercised "sound judgment" and "commonsense." He is seen as "a critic who, by his passion for accuracy and his tremendous grasp of fact, rebuked an age of intellectual dishonesty, and who, by an acumen at times little short of inspiration, enunciated theories to which the scholarly world has finally returned after long and bitter controversies."[17] If Ritson's final work reveals a mature scholar, how can his penultimate work be a sign of his insanity? Because it is being judged by the texts of meat which dismember vegetarian words.

Writing the Literal; Writing Vegetarianism

When women writers include vegetarianism in a novel it will represent a complex layering of respect for the literal and an acknowledgment of the structure of the absent referent. Women writers who include the issue of vegetarianism could be said to be "bearing the vegetarian word." Margaret Homans identifies several recurrent literary situations or practices that reveal women's concern for the literal, which she has called "bearing the Word."[18] For instance, Homans describes how Mary Shelley's *Frankenstein* recalls the language of Percy Shelley's *Alastor;* Mary can be said to be bearing Percy's words in her novel. Mary Shelley bears Percy Shelley's *vegetarian* word as well; *Alastor* features a vegetarian who consumes "bloodless food," as does *Frankenstein.*[19]

The issue of vegetarianism is a touchstone to the literal for it addresses the literal activities of meat eating by discussing what is literally consumed. For instance, toward the end of Shelley's novel, Frankenstein's Monster writes on stones and trees to leave notes for its pursuer. In this action, we are presented with a multilayered evocation of the literal. First our attention is called to the act of writing. Since the Creature has no paper nor pen, it uses nature itself—stones and trees. As a result we have an explicit writing on the literal, which is nature. One of these marks, which violates by writing *on* nature, recalls the violation *of* nature: "You will find near this place, if you follow not too tardily, a dead hare; eat, and be refreshed."[20] Nature itself bears the words that recall, though undoing, Plutarch's admonition to "tear a lamb or a hare in pieces, and fall on and eat it alive." The Creature writes on the literal about the fate of the literal and names the absent referent.

Bearing the vegetarian word in women's fiction re-members texts *and* animals through (1) allusion to the literal words of a vegetarian from an earlier text. Allusion provides credence to one's own position through association. It also renders the literal—actual books—into the figurative framework of one's writings. (2) Figures in novels who recall historic vegetarians such as the vegetarian matriarch married to a leading artist of the time in Iris Murdoch's *The Good Apprentice,* who echoes the cooking ideas of Laura Huxley, widow of Aldous Huxley.[21] Helen Yglesias's *The Saviors* figures a vegetarian, socialist, and pacifist couple—Dwight and Maddy who after years of political activism made "the long retreat to the good life"—who share many similarities to vegetarian, socialist, and pacifist Scott and Helen Nearing, who attested to "Living the Good Life."[22] (3) Translating vegetarian texts. For instance, Plutarch's two essays "On Flesh-Eating"—the quintessential authoritative vegetarian texts—were translated by both Joseph Ritson and Percy Shelley. (4) Language that clearly identifies the functioning of the structure of the absent referent by referring directly to dead animals. For instance, Margaret Drabble's *The Ice Age* opens with a pheasant dying from a heart attack, who "had had the pleasure, at least, of dying a natural death." The hero of the novel demurs from eating the dead bird because he "did not much fancy a bird that had died in so tragic a manner." In witnessing the bird's death, there was no absent referent.[23] (5) A final form of bearing the vegetarian word is found when individuals are prompted by their reading of vegetarian texts to stop eating meat, a goal Ritson had for his *Essay on Abstinence.*

Bearing the Vegetarian Word

Isabel Colegate's *The Shooting Party* demonstrates several aspects of bearing the vegetarian word and provides the opportunity to discern how a vegetarian's privileging of the literal is handled by a woman writer. We meet the vegetarian of the novel, Cornelius Cardew, within the context of meat eating. Tom Harker, a poacher, has caught a rabbit, knifed it, and pocketed it. As he returns home, anticipating the dinner that will soon be his, he encounters Cardew who is completing a twenty-mile hike and requires directions to a local inn. Cardew, invited to walk along with Tom to regain his proper path to the inn, notices Tom's distinctive limp, which is "due to his attempt to conceal the bulge of the rabbit in his pocket."[24] Cardew wonders if it is a war wound and Tom, lying, reports that his limp was caused by a mantrap. Indignant at this outrage, Cardew launches into a discourse on the killing of animals. While the readers and

Tom are aware that Cardew is preaching to a meat eater, Cardew thinks he is conversing with a possible convert. In this conversation the first form of bearing the vegetarian word through allusion appears—the literal words of a vegetarian from an earlier text are invoked. Cardew proclaims, "Until we can recognise the universal kinship of all living creatures we shall remain in outer darkness." Here Cardew recalls the words of Henry Salt who defined a "Creed of Kinship": "the basis of any real morality must be the sense of Kinship between all living beings."[25] To reinforce his ideas, Cardew hands Tom a pamphlet that bears these words, summarizing his viewpoints on the issue of animals.

The next day in the midst of a traditional shooting party, Cardew pickets it and hands his pamphlet on "The Rights of Animals, a Vindication of the Doctrine of Universal Kinship" to the host, which spurs a conversation about printing in general. This common ground of a shared interest in pamphleteering confirms Cardew as a Ritson-like character with a literal interest in writing.

Cardew has multiple vegetarian texts, he bears vegetarian words on both picket and pamphlet, and in these writings bears the literal words of previous writers. Through the title of his leaflet, Cardew is bearing the words of Mary Wollstonecraft's *A Vindication of the Rights of Woman* and Percy Shelley's *A Vindication of Natural Diet.* Colegate summons a third "vindication" of that time as well: *A Vindication of the Rights of Brutes*—the first written response to Wollstonecraft's *Vindication*—which parodied her book by extending her claims to animals. Henry Salt remarked that this response to Wollstonecraft's book demonstrates "how the mockery of one generation may become the reality of the next."[26] Colegate cleverly evokes the sense that efforts for women's rights can be undercut by implying that consideration of animals will be next—the message of the *Rights of Brutes*—through the following mocking response: "Sir Reuben Hergesheimer was describing to Minnie how a lunatic had appeared waving a placard and how he had taken for granted that it must be a suffragette and been astonished to find out that the agitation was on behalf of animals. 'Votes for pheasants, I suppose.' "

The second aspect of bearing the vegetarian word that appears in Colegate's novel is when a character in fiction recalls a historic vegetarian. Colegate's vegetarian character is based on Henry Salt, called by Heywood Broun the "father of modern vegetarianism" because of his influence on Shaw and Gandhi.[27] Besides the interrelated texts, there are many notable biographical parallels between the fictional Cardew and the historical Salt. Colegate makes Cardew, like Salt, involved in the Fellowship of the New Life and the Fabian Society. She has Cardew, like Salt, become a vegetarian while at public school. Salt tells us in his memoirs:

"Thus gradually the conviction had been forced on me that we Eton masters, however irreproachable our surroundings, were but cannibals in cap and gown—almost literally cannibals, as devouring the flesh and blood of the higher non-human animals so closely akin to us."[28] Salt founded the Humanitarian League, a reform-oriented group that, like Cardew, concerned itself with animals' rights, the extension of the franchise, land reform and socialism, among other issues.[29]

The third form of bearing the vegetarian word in this novel appears in language that refers directly to dead animals. Cardew calls the killing of animals "murder," the body of a dead animal is called a corpse rather than the more frequently used term carcass, and the number of dead birds is closely calculated.

The last form of bearing the vegetarian word involves the proselytizing motif, the hope that individuals will be prompted by their reading of vegetarian texts to stop eating meat. Cardew believes his vegetarian word will be made flesh. He imagines the reactions of a family that has received his pamphlet, "words which would strike them first as strange and then as startling and then as scintillating with a fine refulgent light which made everything new and plain and held out to them quite irresistibly the clear necessity that they, the labouring poor, exploited by the rich, should connect themselves by sympathetic alliance with the animals, exploited by all men."[30]

Cardew represents vegetarian writers like Percy Shelley, Joseph Ritson, and Henry Salt who attempt to reproduce their own vegetarian conversion for others by adding texts to the vegetarian canon. They seek multigenerational, multitextual vegetarian readings against the cultural texts of meat. They presume a continuous relationship between text and reader in which the text, protected, left whole, will have an effect on the reader who greets the words literally.

Essentially, the dialectic between vegetarianism and meat eating in the text represents the dialectic between writer and reader. The former seeks to convert the latter through the power of the text. Reversing the image of a text inscribed on and scarring nature pointing to a dead animal as is evoked in *Frankenstein,* they hope that from their image of the inviolate text arises the desire for unviolating diets. The signature of a vegetarian in a vegetarian text, whether Cardew or Shelley, Ritson or Salt, is the signature of someone trying to write on the reader, leave a mark on the reader's own personal text of meat. It is an attempt to make their words flesh and to stop the story of meat. In their expectation of a literal response, they seek no more dismembered texts, dismembered animals, but instead hope for a re-membered text that protects the literal, living animals.

chapter 6

Frankenstein's Vegetarian Monster

> Is it so heinous an offence against society, to respect in other animals that principal of life which they have received, no less than man himself, at the hand of Nature? O, mother of every living thing! O, thou eternal fountain of beneficence; shall I then be persecuted as a monster, for having listened to thy sacred voice?
>
> —John Oswald, *The Cry of Nature,* 1791

Frankenstein's Monster was a vegetarian. This chapter, in analyzing the meaning of the diet adopted by a Creature composed of dismembered parts, will demonstrate the benefits of re-membering rather than dismembering vegetarian tradition. Just as *The Shooting Party* draws upon vegetarian ideas and an individual of Edwardian England, the time in which it is set, so *Frankenstein* was indebted to the vegetarian climate of its day. Therefore this chapter places the themes of vegetarianism within both the vegetarian history of the Romantic period and the implicit feminism of this notable book. In its association of feminism, Romantic radicalism, and vegetarianism, Mary Shelley's book bears the vegetarian word.

For a work that has received an unusual amount of critical attention over the past thirty years, in which almost every aspect of the novel has been closely scrutinized, it is remarkable that the Creature's vegetarianism has remained outside the sphere of commentary. The late James Regier saw "*Frankenstein* as an imaginative ecotype, endlessly adaptable to unmixable seas of thought."[1] By exploring the Creature's vegetarianism and providing a literary, historical, and feminist framework for understanding it, this chapter offers a few more waves of interpretation to the swelling waters.

The Creature's vegetarianism not only confirms its inherent, original benevolence,[2] but conveys Mary Shelley's precise rendering of themes articulated by a group of her contemporaries whom I call "Romantic vegetarians." The references that are central to Shelley's novel and to Romantic writers in general—the writings of Ovid, Plutarch, Milton, and Rousseau—are all united by positive vegetarian associations. The myths of Adam and Eve and Prometheus, clearly evoked in the novel, were interpreted in a vegetarian framework during the Romantic period as being about the introduction of meat eating. Mary Shelley's husband, Percy, was among the group of vegetarians who formulated this interpretation.

Of the numerous areas of exploration that have attracted literary critics, many overlap with the project of recovering the vegetarian meaning in this novel: the novel's narrative strategy; literary, historical, and biographical aspects of the novel; and the novel's feminist/gender issues. In the succeeding sections I consider these three areas and interpret the theme of vegetarianism as it is embedded in each.

Closed Circles and Vegetarian Consciousness

> The moral universe is not just a system of concentric circles, in which inner claims must always prevail over outer ones. . . . The model of concentric circles dividing *us* from *them* remains, however, very influential. One of its most popular forms is the idea that concern for *them* beyond a certain limit—and in particular concern for animals—is not serious because it is a matter of emotion.
>
> —Mary Midgley, *Animals and Why They Matter*[3]

The Creature includes animals within its moral codes, but is thwarted and deeply frustrated when seeking to be included within the moral codes of humanity. It learns that regardless of its own inclusive moral standards, the human circle is drawn in such a way that both it and the other animals are excluded from it.

The Creature's vegetarianism is revealed in the innermost of three concentric circles that structure the novel. The outermost circle consists of the letters of Robert Walton while journeying through the Arctic to his sister Margaret Saville in England. Walton's ship is traveling farther and farther from human society as the story unfolds; but as the story ends,

Walton has agreed to return to the folds of civilization. His reversal occurs after Victor Frankenstein, the Being's creator, is brought half-alive onto Walton's ship. Bent on avenging the deaths of his wife, his friend, and his brother by destroying the Creature, Victor has followed it to the Arctic. His tale to Walton of his movement away from the human circle—through his lone scientific experiments that culminated in the creation of this Being and his subsequent solitary pursuit of the Creature—is situated in the novel as the mediating narrative between Walton's tale of wanderlust and the Creature's woeful story of parental desertion, isolation, and rejection by humans. The inner circle is the Creature's orphan tale of how it gained knowledge and survival skills, and of what precipitated the murder of Victor's little brother. Again and again it tells of being violently refused admittance to human society. At the conclusion of this narrative it proposes the creation of a companion so that it need no longer seek inclusion in the human circle; it will be content with companionship in its restricted inner circle.

In a ringing, emotional speech the Creature enunciates its dietary principles and those that its companion will follow when they accept self-imposed exile to South America. Vegetarianism is one way that the Creature announces its difference and separation from its creator by emphasizing its more inclusive moral code. In its explanation of its vegetarianism, the Creature restores the absent referent: "My food is not that of man; I do not destroy the lamb and the kid, to glut my appetite; acorns and berries afford me sufficient nourishment. My companion will be of the same nature as myself, and will be content with the same fare. We shall make our bed of dried leaves; the sun will shine on us as on man, and will ripen our food. The picture I present to you is peaceful and human."[4] The Creature's vegetarianism serves to make it a more sympathetic being, one who considers how it exploits others. By including animals within its moral circle the Creature provides an emblem for what it hoped for and needed—but failed to receive—from human society.

Through its structural existence as the innermost of three concentric narratives, the Creature's story reinforces the Creature's position in society; it must be self-contained because no one will interact with it. The Creature's litany of rejections by human beings—Victor's rejection of it once it comes to life; villagers fleeing from it; the attack on it after saving a young person's life; the DeLacey's rebuff of its approach—holds up a clue as to what truly embodies the common center of all three tales: Human beings see themselves as their own center, into whose moral fabric neither gigantic beings nor animals are allowed.

The structure reiterates the theme. The Creature must overcome concentricity to be heard, to achieve social intercourse and be assimilated into human society. In this drive to overcome the self-enclosed concentric circles of the novel and of society, the Creature also challenges the concentric circles that philosopher Mary Midgley sees as separating humans from animals. The Creature's inclusion of animals in its moral code symbolizes the idea that it seeks to achieve in human intercourse, breaking through the concentric circles of *us* and *them.*

Bearing the Romantic Vegetarian Word

> It was not until after the age of Rousseau . . . that vegetarianism began to assert itself as a system, a reasoned plea for the disuse of flesh-food. In this sense it is a new ethical principle.
>
> —Henry Salt, *The Humanities of Diet,* 1914[5]

Literary critics identify in *Frankenstein* a distillation of Mary Wollstonecraft Shelley's life and learning, an interweaving of biography and bibliography. Through her father, William Godwin, Mary Shelley met many notable vegetarians, such as John Frank Newton, author of *The Return to Nature; or, A Defence of the Vegetable Regimen,* Joseph Ritson, his publisher Sir Richard Phillips, and, of course, Percy Shelley, who had authored *A Vindication of Natural Diet* and the visionary and vegetarian *Queen Mab.*[6]

Romantic radicalism provided the context for the vegetarianism to which Mary Wollstonecraft Shelley was exposed while growing up. As historian James Turner comments, "Radical politics and other unorthodox notions went hand-in-glove with their vegetarianism."[7] Historian Keith Thomas agrees, "In the 1790s vegetarianism had markedly radical overtones."[8] Turner observes that of all the "novel manifestations of sympathy for animals" that began to appear at this time, "the most profoundly subversive of conventional values was vegetarianism."[9] A clergyman who upbraided Thomas Jefferson Hogg for becoming a vegetarian demonstrated the way in which this subversive reform was greeted: "But this new system of eating vegetables . . . has hung on your Mother as a sort of indication that your determination was to deviate from all the old established ways of the world."[10]

Romantic vegetarians sought to expand the human-centered moral circle that excluded animals from serious consideration. To them, killing animals was murder, brutalizing those who undertook it and those who benefited from it. They argued that once meat eating had redefined humanity's moral relationship with animals, the floodgates of immorality were opened, and what resulted was the immoral, degenerate world in which they and their contemporaries lived. Joseph Ritson thought that human slavery might be traced to meat eating while Percy Shelley suggested that a vegetarian populace would never have "lent their brutal suffrage to the proscription-list of Robespierre."[11] They argued that including animals within the circle of moral consideration was urgently required.[12]

Most of the Romantic vegetarians were sympathetic Republicans; they saw the French Revolution as one of the toeholds into reforming the world, eliminating meat eating was another. John Oswald, whose *The Cry of Nature; or, An Appeal to Mercy and to Justice, on Behalf of the Persecuted Animals* (1791) was the first British book of this time to champion vegetarianism, lost his life in France in 1793 fighting for the Jacobins at the battle of Pont-de-Cé.[13] Ritson visited Paris in 1791, adopted the new Republican calendar and liked to be called "Citizen Ritson." Richard Phillips, publisher for both Ritson and Godwin, and founder of the *Monthly Magazine* supported the Republican cause.

Unlike many animal reform campaigns of the time, which directed their energy to controlling the abuses of animals occassioned by the sports of the lower classes such as bear or bull baiting, vegetarians went after the jugular of the upperclass—meat eating and blood sports. As Percy Shelley vehemently framed the argument: "It is only the wealthy that can, to any great degree, even now, indulge the unnatural craving for dead flesh."[14]

The ideas to which Mary Shelley and the Romantic vegetarians gravitate tantalizingly overlap: each rewrote the myths of the Fall (especially Genesis 3) and the myth of Prometheus. Each ponders the nature of evil and visions of utopia. In the Creature's narrative, Mary Shelley allies herself with Romantic vegetarians who decoded all tales of the primeval fall with the interpretation that they were implicitly about the introduction of meat eating. She precisely situates the vegetarian position concerning these two myths in the Creature's narrative. The two preeminent myths that frame her *Frankenstein,* the myth of Prometheus and the story of Adam and Eve, had both been assimilated into the Romantic vegetarian position and interpreted from a vegetarian viewpoint by Joseph Ritson, John Frank Newton, and Percy Shelley.

The Vegetarian Garden of Eden and the Fall

It was commonly presumed that the Garden of Eden was vegetarian.[15] Proof of the vegetarian nature of the Garden of Eden was said to be found in Genesis 1:29: "And God said, Behold, I have given you every herb bearing seed, which *is* upon the face of all the earth, and every tree, in which *is* the fruit of a tree yielding seed; to you it shall be for meat." ("Meat" at the time of the *King James Version* of the Bible meant food.) Seventeenth-century poet Katherine Philips said of the Golden Age, "On roots, not beasts, they fed."[16] In a phrase that Joseph Ritson would quote, Alexander Pope wrote that in Eden,

> Man walk'd with beast, joint tenant of the shade;
> The same his table, and the same his bed;
> No murder cloath'd him, and no murder fed.[17]

Milton in book 5 of *Paradise Lost* describes Eve preparing "For dinner savoury fruits, of taste to please / True appetite."[18]

The Romantic vegetarians heartily accepted the notion of the meatless Garden of Eden. They infused their peculiar interpretation in their consideration of Genesis 3. They transformed the myth by locating meat eating as the cause of the Fall. For instance John Frank Newton's *The Return to Nature; or, Defence of Vegetable Regimen* posits that the two trees in the Garden of Eden represent "the two kinds of foods which Adam and Eve had before them in Paradise, viz. the vegetables and the animals."[19] The penalty for eating from the wrong tree was the death that Adam and Eve had been warned would befall them. But it was not immediate death; rather it was premature, diseased death caused by eating the wrong foods, i.e., meat.

Approaching the Fall from this interpretation deflects attention from the role of Eve as temptress, and removes the patriarchal obsession with the feminine as the cause of the evil of the world. Because of the vegetarian attention given to the (male) role of butchers, and the presumed manliness of meat eating, the evil that fills the world after the fall is generalized, if not masculinized. In support of Gilbert and Gubar's suggestion that Eve is all parts of the story of *Frankenstein*—especially the Creature[20]—the Creature, unlike Adam, but like Eve in Milton's depiction, must prepare its own dinner of "savoury fruits." And when the Creature envisions its companion, it does not posit food preparation as her role though she will share its fare.

The Myth of Prometheus

Both Mary Shelley and the Romantic vegetarians weave another myth of the Fall into their writings: the myth of Prometheus who stole fire, was chained to Mount Caucasus, and faced the daily agony of having his liver devoured by a vulture, only to have it grow back each night. Besides the standard Romantic view of Prometheus as a rebel against tyranny, Mary Shelley knew of an additional interpretation of the myth. For Romantic vegetarians, the story of Prometheus's discovery of fire is the story of the inception of meat eating. They accepted Pliny's claim in *Natural History* that "Prometheus first taught the use of animal food *(Primus bovem occidit Prometheus).*"[21] Without cooking, meat would not be palatable. According to them, cooking also masks the horrors of a corpse and makes meat eating psychologically and aesthetically acceptable. Percy Shelley provides the Romantic vegetarian interpretation of this myth: "Prometheus (who represents the human race) effected some great change in the condition of his nature, and applied fire to culinary purposes; thus inventing an expedient for screening from his disgust the horrors of the shambles. From this moment his vitals were devoured by the vulture of disease."[22]

It is notable how the Creature in a tale subtitled *The Modern Prometheus* handles its introduction to fire and meat. Finding a fire left by some wandering beggars, it discovers that "some of the offals that the travellers had left had been roasted, and tasted much more savoury than the berries I gathered from the trees." From this, it does not adopt meat eating, but rather learns how to cook vegetable food. "I tried, therefore, to dress my food in the same manner, placing it on the live embers. I found that the berries were spoiled by this operation, and the nuts and roots much improved." The offals figure meat eating; the Creature rejects this Promethean gift.

The Golden Age and the Natural Diet

Descriptions of what the Creature eats reveal Mary Shelley's indebtedness to vegetarian meals described by Ovid and Rousseau. In this, her book bears the vegetarian word through allusion to previous words about vegetarianism. The Golden Age described in book 1 of Ovid's *Metamorphoses* is a time prior to the erection of dwelling places, a time of contentment with acorns and berries, a time when animals were not excluded from the human circle by meat eating:

> Content with Food, which Nature freely bred,
> On Wildings, and on Strawberries they fed;
> Cornels and Bramble-berries gave the rest,
> And falling Acorns furnisht out a Feast.[23]

After the Creature announces its vegetarianism to Victor, it promises that once Victor fashions a companion, the two shall retreat to South

America, and there live faultless lives. Ovid appears to be the source for the precise wording of Shelley's vegetarian-pacifist vision the Creature presents to Victor, in particular, the use of "acorns and berries," quoted earlier, as the source of nourishment. The Creature enters into a fallen world in which it is rejected and seeks to establish a new Golden Age in which harmony through vegetarianism reigns.

The Creature also bears the vegetarian word of Rousseau in his descriptions of food. From the *Discourse on Inequality,* when he first suggested that one of the links in the chains that kept humankind in bondage was an unnatural diet, through *Émile* and *La Nouvelle Heloise,* vegetarianism is Rousseau's ideal diet.[24] Émile, Sophie, and Julie were all vegetarians. Mary Shelley precisely renders Rousseau's ideal diet in the Creature's narrative. Rousseau rhapsodized in *The Confessions,* "I do not know of better fare than a rustic meal. With milk, eggs, herbs, cheese, brown bread and passable wine one can always be sure to please me."[25] Once forced to leave the Promethean fire behind because of the scarcity of food, the Creature's next encounter with food is a paraphrase of Rousseau's favorite meal in rustic surroundings: "I greedily devoured the remnants of the shepherd's breakfast, which consisted of bread, cheese, milk, and wine; the latter, however, I did not like."[26] (Wine was tabooed by Romantic vegetarians as well as meat). In a village, the Creature again responds with pleasure to the ideal foods Rousseau identified: "The vegetables in the gardens, the milk and cheese that I saw placed at the windows of some of the cottages, allured my appetite."

Diet for a Small Planet

Another instance in which the Creature's views of a fallen world intersect with that of the Romantic vegetarians is its observation that cows need food. It remarks about one cow owned by a poor family that she "gave very little [milk] during the winter, when its masters could scarcely procure food to support it." Its reference to the demands that one cow puts on food resources echoes the modern ecological vegetarian position popularized in Frances Moore Lappé's *Diet for a Small Planet.* Lappé argues that the land used to feed livestock would be better devoted to feeding humans.

This was a longstanding vegetarian issue and its first traces appear in Plato's *Republic* when Socrates tells Glaucon that meat production necessitates large amounts of pasture. Resultingly, it will require cutting "off a slice of our neighbours' territory; and if they too are not content with necessaries, but give themselves up to getting unlimited wealth, they will want a slice of ours." Thus Socrates pronounces, "So the next thing will be, Glaucon, that we shall be at war."[27] In 1785, William Paley's *The Principles of Moral and Political Philosophy* raised the economic and agricultural issues associated with meat eating: "A piece of ground capable of supplying animal food sufficient for the subsistence of ten persons would sustain, at least, the double of that number with grain, roots and milk."[28] Richard Phillips's 1811 vegetarian article argues: "The forty-seven millions of acres in England and Wales *would maintain in abundance as many human inhabitants* if they lived wholly on grain, fruits and vegetables; but they sustain only twelve millions *scantily* while animal food is made the basis of human subsistence."[29] Percy Shelley's essay culminates this position: claiming that with vegetarianism "the monopolizing eater of animal flesh would no longer destroy his constitution by devouring an acre at a meal. . . . The most fertile districts of the habitable globe are now actually cultivated by men for animals, at a delay and waste of aliment absolutely incapable of calculation."[30]

The Slaughterhouse as Source for the Creature's Body

The Creature is "born" into a fallen world; but the Creature was also "born" *of* this fallen world—as the Romantic vegetarians viewed it—in that it is made, in part, of items from a slaughterhouse. Unlike many Gothic tales in which a customary raid on the graveyard is obligatory, Victor Frankenstein, in constructing his Creature, makes forays to the slaughterhouse as well: "The dissecting room and the slaughter-house furnished many of my materials." How was it that Mary Shelley extended grave robbing to invading the slaughterhouse? Her familiarity with the ideas of Romantic vegetarianism may have influenced her. The slaughterhouse was one of the consequences of the fall from vegetarianism and Romantic vegetarians could not avoid considering it, even if, like John Oswald, they deliberately took long detours to avoid passing slaughterhouses and butcher shops. Sir Richard Phillips traced his vegetarianism to his experience at twelve years of age, when he "was struck with such horror in accidentally seeing the barbarities of a London slaughter-house that since that hour he has never eaten anything but vegetables."[31]

The Anatomically Correct Vegetarian

That Victor goes to slaughterhouses not only incorporates into the novel the anathema with which vegetarians beheld it, but suggestively implies the Creature was herbivorous. Since it is only herbivorous animals who are consumed by humans, the remnants gathered by Victor from the slaughterhouse would have been parts from herbivorous bodies. Thus, at least a portion of the Creature was anatomically vegetarian. Romantic vegetarians held that humans did not have a carnivorous body; ill health consequently resulted from meat eating. In what would become a standard vegetarian argument, Rousseau discussed the physiological disposition of the body to a vegetable diet. Like herbivorous animals, humans had flat teeth. The intestines, as well, did not resemble those of carnivorous animals. By positing the Creature's creation in part from the slaughterhouse, Mary Shelley circumvents the anatomical argument that vegetarians of this time found compelling and their critics ludicrous.

When the vegetarianism of the novel is considered separate from its vegetarian context, it is shorn of the literary allusions it carries and its adherence to the novel's project of echoing earlier texts goes undetected. In *Frankenstein* we find a Creature seeking to reestablish the Golden Age of a vegetarian diet with roots and berries; a Creature who eats Rousseau's ideal meal; a Being who, like the animals eaten for meat, finds itself excluded from the moral circle of humanity.

Deciphering Muted Meanings

> We did transcription, copied out set passages in this arching, long-looped hand. I wrote out, over and over, with a calm satisfaction: "I should like to live among the leaves and heather like the birds, to wear a dress of feathers, and to eat berries." This sentence seemed to me to possess an utter and invulnerable completeness.
>
> —Denise Riley, "Waiting"[32]

The Creature embodies both vegetarian and feminist meaning. While the women in *Frankenstein* enact Mary Shelley's subversion of sentimentalism by fulfilling feminine roles and dying as a result, and the men represent inflexible masculine roles, it is the New Being who represents the complete critique of the present order which Shelley attempted. The nameless Creature, who Gilbert and Gubar see as seeking for a maternal principle in the midst of a world of fathers, resolutely condemns the food of the fathers as well as their mores; in this sense its vegetarianism carries feminist as well as pacifist overtones. Those who overtly reviled the meat diet of that day failed to see that they were covertly criticizing a masculine symbol The maternal principle would be present in the Creature's vegetarian paradise; indeed, the maternal principle is the missing aspect of Romantic vegetarianism.

Recalling the exclusions enforced by the outer narratives upon the Creature's inner circle, we find a paradigm for interpreting not only the Creatures' vegetarianism but one of the feminist aspects of the novel. Embedded within the Creature's story is yet another story, that of the DeLacey family. Within that family story, we find the story of Safie's independent mother. It is in fact "the structurally central element of the narrative."[33] Safie had been taught by her mother "to aspire to higher powers of intellect, and an independence of spirit, forbidden to the female followers of Mahomet."[34] Marc Rubenstein observes that Safie's mother "is surely a cartoon, distorted but recognizable, of the author's mother, Mary Wollstonecraft."[35] In fact, on the second page of the introduction to *A Vindication of the Rights of Woman,* Wollstonecraft comments of women in her own country that "in the true style of Mahometanism, they are treated as a kind of subordinate beings, and not as a part of the human species."[36]

Women's anger at confinement and their vision for independence are themselves confined in this novel within numerous layers of concentric circles that represent a society that excludes these issues. Though located at the center of the book, the issues there represented—central to both Mary Wollstonecraft and her daughter—have been closed off by the dominant world order. Among other things *Frankenstein* became a cathartic vehicle for a woman suppressing great anger at being made subordinate.

The Creature's vegetarian proclamation is a cipher in the text; though it has been treated in the sense of being without meaning, it is rather a key to Mary Wollstonecraft Shelley's feelings about discourse and the cipherlike role—that is, the nonentity role—permitted to women by male discourse. As Shelley's mother proved, women were excluded from the closed circle of patriarchy. In describing the events that led up to the conception of *Frankenstein* in the 1831 edition, Mary Shelley creates an image of herself as cipher by portraying herself as outside the circle of discourse of the men in her party: She casts herself in the role of faithful listener. "Many and long were the conversations between Lord Byron and Shelley, to which I was a devout but nearly silent listener."[37] During the time that *Frankenstein* was conceived, Byron and Percy Shelley's many companionable hours were achieved at the exclusion of Mary. Marcia Tillotson, who examines this exclusion, and suggests that the Creature's rage mirrors Mary Shelley's own rage over being excluded, queries:

> The question I cannot answer is whether Shelley was fully aware of what she was doing: did she deliberately use the monster's self-defense to protest against men's behavior toward women, or did she merely make the monster speak for her without knowing herself that the source of his rage was her own?[38]

The Creature's situation matches that of many women characters for whom tragedy "springs from the fact that consciousness must outpace the possibilities of action, that perception must pace within an iron cage."[39] Yet the Creature's style of speaking differs greatly from the characteristic forms of speech attributed to women. It is not hesitant, self-effacing, tentative, weak, polite, restrained. Its speech is not characterized by hedges, maybes, perhaps, possibly, if you please.[40] The Creature does not avoid confrontation. It is excited, impassioned speech, but clear, unambiguous, direct. It demands, it entreats, it implores, it commands, it prophesies. The Creature is a powerful speaker, it transgresses conversations mightily and fearlessly. It embodies patterns of speech that would have been foreign to many women of that time. Yet like feminists, its speech was muted by the dominant social order; as is vegetarianism. Vegetarianism, like feminism, is excluded from the patriarchal circle, just as Mary Shelley experienced herself as being excluded from the male circle of artists of which she saw herself a part.

It may be that the compressed form of the Creature's vegetarian statement causes it to be elided from our collective memory. Since vegetarianism is not a part of the dominant culture, it is more likely, however, that the vegetarian revelations, terse as they are, are silenced because we have no framework into which we can assimilate them, just as the feminist meaning at the center of this novel failed to be analyzed extensively for more than a hundred years. The Creature's futile hopes for admittance to the human circle reflect the position of that time's vegetarians and feminists; they confront a world whose circles, so tightly drawn, refuse them admittance, dividing *us* from *them*.

chapter 7

Feminism, the Great War, and Modern Vegetarianism

> What is civilization? What is culture? Is it possible for a healthy race to be fathered by violence—in war or in the slaughter-house—and mothered by slaves, ignorant or parasitic? Where is the historian who traces the rise and fall of nations to the standing of their women?
>
> —Agnes Ryan, "Civilization? Culture?"

After Frankenstein's Creature describes its diet of acorn and berries, and its hope of retreating to South America with its companion, it remarks to Frankenstein, "The picture I present to you is peaceful and human."[1] The Creature's idyllic pacifist and vegetarian utopian vision intersects with the themes of a number of novels by twentieth-century women that in challenging patriarchal society hearken to a Golden Age of feminism, pacifism, and vegetarianism. The context against which these more recent novels must be read is World War I—for it was then that the peaceful, vegetarian life envisioned by the Creature and many others encountered its starkest contrast, catalyzing the assimilation of vegetarianism into the antiwar vision of women writers. As Edward Carpenter put it after World War I: "When we think of the regiments and regiments of soldiers and mercenaries mangled and torn . . . when we realise *what* all this horrible scramble means, including the endless slaughter of the innocent and beautiful animals, and the fear, the terror, the agony in which the latter exist," we must "pay homage" to Percy Shelley's androgynous vision, for he "saw that only a new type of human being combining the male and the female, could ultimately save the world—a being having the feminine insight and imagination to perceive the evil, and the manly strength and courage to oppose and finally annihilate it."[2]

Just as the Great War is the context for Carpenter's statement about the need for an androgynous vision to challenge war and animal slaughter, in the wake of World War I many modern women writers trace the causes of both war and meat eating to male dominance. Events of the Great War yoked the heretofore sporadically linked notions of pacifism and vegetarianism. The Great War quickened vegetarianism, propelling it as a movement into the twentieth century and as a subject into the novels of women writers.

As an attribute of fictional characters, few literary examples of vegetarianism antedate the Great War, with the notable exception of Frankenstein's Creature. The modernization of vegetarianism occurred when it began to figure, as a theme or incidental element, in novels. The last chapter examined the significance of vegetarianism and its historical manifestations as it appears in one novel; this chapter applies that same approach to consider vegetarian themes that recur in a series of novels. As with *Frankenstein,* these novels, too, enact a narrative strategy that highlights vegetarian meaning.

In this chapter I will propose that the textual strategy of "interruption" allows modern women writers to introduce vegetarian incidents into their novels. Four themes arise when a vegetarian "interruption" occurs. These themes include rejection of male acts of violence, identification with animals, repudiation of men's control of women, and the positing of an ideal world composed of vegetarianism, pacifism, and feminism as opposed to a fallen world composed in part of women's oppression, war, and meat eating.

The novels to be considered in this chapter adhere to patterns previously discussed in chapter 5, "Dismembered Texts, Dismembered Animals." They bear the vegetarian word through allusion to earlier vegetarian ideas, through language that clearly identifies the functioning of the structure of the absent referent, and through the assumption that people who read vegetarian writings become vegetarian. We will see that the idea of meat is used as a trope for women's oppression; this trope identifies the overlap of the oppression of women and animals.

A feminist perspective in these novels links violence against people and violence against animals. It is this unique perspective that will be closely examined, for it demonstrates how vegetarian insights can be applied to analyses of other forms of political violence. The apparently unrelated critiques of women against war and vegetarians against meat eating become intimately related. From this perspective of the interrelationships of violence, vegetarianism can be seen as a challenge to war, pacifism as a challenge to meat eating. This interrelationship becomes visible when women articulate a connection with animals—beings who are also made absent referents by patriarchal society—thus correlating male acts of violence against people and animals. In deliberately bearing the vegetarian word, they challenge a world at war.

After briefly summarizing a feminist analysis of political violence and the ways by which the Great War effected the modernization of vegetarianism, we will consider the narrative strategies and thematic concerns of several illustrative works. This consideration will suggest the depths of the linkage between vegetarianism and pacifism in women's writings of the twentieth century and extend our understanding of the sexual politics of meat.

The Sexual Politics of War

During the Great War some anti-war feminists argued, like Edward Carpenter, that women had unique traits that caused them to be more peace-loving than men. This emphasis on gender distinctions, called by one historian the "argument for ameliorative influence," focused on women's role as nurturers and mothers. As historian C. Roland Marchand describes this viewpoint: "Women embodied the 'gentler traits of tenderness and mercy' and therefore had a special contribution to offer to government. . . . Destructive masculine ideas of physical force would only be overcome, militant suffragist Harriet Stanton Blatch argued, when the 'mother viewpoint' forced its way into international diplomacy."[3]

In a chapter entitled "Woman and War," from her 1911 book *Woman and Labour,* Olive Shreiner provides an illustrative example of this argument for ameliorative influence. She posits that women oppose war *and* the killing of animals for sport because of their child-bearing:

> The relations of the female towards the production of human life influences undoubtedly even her relation towards animal and all life. "It is a fine day, let us go out and kill something!" cries the typical male of certain races, instinctively. "There is a living thing, it will die if it is not cared for," says the average woman, almost equally instinctively.[4]

Other feminists decried political violence by arguing that it was male domination, not male traits, and the absence of female power that caused war. Women's exclusion from powerful positions in patriarchal society provides Virginia Woolf with the opportunity to propose in her brilliant anti-war feminist essay, *Three Guineas,* the creation of an Outsider's Society. As she develops her argument linking male power, the exclusion of women, and bellicose militarism, she, like Carpenter and Schreiner before her, connects the deaths of people and of animals: "Scarcely a human being in the course of history has fallen to a woman's rifle; the vast majority of birds and beasts have been killed by you, not by us."[5]

Agnes Ryan and her husband Henry Bailey Stevens, both editors of the *Woman's Journal* and pacifists, became vegetarians during the Great War. They decided that the responsibility for both war and meat eating rested with men, and were influenced in their analysis by their friendship with Emarel Freshel. Ryan describes Freshel's address on war and meat eating to a 1915 Fabian Society meeting: "Here was a new type of woman; here was a new spiritual force at work in the universe. . . . She clearly stressed the idea that wars will never be overcome until the belief that it is justifiable to take life, to kill—*when expedient,*—is eradicated from human consciousness."[6] In 1917, Freshel, author of the definitive vegetarian cookbook for that time, *The Golden Rule Cookbook,* resigned from the Christian Science Church when it supported the entry of the United States into World War I.

If feminist vegetarians argued that killing animals becomes a justification for killing human beings, some who adhere to the dominant viewpoint persuade children to eat meat by justifying the necessity, at times, to kill even human beings. Lawrence Kohlberg, well-known scholar on the moral development of children, reports that his four-year-old son "joined the pacifist and vegetarian movement and refused to eat meat because, he said, it is bad to kill animals." Kohlberg's response was an attempt to "dissuade him by arguing about the difference between justified and unjustified killing,"[7] thus establishing a morality that recognizes some forms of killing as legitimate. It is as though the way to create a child's acceptance of animals' deaths is by convincing him or her that sometimes humans must be killed, too. "Just" wars then justify meat eating. This phenomenon is figured in Walter de la Mare's "Dry August Burned": a small girl is weeping at the sight of the absent referent, a dead hare that lies lifeless on the kitchen table. A team of field artillery "thudding by" interrupts her mourning. She watches the wonderment and tumult of it all, returns to the kitchen and with flushed cheeks asks to watch the rabbit be skinned.[8] The soldiers have intervened; in their presence, the dead rabbit has now become an accepted fact, no longer mourned.

"Dry August Burned" figures a transition in an attitude toward an animal killed for food, a transition caused by the reminder of war. This response enforces a relationship between eating animals and killing humans. If the wartime killing of human beings is used to establish the legitimacy of meat eating, then challenging meat eating challenges a world at war.

Individual women took the insights of the connected brutalities of war and of meat eating to heart. For instance Mary Alden Hopkins remarked: "I reacted violently at that time against all established institutions, like marriage, spanking, meat diet, prisons, war, public schools, and our form of government."[9] Many feminist-vegetarian pacifists can be found during World War I. During the Great War, feminist, pacifist, and vegetarian Charlotte Despard provided vegetarian meals at the cheap meals service she offered on her property.[10] At least four American vegetarian feminists traveled on the Ford Peace Ship in 1915.[11]

In the wake of the war, the position that the absence of female power caused war intersected with the view that meat-eating cultures were war cultures (even though not all meat-eating cultures were then at war). As feminists and vegetarians acknowledged their shared critical positions, they discovered that the destructive values of patriarchal culture were not limited to the battlefront.

The Great War: Modernizing Vegetarianism

> When times are normal people and governments are inclined to pursue lines of least resistance; that is, to continue practices and customs not because they are best but because of habit, but it is during abnormal periods that we do our best thinking. . . . I have long had in mind a book on "Wheatless and Meatless Menus," but the time to bring it out was not ripe until now.
>
> —Eugene Christian, *Meatless and Wheatless Menus,* 1917[12]

Just as antiwar feminists believed that empowering women would end war, so vegetarians believed that eliminating meat eating moved the world closer to pacifism. Indeed, they would say, the Vedic word for war "means 'desire for cows.' "[13] Anna Kingsford, when discussing Women's Peace Conventions of the nineteenth century bemoaned that "These poor deluded creatures cannot see that universal peace is absolutely impossible to a carnivorous race."[14] Percy Shelley thundered that "the butchering of harmless animals cannot fail to produce much of that spirit of insane and hideous exultation in which news of a victory is related alto' purchased by the massacre of a hundred thousand men."[15] In 1918 the Federation of Humano-Vegetarians in America wrote to President Woodrow Wilson seeking equivalent treatment for "adherents of the Vegetarian Cult" as for conscientious objectors because "we vegetarians, reaffirming our faith in the Universal Kinship of the 'Animal Kingdom' and the 'Brotherhood of Man,' adhere in our allegiance to the elementary human commandment, 'Thou Shalt Not Kill.' "[16] Douglas Goldring, in discussing the conscientious objectors who joined the 1917 Club, remarks that they "were certainly the oddest lot of people ever temporarily united under one banner. Some of them carried their dislike of killing so far that they existed only on vegetables."[17] Notably, after the Great War, insights into the possible connections between war and meat eating can be found in writers other than ethical vegetarians.

One reason that insights into these connections are now found in other writers is because of the revelations of the war itself. During the war, soldiers' imaginations became alerted to what Bernard Shaw and other vegetarians had claimed for decades: corpses are corpses. How could the soldier avoid thinking of his commonality with animals as he sat in the trenches watching large black rats consume soldier and horse? The horrors of this war were also found in the slaughterhouse. The editor's introduction to L. F. Easterbrook's article on "Alcohol and Meat" explains, "In 1918 the spectacle of a herd of scared and suffering cattle hustled together in a van, and being conveyed to a slaughter yard, struck the writer of this note as being at least as abominable, and as degrading to our civilisation, as anything he had recently witnessed on several hard fighting fronts in France and Italy."[18]

Philosopher Mary Midgley views the Great War as a turning point in attitudes toward animals, suggesting that after the war there was an upsurge of interest in and scientific proof of the continuities between the other animals and human beings. After citing examples of good-hearted tolerance of egregious acts of hunting, she writes, "For most of us, however, the light seems somehow to have changed—indeed, it probably did so during the First World War."[19]

The Great War also provided a positive, though transitory, vegetarian environment for civilians, especially women, through the rationing of food.[20] Civilians could turn to books such as *Meatless and Wheatless Menus* or *The Golden Rule Cookbook*. This rationing provided one researcher the largest survey population attainable, the entire nation of Denmark. Dr. Mikkel Hindhede describes it as "a low protein experiment on a large scale, about 3,000,000 subjects being available." After directing the rationing program necessitated by the war—"a milk and vegetable diet" along with bran bread, barley, porridge, potatoes, and greens—Hindhede, who had been conducting experiments on low protein, mostly vegetarian, diets since 1895, found that it had improved the Danish people's mortality rates.[21] As a result of vegetarianism's increased attractiveness, the time between the Great War and World War II has been called the "Golden Era of Vegetarianism."[22]

Whereas civilians encountered government encouragement for meatless diets, the epitome of the masculine men, soldiers, received meat, as I discussed in chapter 1. The late Marty Feldman reported that during World War II when his father "was in the Army, [he] could not eat meat because he was an Orthodox Jew. He practically starved to death and was treated with great contempt by the other soldiers because a soldier should eat steak."[23] This emphasis on meat for the male population at the war front may have clarified connections between feminism, vegetarianism, and pacifism at home.

"The lesson of the past six years is this," Henry Salt observed in 1921, "As long as man kills the lower races for food or sport, he will be ready to kill his own race for enmity. It is not *this* bloodshed, or *that* bloodshed, that must cease, but *all* needless bloodshed—all wanton infliction of pain or death upon our fellow-beings."[24] In this observation, Salt expands the notion of the "front" at which deplorable killing occurs. Vegetarians are not alone in postulating an expanded front that includes animal victims. Some twentieth-century British and American women writers strategically expand the terrain of war while exploring the issue of male dominance. The front, they suggest, exists not only in traditionally viewed warfare, but also in what they view as the war against nonhuman animals, typified in hunting and meat eating. Thus they apply insights about wars to the sexual politics of meat.

Women's Fiction and the Expanded Front

> Wars will never cease while men still kill other animals for food, since to turn any living creature into a roast, a steak, a chop, or any other form of "meat" takes the same kind of violence, the same kind of bloodshed and the same kind of mental processes required to change a living man into a dead soldier.
>
> —Agnes Ryan, "For the Church Door," March 1943[25]

> I expect after you have many times seen a deer or woodchuck blown to bits, the thought of a human being blown to bits is that much less impossible to conceive.
>
> —Medieval scholar Grace Knole in *The James Joyce Murders*[26]

Does a man revisit the Great War by recalling his days as a fox hunter? Yes, according to Siegfried Sassoon, whose *The Memoirs of George Sherston,* which culminates in 1918, begins with *Memoirs of a Fox-Hunting Man.*[27] Is sport a training for war, as Henry Salt argued in 1914?[28] How else should Robert Graves begin his farcical, satirical, humorous memoir—his book that turned the war and everything else on its end—but by introducing us to a vegetarian?[29] Can there be *A Case for the Vegetarian Conscientious Objector,* as Max Davis and Scott Nearing believed in 1945? Where else should a novel anticipating the Great War begin but with a male-only shooting party? All of these works suggest a connection between eating meat (and/or hunting) and war. This sense of connection was both verified and intensified once examined through a feminist lens. For then one saw that it was *Man* the Hunter and *Man* the Soldier—the phrases are Charlotte Perkins Gilman's from a poem that opens her penultimate book, *His Religion and Hers,* written after, and influenced by, World War I.[30]

Man the hunter, man the soldier: this refrain not only links disparate acts of violence—the killing of people and the killing of animals—but also focuses on the sex of the killer. The tradition of vegetarian feminist novels by women writers that I explore in this chapter recalls this approach. This tradition originates with the recognition of an expanded front that exists wherever animals are killed. A constellation of feminist insights seems to follow this recognition, which I have isolated into four distinct themes. (1) The theme of rejection of male acts of violence: While their complicity in meat eating locates women *at* the front, a heightened sensitivity to the consumption of animal flesh also generates a comprehensive antiwar critique *from* the front. (2) The theme of identification with animals: Women are allied with animals because they too are objects of use and possession. Women's oppression is expressed through the trope of meat eating. (3) The theme of vegetarianism as rejection of male control and violence: Through the adoption of vegetarianism women simultaneously reject a warring world and dependence on men. This dependence not only manifests itself in the need to be protected by men, but also the need to project on men tasks that women prefer not to think of themselves as doing, such as functioning as killers. (4) The theme of linked oppressions and linked ideal states: Human male dominance is seen to cause women's oppression, war, and meat eating; conversely, in discussions of that perfect world before the Fall, vegetarianism and pacifism become linked with women's equality. While the works in this tradition are unified by their inclusion of animals, none of them attempts to include all four themes in any one text, nor is there any chronological order to the development of these themes. In essence, while the texts are united by a recognition of an enlarged war front, they vary according to the distinct themes evolving from the particular configuration they choose to explore.

Isabel Colegate's Great War novel *The Shooting Party* anchors the texts securely within the antiwar tradition. By exploring the connection between hunting and war from a woman's perspective, Colegate demonstrates, like Sassoon, that hunting is the perfect prelude and pattern for judging a warring world. Colegate provides a female twist, however, by including women in the expanded front. If hunting is the appropriate mirror against which to judge war, then women can gain a voice in judging what they do not share—the battlefront—by judging what they do share as spectators—the experience of the hunt.

Colegate's tightly constructed novel depicts the evening of the second day and the third day of a traditional shooting party. It is a stunning evocation of prewar innocence and a dark foreshadowing of a bloody war. But the shooting party—with its army of uniformed beaters following campaign plans, moving from the bivouac of lunch to the front line of the shooting, with the loaders scurrying in a no-man's-land retrieving the thickly strewn corpses—is not a mere intimation of things to come, but a depiction of a war itself. "War might be like this," thinks Olivia, "casual, friendly and frightening."[31] Indeed, male competition, culminating in the accidental death of a beater, who propelled the frightened pheasants forth to their slaughter at the guns of the upper-class shooters, represents the eternal cause of war. A hunter eager for the most animals "bagged" mistakenly shoots the beater.

Colegate places more spectators at the "front" than shooters. We find there the beaters, the upper-class women, an activist vegetarian, a young child worried about his pet duck, a maid. Their thoughts about the shooting act as counterpoints to the escalating competition of the male shooters.

By positioning her women at the shooting party, Colegate establishes their right to voice criticisms such as Olivia's: "And I am often aware at shooting parties how differently I feel from a man and how, more than that, I really would like to rebel against the world men have made, if I knew how to." Olivia articulates Colegate's theme of rejection of male violence. In Colegate's novel, women's presence in, but opposition to, the violent world men have made is constantly reiterated.

Through the analogy of the shooting party as war, Colegate expands the front to where women are, empowering their articulations. When the war is referred to as "a bigger shooting party [which] had begun, in Flanders," empowerment to speak of *this* front implicitly exists. Thus, *The Shooting Party* becomes one answer to the recurring twentieth-century question posed to women writers: how does a woman condemn war if she cannot be a soldier?[32] This issue is dissolved if she criticizes war by criticizing its equivalent, of which she *is* a part, as witness as well as subsequent consumer: the shooting party.

During the Great War the chasm between the soldier at war and the woman spectator was intentionally widened by soldier-writers who condescendingly dismissed—for lack of experience at the front—any writings by noncombatants. This legacy of condescension and dismissal carried into World War II as well. By showing that women, prior to the Great War, had a right to voice their perspective on war through the corollary experience of participating in, and responding to, a shooting party, Colegate brilliantly restores a right of articulation. The suggestion her novel leaves, therefore, is not that one must be at the war front to have the right to speak, but that one may speak by linking one's own experience *to* war, through making the connection between hunting and/or meat eating and war. So, one can claim one's voice. Wilfred Owen and other writers of World War I erred not by restricting authentic experiences to the front alone, but by their too-limited definition of where the front can be found.

At the expanded front, the theme of identification with animals arises: With whom do the women located there align themselves, the hunter or the hunted? Identification with animals is a pivotal moment for two novels in this tradition of women writers. For Margaret Atwood's and Marge Piercy's characters, meat eating becomes a trope of their own oppression. Women come to see themselves as being consumed by marital oppression at the domestic front; they realize that their bodies are battlegrounds and view animals with the new awareness of a common experience. The third theme, related to their identification with animals, expresses their sense of shared violation. Linking sexual oppression to meat eating, Atwood's and Piercy's women forego the traditional romantic ending by giving up marriage and associating male dominance in personal relationships with meat eating.[33] Thus, they give up meat as well.

The character who most successfully rejects both meat and marriage is Beth, in Marge Piercy's *Small Changes*. Newly married, she finds herself one night eating meat loaf at the kitchen table. Though shaken by a vehement argument during which her husband, angered by her apparent independence, had flushed her birth control pills down the toilet, she sits and contemplates her situation. As she chews the meat loaf she realizes her status as simultaneously victim and victimizer: "A trapped animal eating a dead animal."[34] She restores the absent referent: "Remember the cold meat loaf. From the refrigerator she got the ketchup and doused it liberally. Then it was less obnoxious. Meat, a dead animal that had been alive. She felt as if her life were something slippery she was trying to grab in running water." Grasping her life, she flees her domestic front, becoming a conscientious objector to the war against women and animals.[35] Beth undergoes numerous "small changes" on which Marge Piercy centers her novel. Beth's first and abiding change is her rejection of meat: "The revulsion toward eating flesh from the night of the meat loaf remained. It was part superstition and part morality: she had escaped to her freedom and did not want to steal the life of other warm-blooded creatures." (Her refusal of meat did not include fish.) Her insights of an expanded front catalyze her education into feminism, her evolution into lesbianism, and, finally, her important enactment of antiwar activism through a Traveling Women's Theater. Inevitably she denounces all war fronts.

Though Margaret Atwood's *The Edible Woman* takes place far from war it is in the midst of a war zone. Atwood's character, Marian, discovers there are no civilians there, only hunter or hunted, consumer or consumed. Marian's job is to assess the impact of a Moose beer ad that features hunting: "That was so the average beer-drinker, the slope-shouldered pot-bellied kind, would be able to feel a mystical identity with the plaid-jacketed sportsman shown in the pictures with his foot on a deer or scooping a trout into his net."[36] But Marian identifies with the victim and cries after hearing her fiancé describe his experience at the "front" as a hunter killing and eviscerating a rabbit.

An emotional argument over dinner propels Marian to realize that not only is she *at* the front, she is *the* front: She watches her fiancé skillfully cut his meat, and remembers the Moose beer ads, the hunter poised with a deer, which reminds her of the morning newspaper's report of a young boy who killed nine people after going berserk. Again she ponders her fiancé carving his steak and recalls her cookbook's diagram of a "cow with lines on it and labels to show you from which part of the cow all the different cuts were taken. What they were eating now was from some part of the back, she thought: cut on the dotted line." Then she casts her eyes at her own food.

> She looked down at her own half-eaten steak and suddenly saw it as a hunk of muscle. Blood red. Part of a real cow that once moved

> and ate and was killed, knocked on the head as it [*sic*] stood in a queue like someone waiting for a streetcar. Of course everyone knew that. But most of the time you never thought about it.

After this, Marian's unconscious attitude toward food changes: her body rejects certain foods and she realizes to her surprise that she is becoming a vegetarian, that her body has taken an ethical stand: "It simply refused to eat anything that had once been, or (like oysters on the half-shell) might still be living." Both meat eating and first-person narration are suspended once Marian intuits her link to other animals, suggesting that a challenge to meat eating is linked to an attack on the sovereign individual subject. The fluid, merged subjectively of the middle part of the book finds mystical identity with things, especially animals, that are consumed.

Only when she can deal with her own sexual subjugation is Marian released from her body's refusal to eat. She confronts her fiancé with a truly edible woman, a cake she has made, and accuses: "You've been trying to destroy me, haven't you. . . . You've been trying to assimilate me."[37] Domestic dynamics, a sexual war, led to vegetarianism. But so profound a challenge to the status quo seems too much to sustain. After breaking her engagement and freeing herself from subjugation to her fiancé, Marian reclaims both first-person narration and regains control over her body's selection of foods. Freed from domestic oppression, she has difficulty sustaining insights in opposition to the dominant worldview, and the pleasure of her own autonomy renders her less sensitive to others' oppression. Her consciousness of being (at) the front subsides. She begins to eat meat and to date men again.

If male dominance catalyzes the feminist insight of an expanded front and resultant vegetarianism, feminist vegetarianism offers men a way to reject war by rejecting meat eating. As opposed to Piercy's and Atwood's controlling, masculine men, whose relationships with women catalyze the ineluctable insight that meat eating and sexual oppression are linked, Agnes Ryan's unpublished novel, "Who Can Fear Too Many Stars?" figures a romance of vegetarian conversion for a liberated man. Writing in the 1930s, Ryan introduced an unusual motivation for vegetarianism: love of a New Woman. Vegetarianism is the standard against which the new man is measured. As Ryan described her work in a letter to the author of *The Golden Rule Cookbook,* "I would like to make it a ripping love story, hinging on meat-eating."[38]

Ruth, an independent, professional woman, is opposed to marriage yet finds herself in love with John Heather. Fearing that it will make their love "go asunder," Ruth withholds from John one vital piece of information. She will not "take anybody into [her] inner circle who can think and know—and still eat flesh." Unfortunately, John is a meat eater. He struggles to become a vegetarian for the woman he loves, but, at Christmas, all romance collapses when he sends Ruth fox furs. Horrified by the gift and the lack of comprehension it reveals—John has not really understood her complete rejection of animal exploitation—Ruth sends them back and flees. Deeply in love, John resolves to learn as much as possible about vegetarianism by reading, among others, nineteenth-century vegetarian Anna Kingsford and Bernard Shaw. The journal he keeps during this time reveals to Ruth that he is now fully a vegetarian, and as a result they can be married.

Vegetarianism and feminism act as antiphonal voices in this novel, not as a unified vision, except to demonstrate Ryan's theme "that there are many modern thinking women who mean to stiffen the case for men—or not marry."[39] While John reads vegetarian writings, Ruth receives a tract against marriage that warns "To be a bride is to become a slave, body and soul."[40] Ryan introduces vegetarian and feminist arguments into the novel through references to books, diaries, pamphlets; for her, texts mediate the conversion to vegetarianism and feminism. This adheres to the tradition of bearing the vegetarian word, believing that reading will bring about revelation and change. Whatever John and Ruth read, we must read as readers of Ryan's novel, thus we encounter both the literal and literary arguments for vegetarianism and feminism. But in this an imbalance exists. Whereas John reads his way into vegetarianism, Ruth avoids confronting the implication of romantic love. His fate as a male in love with a "modern thinking woman" is redemption. The word becomes flesh as he becomes a vegetarian. Ruth's fate as a modern thinking *married* woman will be to live in oppression. Ryan thus acknowledges there are some things that vegetarianism cannot redeem and that reading cannot accomplish. The text fails at this point. What can be the fate of a woman in a ripping love story hinging on meat eating? As a vegetarianism redeemed through romantic love is written into the text, *she* is written out of it. The novel collapses into itself and becomes a tract such as the ones that John and Ruth encounter.

Ryan's novel presents a variant formulation of vegetarianism as rejection of male control and violence. Rather than portray a woman who simultaneously rejects violence and dependence on a man, like Piercy's and Atwood's heroines, it figures a man who, through his love for a woman, discovers the ability to reject a warring world. John represents Ryan's husband, Henry Bailey Stevens, who held that humanity was initially vegetarian, goddess worshiping, and pacifist. These characteristics embody the fourth theme of the expanded front, the Golden Age of vegetarianism.

The Golden Age of Vegetarianism and Women's Fiction

> Rynn Berry, Jr.: *Do you think if more and more people become vegetarians, it will usher in a new Golden Age?*
> Brigid Brophy: No, not of itself. Bernard Shaw pointed out that human vegetarians were often very fierce people, and vegetarian animals also are often quite fierce. No, there is no direct connection. If, however, human beings work it out and decide to renounce violence then, obviously, if you renounce violence against chickens, cows, lambs, etcetera, you likewise renounce it against human beings. And then, yes—if we could all manage it—straight into the Golden Age.[41]

In *The Recovery of Culture,* Henry Bailey Stevens proposes that a plant culture—which he considers anthropologically and horticulturally verified—was replaced with a "blood culture." In a section entitled "The Rape of the Matriarchate" he writes: "The truth is that animal husbandry and war are institutions in which man has shown himself most proficient. He has been the butcher and the soldier; and when the Blood Culture took control of religion, the priestesses were shoved aside."[42] Novelists and short story writers join Stevens in locating the cause of meat eating and war in male dominance; some twentieth-century women writers imagine a Golden Age before the fall that was feminist, pacifist, and vegetarian.

In the short story "An Anecdote of the Golden Age [Homage to *Back to Methuselah*]" Brigid Brophy suggests that men's behavioral change is at the root of war, women's oppression, and the killing of animals. Brophy's Golden Age is one in which immortals consume bounteous food from the garden. Naked women menstruate openly and their blood is admired by everyone for its rare beauty. However, men discover that they too bleed when two men engage in a blood-letting fist fight, and paradise is lost. Menstruation is tabooed and fruit, moments ago cherished food, is now disdained by one of the men, Strephon. He bombs another man's pagoda and offers this justification: " 'Corydon was a murderer,' Strephon said sulkily. 'He was fair game. Which reminds me: I shall kill the animals next.' "[43] Strephon confines his menstruating woman to the house, "and preferably the kitchen, in which unglamorous setting she would be least attractive to other men." Brophy concludes her cautionary tale: "Strephon, the only one of the group to be truly immortal, is in power to this day."

Though obviously having a romp in this piece, Brophy's viewpoint is consistent with her other writings on the subject of the oppression of woman and animals.[44] Brophy suggests that as long as men are in power, patriarchal violence and its attendant oppressions of women and animals will continue. This theme of the male overthrow of a prepatriarchal vegetarian era also appears in June Brindel's *Ariadne: A Novel of Ancient Crete.* Blood sacrifice here is associated with male control. Ariadne, called by her author "the last Matriarch of Crete," attempts to introduce the ancient worshipful rituals featuring milk and honey but no blood. Brindel's feminist-vegetarian-pacifist mythopoesis figures a vegetarian time of powerful priestesses worshiping goddesses. The triumph of patriarchal control simultaneously introduces the slaughter of animals and the worship of male gods: "Daedulus would ask a question about the ritual, cautiously. 'The invocation to Zeus, when was that introduced into the ceremony? I do not find it in the oldest texts.' Or, 'The earliest records of offerings to the Goddess list only grains and fruit. When was the slaughter of animals added?' "[45] Brindel's dependence on early twentieth-century scholar Jane Harrison is evident in her description of the rituals followed by Ariadne. As women's power is displaced, Ariadne escapes to the mountains and pronounces that the labyrinth of Theseus is patriarchal thought that has killed the center, the Mother Goddess. Brindel continues this theme in *Phaedra: A Novel of Ancient Athens,* in which Phaedra, despite living in a hostile atmosphere, attempts to live a peaceful, vegetarian, goddess-worshiping life.[46] Brindel, like Brophy, evokes a female-oriented Golden Age where there are no fronts and no wars.

Through diets for a peaceful vegetarian life, feminist utopias enact the critique of the expanded front, imagining a world without violence. This aspect of the fourth theme is initially depicted in the first feminist, vegetarian, pacifist utopia written by a woman, Charlotte Perkins Gilman's *Herland,* published during the Great War.[47] In *Herland,* we find menus recalling *The Golden Rule Cookbook:* "The breakfast was not profuse, but . . . this repast with its new but delicious fruit, its dish of large rich-flavored nuts, and its highly satisfactory little cakes was most agreeable."[48] Fruit- and nut-bearing trees, grains and berries, citrus fruits, olives and figs are carefully cultivated by the women inhabitants. Gilman's narrator, the American intellectual male of 1915, at once notices the absence of meat in *Herland* and queries: "Have you no cattle—sheep—horses?" In a novel that demonstrates the need for a feminist loving kindness, what Gilman called Maternal Pantheism, we might expect that their vegetarianism is one expression of mother love and the corollary belief that meat eating causes aggressive behavior such as male dominance and war. But it is not. Instead, it is a politically astute and ecologically sound conclusion: wars can be avoided if meat eating is eliminated. They did not have any cattle, sheep, or horses because they did "not want them anymore. They took up too much room—we need all our land to feed our people. It is such a little country, you know." What wartime had required of Denmark, the potential causation of war required of *Herland*.

Gilman's *Herland* is a feminist gloss on the ecological position enunciated in Plato's *Republic*.[49] Gilman's subtext about land use resulting in war is in opposition to the overt text, which suggests that motivations arising from Mother Love determine Herland's policies. Through her use of the classical ecological argument of preventing wars through controlling diet, Gilman acknowledges that women living on their own would still have a potential for violence against each other *if* they left their diet uncontrolled. Thus women are not exempted from future wars, as Maternal Pantheism would imply. By extension, the Great War could not be the war that ends all wars if meat eating continued. The issue of vegetarianism is an inevitable part of *Herland* because Gilman, while emphasizing women's strengths and abilities, deconstructs the essentials of patriarchal culture at its many fronts.

Whereas *Herland* is the initial text in which a modern woman writer posits the configuration of feminism, vegetarianism, and pacifism, Dorothy Bryant's more recent *The Kin of Ata are Waiting for You* extends Gilman's treatment by situating animals within the moral order. *The Kin of Ata* depicts an egalitarian utopian society in which men and women share child care, gardening, and cleaning. Dried fruits and nuts, grains and legumes, root vegetables and herbs provide great variety to the diet. And the reason for the diet is Bryant's 1970s equivalent to Maternal Pantheism: "I knew better than to suggest that we eat birds or animals, or even fish. They would have reacted the same way as if I had told them we should eat the children. . . . No one would have thought of killing any of them."[50]

Because Gilman, Bryant, Ryan, and other women writers perceived connections between male dominance, war, and meat eating, they figure men who demonstrate the ability to change. We find in their novels men who are adaptable, who forswear certain masculine and human-centered privileges, including meat consumption. In addition, sensitive male writers such as Shelley, Shaw, Salt, and Stevens explored the issues of animals' and women's otherness. Indeed, the conclusion to be drawn from their writings and their lives is that men as well as women can enact lifestyles sensitive to issues of feminism, pacifism, and vegetarianism.

Rachel Blau DuPlessis comments that the "erasure of the dualism of public and private spheres is one part of the critique of ideology in women's writings."[51] Together the four themes arising from the insight of the expanded front exemplify this erasure. The meaning of the public front invades the private sphere, prompting a redefinition of the location of the front. Additionally, taken together these themes challenge the dualism separating the consequences of violence for animals and human beings. These works argue that domestic oppression and meat eating, usually considered private occurrences, are vitally connected to waging war, while vegetarianism, an apparently private act, constitutes the public rejection of war as a method of conflict resolution. At the front, the connections between male dominance, the killing of animals, and the killing of human beings become clear.

The Narrative Strategy of Interruption

> Central to all [Woolf's] thinking is the revelation of interruption, heralding change, and the growing expectation that society is on the verge of radical transformation.
>
> —Lucio Ruotolo, *The Interrupted Moment*[52]

> The symbolism of meat-eating is never neutral. To himself, the meat-eater seems to be eating life. To the vegetarian, he seems to be eating death. There is a kind of gestalt-shift between the two positions which makes it hard to change, and hard to raise questions on the matter at all without becoming embattled.
>
> —Mary Midgley, *Animals and Why They Matter*[53]

We have examined novels in which feminist insights catalyze connections between vegetarianism and political violence. Each of these novels appears to employ the same literary technique for summoning these connections—a technique I call *interruption.* Interruption provides the gestalt shift by which vegetarianism can be heard. Technically, it occurs when the movement of the novel is suddenly arrested, and attention is given to the issue of vegetarianism in an enclosed section of the novel. The author provides signs that an interruption has occurred. Dots or dashes; the use of the word "interruption"; stammering, pauses, inarticulateness, or confusion in those who are usually in control; the deflection of the story to a focus on food and eating habits; or the reference to significant earlier figures or events from vegetarian history: all become the means for establishing an interruption, a gap in the narrative in which vegetarianism can be entertained.[54] Although the interruption is set apart, the meaning it contains speaks to central themes of the novel, unifying the interruption and the interrupted text through acute critical comments about the social order and meat eating.[55]

In the works of modern women writers the intrusion into the text of a vegetarian incident announces a subversion of the dominant world order, enacted through the subversion of the text itself by the textual strategy of interruption. What was once silenced breaks into the text, deflecting attention from the forces that generally silence it, both thematically and textually. Interruption provides an opportunity for refocusing the trajectory of the text, as well as providing a protected space within the novel for expanding the front. Interruption does battle with the novel for meaning, wresting meaning from the dominant culture as represented in the text itself.[56] In essence, expanding the front requires extending the scope of the novel, taking it to new topical territory, and this is the function of interruption, which provides the needed space for such expansion. A vegetarian presence destablizes patriarchal concerns.

Isadora Duncan's meditation on the connection between war and meat eating in her autobiography *My Life* exemplifies the interruption of narrative. She interrupts a discussion about her life during the Great War to assert: "Bernard Shaw says that as long as men torture and slay animals and eat their flesh, we shall have war. I think all sane, thinking people must be of his opinion." From her wartime experience she concludes:

> Who loves this horrible thing called War? Probably the meat eaters, having killed, feel the need to kill—kill birds, animals—the tender stricken deer—hunt foxes. The butcher with his bloody apron incites bloodshed, murder. Why not? From cutting the throat of a young calf to cutting the throat of our brothers and sisters is but a step. While we are ourselves the living graves of murdered animals, how can we expect any ideal conditions on the earth?[57]

Duncan's interruption is clearly announced to readers by her beginning reference to Shaw and her ending with a literal invocation of what she believed to be his words.[58] However, she provides a distinctly feminist interpretation to Shaw's insights. By positioning the masculine pronoun between the butcher and the bloody apron, she implicitly indicts male behavior.

The most notable interruption in a text occurs during a Thanksgiving dinner in France, described in Mary McCarthy's *Birds of America*, a novel referred to briefly in chapter 1. The novel moves forward without much regard to any specific ethics of consumption. Suddenly, a vegetarian speaks, attention becomes riveted to what the vegetarian is saying and not eating. The interruptions occur on many levels. Roberta Scott, a young American, refuses both dark and light meat from her host, a NATO general. Shocked, he must set down his carving knife before he can say, "*No turkey?*" With the carving knife he has arrogated power, and each slice of speared meat reinforces his military presence. Her refusal challenges his use of these symbolic implements and thus his power. His implements remain unused as he learns of her vegetarianism, and he must resort to playing "impatiently" with them as he solemnly informs his guest, "This is Thanksgiving!"[59]

Later, his wife asks, "What made you decide to take up vegetarianism? I don't mean to be intrusive, but tell us, do you really think it's cruel to kill animals?" Again, the general's actions are arrested by the presence of vegetarianism: "The general, who was carving seconds, paused with his knife in mid-air to await the verdict." In the midst of this interruption we find Miss Scott's precise echoing of the vegetarian position on warfare, artfully introduced into the text prior to a heated argument about the war in Vietnam: "Why, some people actually claim that it's a flesh diet that's turned man into a killer of his own kind! He has the tiger's instincts without the tiger's taboos. Of course that's only a hypothesis. One way of testing it would be for humanity to practice vegetarianism for several generations. Maybe we'd find that war and murder would disappear."

McCarthy's chapter uses domestic events to figure the claim that meat eating causes war, as it traces the slowly escalating rage of the general for whom carving recalls his military might. He announces that he is "in command here," and discounts Miss Scott's refusal by giving her turkey anyway. But she will not eat it, nor any of the gravy-polluted foods he proffers. Her refusal implies that if meat eating and war are related, as *some* people claim, then the dining-room table is a part of the extended front; her vegetarianism functions as a condemnation of war. The table soon becomes a site of simulated warfare, as an enlistee makes the sounds of an automatic machine gun. Meanwhile, the general perceives the subtle condemnation and escalates the verbal battle as he argues for the bombing of Hanoi. Pinpointing the cause of his bellicosity his wife confides, "Between you and me, it kind of got under his skin to see that girl refusing to touch her food, I saw that right away." McCarthy's novel pursues the question of how far moral obligations should extend; this interruption suggests that they extend to the quintessential bird of America.

The interruptions of *The Shooting Party* are caused by the appearance of Cornelius Cardew, who actually interrupts the shooting by bearing the vegetarian word through picketing. He shoulders his "Thou Shalt Not Kill" banner and marches "straight down the line in front of the guns."[60] Some of the shooters refuse to cease their firing, especially the most competitive one: "The interruption had not caused him to lose a single shot," but for the others, "their concentration had been broken by the interruption." By Cardew's interruption, the historical alliance between feminism and vegetarianism is suggestively summoned; he hands out his own pamphlet which as we saw in chapter 5 evokes past writers of vindications—Mary Wollstonecraft's *A Vindication of the Rights of Woman* and Percy Shelley's *A Vindication of Natural Diet.*

As these examples demonstrate, the interruptions contain their own legitimating mechanism by summoning historical figures who endorsed what the interruptions convey—the message of the expanded front. Essentially, vegetarian tradition provides the authority for interrupting the text with vegetarianism. Shaw is summoned by Duncan and Brophy, Salt by Colegate, the Doukhobors (Russian pacifist-vegetarians who migrated to Canada) by McCarthy and Atwood, and Kingsford by Ryan. It is striking that two different texts linking vegetarianism and pacifism insert the name of the Doukhobors, who maintained their vegetarianism and pacifism in rigorous circumstances, persecution, and banishment in Russia as well as migration as a group (estimated as high as 7,500 individuals) to Canada. The Doukhobors become grounding figures. This tradition of providing additional authority through historical references is a version of what any embattled group does—that is, evoke touchstone figures who in feminist terms we might consider "role models."

This historical invocation of past vegetarians imprints a distinctly feminist hermeneutic: Duncan's view of male butchers as inuring the world to bloodshed; McCarthy's female challenge to male bellicosity through dietary choice; Colegate's allusions to Wollstonecraft and Shelley as well as Salt. Situating historical reference within the interruption suggests that the notion of an expanded front is one that recurs in history. And through the feminist hermeneutic brought to vegetarian history, a causal link with male dominance and war is effected. Interruption destabilizes the text and the culture it represents.

Overcoming Dominant Viewpoints

> There is not always encouragement and acceptance for those who try to introduce meanings for which there is no conceptual space in the social order.
>
> —Dale Spender, *Man Made Language*[61]

> There is a kind of seductiveness about a movement which is revolutionary, but not revolutionary enough.
>
> —Mary Daly, *Beyond God the Father*[62]

How can we explain the heightened sensitivity by twentieth-century women writers to violence against animals and the failure among literary critics to remark on this sensitivity? When female marginality is "in dialogue with dominance" it invokes the position of animals, who are also on the margins, who are also absent referents.[63] Part of the otherness with which women writers identify is the otherness of the other animals; both are caught in the overlapping structure of oppression in which each functions as absent referents for the other. The "assertive repossession of voice" includes the expression of voice through identification with those who have none.[64]

Through specific female identifications catalyzed by male oppression, the character reflects on the question "How would you like it if this were done to you?" When Margaret Atwood's Marian cannot think of herself as *I*, when her first-person-singular identity is interrupted, her body becomes alert to the oppression of the other animals. What evolves is a poetics of engagement between women and animals, and a belief that violence against other animals carries the same seriousness as violence against people; where meat eating is, there is the front. Vegetarianism becomes, then, a necessary accompaniment to pacifism. Challenging the dominant ethos that animals exist for human consumption by extension challenges a world at war.

Generally women as well as men hold to the powerful, dominant ethos regarding animals, just as Marian returns to eating meat once she is able to think again in the first-person singular. This causes the muting of a tradition that does not hold to the dominant ethos.

The tradition in which modern women writers confront the meaning of meat eating within the context of war is one of a dialectic between silencing and risking speech. It is a tradition that speaks through specificity (i.e., naming what is eaten): interrupting a meal, interrupting a man's control, interrupting the male tradition with female voices. When women writers raise the issue of vegetarianism, they touch upon their dilemma of being silenced in a patriarchal world. Vegetarianism becomes a complex female meditation on being dominated and dominator.

While modern vegetarianism interrupts modern women's writing and hence disrupts it as a way of finding space and power to speak, on a deeper level it confirms women's work. By redefining the front and locating it wherever meat eating is, modern women writers make a powerful statement on the rights of women and women writers to have a voice during wartime. And this feminist, vegetarian, pacifist tradition—tracing its genesis to the Great War—would argue that an aspect of the war that gave it voice continues today.[65]

Figure 7

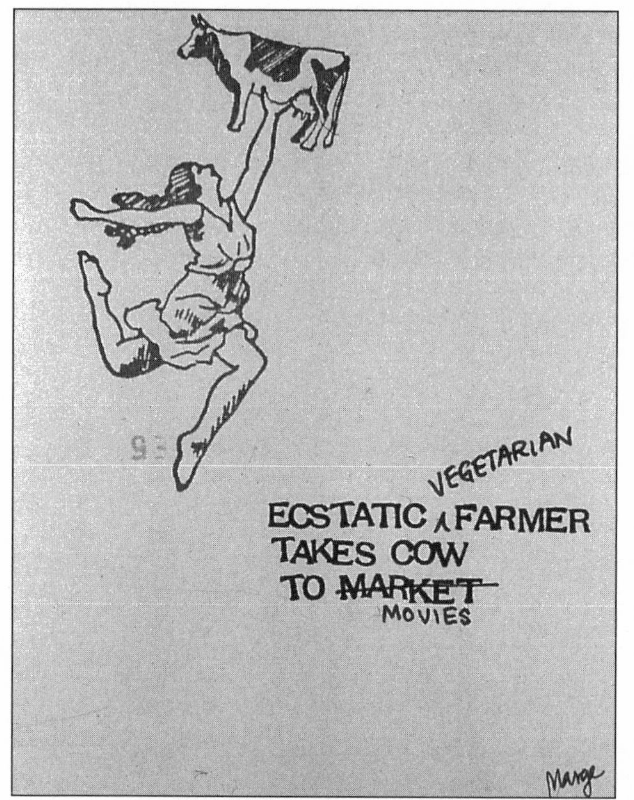
ECSTATIC VEGETARIAN FARMER
TAKES COW
TO MARKET
MOVIES
Marge

FEMINIST
VEGETARIAN

ANIMAL
LIBERATION
is a
FEMINIST
ISSUE

WOMEN AND TURKEYS
AGAINST CHRISTMAS

part three

Eat Rice Have Faith in Women

The enlightened mortals of the twentieth century will surely be vegetarians.

—Frances Willard, 1839–1898
feminist, vegetarian, and temperance leader

eat rice have faith in women
what I dont know now
I can still learn
if I am alone now
I will be with them later
if I am weak now
I can become strong
slowly slowly
if I learn I can teach others
if others learn first
I must believe
they will come back and teach me
. . . .
slowly we begin
giving back what was taken away
our right to the control of our bodies
knowledge of how to fight and build
food that nourishes
medicine that heals
. . . .
eat rice have faith in women
what I dont know now
I can still learn

—Fran Winant, "Eat Rice Have Faith in Women"

chapter 8

The Distortion of the Vegetarian Body

My journal entry, May 4, 1976:

For my frustration about not finding readily accessible information about fem[inists] who were veg. in the past—write an article on Veg. and Fem. Historiography use Mary's [Daly] analyses from *B[eyond] G[od] t[he] F[ather]*—how people don't take seriously thru trivialization, erasure, how does one find a connection when not indexed?

—Frances Willard (glancingly mentioned), Lou Andreas-Salome, Agnes Ryan's involvement in "lunatic fringe" groups according to the archivist at Radcliffe [Schlesinger Library] 20 yrs ago.

veg—a conscious decision effecting every day of your life. not simply a reform fad

one has to approach your reading material w/ a hopeful, faith-filled attitude, hoping for one small mention.

left Schlesinger at 3:45. Bicycled for an hour along Charles River. Dinner was marvelous—Middle Eastern bread, tomato, avocado, sprouts, garbanzo beans; sunflower butter on toast w/ bananas. At CSR's [Carroll Smith-Rosenberg] I couldn't pass up pound cake and ice cream. Discussed whether Agnes Ryan would be a good candidate for 4th volume of *NAW [Notable American Women]*. Returning here at 9:00 I read Kate Millet and didn't do my yoga.

Before finishing this book, you will have eaten at least one meal. Before I finished writing this book, I ate several hundred meals. Before the people whose histories we reconstruct died, they had eaten tens of thousands of meals. If I ate a veggie burger instead of a hamburger this choice says something about me as an historical actor. For I will have had to act in response to these questions:

- How informed am I about what I eat?
- What are my interests in the preparation and aesthetic presentation of vegetable food?
- What are my resources?
- Did I eat at a vegetarian restaurant?
- Did I have available a fast food mix?
- Did I use a vegan cookbook?
- Why did I leave meat out of my diet?

Whenever people consciously excluded meat from their diet, similar questions may be asked of them as well.

Vegetarianism reveals how people live with the often difficult consequences of their decisions. Meat has to do with coded expectations, patterns of responses. I am intrigued by excesses in interpretation that seek to account for who has left meat out of their diet and why, as well as the gaps in interpretation that completely ignore the question. We cannot understand those things for which our historical or fictional sisters are most noted unless we recognize those things for which they are least noted.

This chapter will analyze reasons for the tendency of many scholars to ignore the signs of the alliance between feminism and vegetarianism. To counter the gaps in interpretation, I propose that not only was vegetarianism a logical enacting of a moral viewpoint, but it also resonated with feminist theory and female experience. I begin by defining the "vegetarian body" as both a body of writings and the idea that many vegetarians hold that we are physiologically predisposed to vegetarianism. In this I use as a basepoint the insight articulated by ethicist Beverly Harrison that asserts the moral importance of being in touch with our bodies:

> If we begin, as feminists must, with "our bodies, ourselves," we recognize that all our knowledge, including our moral knowledge, is body-mediated knowledge. . . . Failure to live deeply in "our bodies, ourselves," destroys the possibility of moral relations between us.[1]

Vegetarians identify a connection between a healthy body and a diet that honors the moral relations between us and the other animals.

Defining the Vegetarian Body

> I take no credit for abstaining from flesh eating. I was born without any desire or relish for meat.
>
> —Lucinda Chandler after 45 years of being a vegetarian[2]

Feminist fundraising dinners and conferences often serve flesh food; some feminists lecture in leather or fur. This is the literal distortion of the vegetarian body. Ethical vegetarianism is a theory people enact with their bodies. "The Vegetarian Body" is a concept that incorporates this understanding and many others. We find a body of literature celebrating vegetarianism that has been distorted because of lack of appreciation by a dominant culture.

A major theme of this body of vegetarian protest literature proposes another level of meaning to these words: the argument that humans have bodies that resemble the bodies of herbivores rather than bodies of carnivores. Marshaled in support of this definition of the human vegetarian body was evidence from the teeth, saliva, stomach acids, and length of the intestines. This argument was often the one which undercut the ethical issues concerning the eating of animals; meat eaters of the past greeted the claims for a physiological disposition to vegetarianism as such a wild stretching of a point that all other arguments were seen as untrustworthy. *A Vindication of the Rights of Woman,* Mary Wollstonecraft's angry attack on Rousseau's opinions about women, begins not with a focused review of his misogyny, but with a footnote to assail his vegetarian-anatomical argument. When she first directly names Rousseau, she cannot resist discussing the absurdity of his position: "Contrary to the opinion of anatomists, who argue by analogy from the formation of the teeth, stomach and intestines, Rousseau will not allow a man to be a carnivorous animal."[3]

That vegetarian converts also argued the connection between diseases such as meat eating and cancer only made them more laughable. Now such a connection is confirmed in countless medical studies. The Western omnivorous diet is associated with higher levels of diabetes, heart disease, hypertension, and cancer. On the other hand, a plant-based diet provides the protective benefits of phytochemicals, antioxidants, fiber, and no cholesterol.

A reconceptualization of the vegetarian body of literature is necessary in the light of the growing medical information about the human body. In addition, anthropological sources indicate that our earliest hominid ancestors had vegetarian bodies. In the records of their bones, dental impressions, and tools, these anonymous ancestors reveal the fact that meat, as a substantial part of the diet, became a fixture in human life only recently—in the past 40,000 years. Indeed, it was not until the past two hundred years that most people in the Western world had the opportunity to consume meat daily.

Archaeological remains provide evidence of our early plant-based dietary. The masticatory system of the early hominids include teeth that could pulverize plant foods rather than rip into flesh. Scratch marks such as are found on the teeth of carnivores are absent. Instead, fossil teeth bear patterns of wear consistent with consumption of large quantities of plant food. In addition, sharp flakes that have survived—originally credited with use in skinning and cutting up animal flesh—bear chips and damage on the edges of the flakes consistent with digging activities. Analyses of fossilized human fecal matter confirm a diet of plant foods as well. From this, vegetarians argue that we are the meat eaters who never evolved a body equipped to digest meat. We have first-stage bodies with a fourth-stage diet. The primary distortion of the vegetarian body, in their eyes, occurs each time a person eats meat and forces the body to digest high-fat, protein-loaded, cholesterol-rich, animal-based foods.

It is not just in our early history that a plant-based diet is suggested. The internal signs that are read to proclaim our anatomical disposition to a vegetarian diet are many. Our saliva "contains the ferment pytalin, for digesting starch, characteristic of the herbivore."[4] The special saliva proteins found in apes and humans "are thought to make tooth enamel more resistant to decay caused by large amounts of plant carbohydrate and/or a high variety of texture in the diet."[5] Jane Brody discusses at length the difference between our "canine teeth" and the canine teeth of carnivores. She concludes: "Our teeth are more like those of herbivores than of flesh eaters. Our front teeth are large and sharp, good for biting; our canines are small—almost vestigial compared to a tiger's; our molars are flattened; and our jaws are mobile for grinding food into the small bits we are able to swallow."[6] We lack the carnivore's rasping tongue, and compared to the amounts in a carnivore, our gastric juices have only a small amount of hydrochloric acid.[7] The intestines of carnivorous animals are short, only three times the length of the animal's body. We, on the other hand, have an intestinal length twelve times the length of the body.

If our anatomical makeup suggests more of a similarity to herbivores than to carnivores, what occurs when meat is ingested? We might argue that the absent referent of the animal is not ever actually absent at all: just redefined. The absent referent makes herself present in one's body through the effects that meat has in the form of disease, especially heart disease and cancer. More than one hundred people die every hour in this country from heart disease. Vegetarians are about fifty percent less likely to die from heart disease than are meat eaters. According to studies in developed countries, vegetarians have lower cancer mortality rates than meat eaters. While other factors increase cancer risk, "the National Cancer Institute estimates that one-third of all cancer deaths in this country and eight out of ten of the most common cancers are related to diet."[8]

For at least two hundred years vegetarians have argued that a connection exists between meat eating and cancer. Sarah Cleghorn, early twentieth-century vegetarian and feminist, mentioned the writings of a Dr. Leffingwell who suggested "a carnivorous origin for cancer. I wish the national cancer society would ascertain the percentage of cancer among vegetarians."[9] After World War II, Agnes Ryan wrote a manuscript entitled "The Cancer Bogy." In it she claimed that

> I became sufficiently convinced in my own mind as to the root cause of cancer to put into effect such a complete right-about-face in my mode of living as to produce a very drastic effect on my own health. . . . I am thoroughly convinced that cancer is preventable now, cheaply, with our present knowledge, by means easily within our reach.[10]

"The Cancer Bogy" is perhaps the first modern vegetarian self-help guide to good health. Ryan begins by establishing a correlation between the number of deaths from cancer with meat eating. Her formula for predisposing one's body to cancer is: "Poison Intake [by which she means 'all flesh foods' as well as tobacco, intoxicants, and drugs] plus Vitamin Starvation plus Faulty Elimination." Conversely, her formula for health is "Natural foods plus Proper Elimination plus Exercise over the period of one's life."[11]

The gestalt shift in which vegetarians see meat as death and meat eaters see meat as life influences the receptivity of each group to information that suggests associations between meat consumption and disease. Vegetarians literally see vegetarianism as giving life and meat as causing death to the consumers. They know that the heart of the average meat eater beats faster than that of the vegetarian. They know that the cancer-preventive benefits of consuming vegetables such as broccoli, brussel sprouts, and cabbage have been demonstrated, from which they conclude that a vegetarian immunity to the degenerative diseases that plague our culture may arise. They see meat as causing death because of the effects of high-fat diets on one's susceptibility to cancer and heart disease.

Many who stop eating meat for a limited period of time comment on the differences they felt. They were no longer sleepy after a meal, a certain undefinable lightness replaced a heaviness or grossness they had associated with food consumption. Others have found that vegetarianism improves their health. When she attended medical school in Paris in the late nineteenth century, Anna Kingsford's vegetarianism helped her overcome "many obstacles and trials, physical and moral, rendered specifically hard by the artifical disabilities of my sex, and by a variety of personal circumstances."[12] In experiencing body-mediated knowledge, many have concluded that the word the human body speaks is vegetarian.

Critical Distortions

> With your immense knowledge of women's activities, can you give me any information about Anna Kingsford, so far as I know the world's first woman vegetarian? I can not find anything about her anywhere.
>
> —Agnes Ryan to Alice Park, 1936[13]

> When I speak for my friends the Anti-Vivisectionists, the Anti-Vaccinationists, the Spiritualists, or the advocates of freedom for women. . . . I always feel that such of these as are not abstainers from flesh-food have unstable ground under their feet, and it is my great regret that, when helping them in their good works, I cannot openly and publicly maintain what I so ardently believe—that the Vegetarian movement is the bottom and basis of all other movements towards Purity, Freedom, Justice, and Happiness.
>
> —Anna Kingsford[14]

In attempting to interpret vegetarianism from the dominant perspective, historians often explain it away rather than explain it. Numerous texts of meat that distort the radical cultural critique of vegetarianism appear. For instance, reasons offered for the rise in the interest in vegetarianism during the time of the French Revolution and afterwards dwell on personal responses to cultural change. Historians have suggested that vegetarians were attempting to subdue their animal nature and disown their (feared) beastliness by their focus on the cruelty of meat eating. They neglect to discuss the uniquely human inventions of meat eating for which there are no animal parallels: the use of implements to kill and butcher the animal, the cooking and seasoning of meat.

Vegetarian writers of the past, starting with Plutarch through Percy Shelley to Anna Kingsford and into the twentieth century, were not troubled by the fact that the other animals ate meat, they were concerned that humans in eating meat did so in ways very unlike the other animals. As we saw in chapter 2, the classic line in the vegetarian body of literature goes something like this: *animals do not need to cook their meat before they eat it, and they do not need help ripping meat off of a bone. If meat eating is natural, why do we not do it naturally, like the animals?* Vegetarians did not fear what was natural to humans, they bemoaned the acceptance of an unnatural, and to them, unnecessary practice.

Vegetarians recognize the cultural aspects of meat eating, what I have been calling the texts of meat. Since meat is not eaten in its "natural" state—raw, off of the corpse—but is instead transformed through cultural intervention, vegetarians have directed their energy toward analyzing the specifics of this cultural intervention. They claim that the structures that transform flesh as it is eaten by the other animals into meat as it is eaten by human beings are not unimportant or trivial, especially as they signal the degree of distancing that our culture has determined is necessary for consumption of animals to proceed. Even a steak tartare is a result of cultural intervention in the form of haute cuisine.

If the vegetarian body is not distorted by the claim that vegetarians feared the animal aspects of being human, historians have argued that vegetarians reflected a conservative impulse, and sought to recapture the fading pastoral society of a pre-Industrial Revolution Europe. But many vegetarians saw themselves responding to repression and oppression, not as agents of regression. In chapter 6 we learned of the numerous Romantic vegetarians who linked their radical politics with their concern for animals. In 1845, Maria Loomis, resident of the Skaneateles utopian community, wrote that vegetarianism "is the beginning place for Reformers. I have little confidence in any very considerable reform that does not commence here."[15] At the end of the century, Henry Salt in *The Logic of Vegetarianism* concurred: "Vegetarianism is, in truth, *progressiveness in diet.*"[16] His associates in the Fabian Society of the 1890s, such as Bernard Shaw and Annie Besant, agreed in substance as most were vegetarians.[17]

A history of distortion is required that would examine the problems embedded in how we judge social activism on behalf of animals; the person is viewed as dysfunctional rather than society. The explanations provided such as status displacement, the erosion of rural society, or a strong identification with pets are obvious attempts to eviscerate the critique of the dominant culture by attributing psychological motives rather than political motives to those who protest the activities of the dominant culture.

One way that the dominant culture avoids the radical critique of vegetarianism is by focusing on individuals who seem to disprove the claims of vegetarians. Thus, meat eaters refer to Hitler's "vegetarianism." In fact, Hitler was not a vegetarian.[18] But many meat eaters need to believe that Hitler was a vegetarian to comfort themselves with the idea that vegetarianism does not necessarily make you a better person. The message appears to be: "I don't have to deal with this issue since Hitler was a vegetarian." But so was Mohandas Gandhi. So was Isaac Bashevis Singer. After a woman commented to Singer that her health had improved when she stopped eating meat, Singer replied, "I do it for the health of the chickens."[19]

Singer's statement is a reminder that the health benefits of vegetarianism—the arguments from the vegetarian body—should not be severed from body-mediated knowledge that gives rise to our moral knowledge. Otherwise, the result is self-absorption. One finds in the writings of vegetarians like Percy Shelley the concern that any illness would be used to judge the appropriateness of their diet and the efficacy of their arguments. As with Singer, the health of the chickens was the primary moral concern. In his preface to *Heartbreak House,* Bernard Shaw reiterates Singer's point: "Being an idle house it was a hypochondriacal house, always running after cures. It would stop eating meat, not on valid Shelleyan grounds but in order to get rid of a bogey called Uric Acid."[20] Finding organic meat acceptable can arise from the tendency to focus solely on health concerns. Like the focus on Hitler's so-called vegetarianism, it evidences a resistance to examining one's own acceptance of the structure of the absent referent. And defending vegetarianism solely for its health benefits diminishes the potential of body-mediated knowledge.

The distorting perspective of the dominant culture is evident in the accusation that vegetarianism is racist. Because people of color, like white women and vegetarians, experience muting by the dominant culture, exploring this issue is neither easy nor simple. Yet just as most women adhere to the prevailing texts of meat of the dominant culture they are both a part of and yet separate from, so do other oppressed groups. Thus, the encounter the late Pat Parker describes in her poem "To a Vegetarian Friend" is troubling yet revealing. Apparently her vegetarian friend was critical of Parker's meat consumption. Parker reminds her friend that the chitterlings and greens, neckbones and tails she was eating connected her to her ancestors who had survived generations of slavery and racism: "This food is good for me," Parker writes. "It replenishes my soul." Do us both a favor, Parker suggests, if you cannot keep quiet about my food, stay home.[21]

Parker's poem implies that two oppressions—racism and the eating of animals—are in opposition to each other. The implication is that vegetarianism must accommodate meat eating so as not to accommodate racism. But if Parker's poem is one form of representation, meat is another. The conflict she depicts is not a conflict between anti-racism or black tradition and vegetarianism but a conflict between the role of meat as representation and the reality of meat eating. For Parker, the meat represents her ancestors' food and provides a sense of continuity. However, Parker's support of meat is not the same meat as that consumed by her ancestors, though they are classified as such. The meat she is eating comes from a commodity, capitalist world in which the fourth stage of meat eating prevails. Contemporary meat-production methods that imprison animals and overmedicate them create an extreme difference between the dead animals, which Parker's ancestors would have eaten, and Parker's meal.

Parker explains the meaning of her meat meal in words that demonstrate the functioning of the absent referent. The chitterlings, neckbone, and tail do not refer to the animal from whom they were taken but metaphorically embody a connection with ancestors oppressed, as is Parker, by a system of white racism. Parker is positing the importance of ritual meaning; I do not disagree with its importance. But to posit the meaning of meat as referent to something other than the animal—i.e., that it operates as her linkage to her ancestors—is to participate in the structure of the absent referent. I do not propose what the ritual food should be that connects one with ancestors who were victimized by an oppressive system; but it is important not to dismember the meaning of meat from the animals' lives. In fact, the vegetarian body of literature demonstrates that soul food can be vegetarian and that knowledge of enslaved and oppressed ancestors need not be at the expense of the enslaved oppressed animals.[22]

As much as white people determine what is normative and important while ignoring the culture and experience of people of color, so have meat eaters of all races, sexes, and classes presumed the normativeness and centrality of their activity. Consequently, feminist historians and literary critics have absorbed the dominant culture's view of vegetarianism though women writers and activists have often demonstrated an alternative perspective.

I wish this book could offer a definitive history of the long and fascinating connection between feminist-activist thinkers and vegetarianism. No book can detail that history yet since the scholars themselves who have access to primary materials that indicate women's concerns for animals—either through activism or the individual choice of vegetarianism for ethical reasons—usually ignore this information. How do I know this? Because I have interrogated them or consulted their writings.

I asked a suffrage worker, still active in radical politics in the 1970s and recording her oral history, if she had ever discussed vegetarianism with her friend, Agnes Ryan. No, she replied, it seemed relatively unimportant to her. I asked a leading feminist historian if she had noticed references to vegetarianism in the letters she had just finished reading of women pacifists of World War I. Frankly, she admitted, she would not have noticed. Ida Husted Harper who edited the last two volumes of the mammoth *History of Woman Suffrage* omitted any discussion of a confrontation between a vegetarian milliner and an officer of the National American Women's Suffrage Association over an aigretted hat and a chicken dinner. Harper could have included the impassioned statement made by the milliner on behalf of animals that occurred during the 1907 National Convention: "Nothing would persuade me to eat a chicken, or to connive at the horror of trapping innocent animals for their fur. It causes a thrill of horror to pass through me when I attend a woman's suffrage convention and see women with ghastly trophies of slaughter upon their persons."[23] But Harper silenced her instead.

Women's alliance with vegetarianism in history and literary texts has been distorted. The result is the failure to sketch an inspiriting network of feminist vegetarians. Past women vegetarians who were feminist theorists have had a part of their feminist theory silenced. What we have is a double hidden history: the hidden history of women, and the illusive history of animal activism and women's vegetarianism.

The absence of references to vegetarianism by historians and literary scholars is part of the history of women. Distortions occur in history and literary criticism not only because historians and literary critics fail to take seriously the vegetarianism they encounter in their texts, but also because they fail to take seriously their own meat eating. They fail to confront the meaning of their own possible vegetarian body.

Feminist-vegetarian texts are the absent referent in feminist criticism and history. Vegetarianism is trivialized, seen as a distraction from or incidental to the important aspects of history and biography, or relegated to the realm of the individual and seen from the lens of male experience. And in contrast to the pressing difficult topics of sexuality, politics, family, work, racism, sexual and domestic violence, vegetarianism is judged as irrelevant to a serious study of women's lives. The silencing of women's vegetarianism is a critical theoretical act because as feminist-vegetarian texts and history are lost to us, so are our foundations for new insights. This silencing of feminist-vegetarian texts parallels my own silencing; after all, thirteen years have intervened since I identified in my journal entry the issues this chapter examines.

Why should we learn to recognize the distortions of the vegetarian body? First, our historical record is inadequate. Second, one way to delegitimate a reform movement is by calling it a fad. A historical cliché which pervades books is that vegetarianism is faddish. But can something be a fad—something that enjoys *brief* popularity—if it recurs throughout recorded history? In the following quotation from *Notable American Women* concerning Abigail Kelley Foster, notice how the author creates a dichotomy between such things as vegetarianism and the "major" purposes of Kelley's life: "Like many reformers of her day, she was attracted to dietary novelties, water cure, homeopathy, phrenology, and spiritualism: yet these faddish interests never diverted her from the major purposes of her life."[24]

Since the connection between feminism and vegetarianism is being argued by some today, its history also carries significance for interpreting present day culture. The silencing of vegetarianism is related to the larger silences concerning women and are of interest for what they reveal of how dominant cultures enforce that dominance. Those who live deeply in their bodies may overcome the separations enforced by the dominant morality. In the following sections I will juxtapose the traditional view of vegetarianism with a more positive approach. Our failure to acknowledge the importance of body-mediated knowledge and how it may be informed by the vegetarian body has caused us to distort our past and to misunderstand why women became vegetarians.

Sexuality and the Vegetarian Body

> Victorian purity was the creation of a self-defined group of male sexual reformers who advocated a variety of reforms, all involving a fusion of bodily and social control: temperance, vegetarianism, health and food reform, phrenologically based eugenics. . . . All, indeed, chose the body as the focus of their reform efforts.
>
> —Carroll Smith-Rosenberg[25]

> Why should we not, at the same time, liberate ourselves from many inconveniences by abandoning a fleshly diet?
>
> —Porphyry[26]

Now that the claims of vegetarians about the healthfulness of their diet have been confirmed, will we create a different analysis of women's decisions about their vegetarian bodies of the past? It is of interest that the vegetarian anatomical/health argument is not aimed at fetishizing sex organs as essential factors in the makeup of human beings; the theories of the vegetarian body do not gravitate to an essentialist feminine/masculine makeup. They are protesting activities that they believe are not consonant with the *human* body.

Yet nineteenth-century vegetarian popularizer Sylvester Graham bequeathed to feminism a mixed legacy. On the one hand, the predominantly vegetarian diet that gained his name and gave him his reputation proved immensely popular to the feminist reformers of his time. On the other hand, the emphasis that he and his medical followers gave to meat's supposed influence on the male sexual organs has caused these ideas to be exposed as yet another instance of the buffoonery of dissenting ideas. That followers of Graham called meat "animalized protein" suggested to critics that vegetarians were denying their animal nature. From this the idea was extrapolated that other aspects of our "animal" nature were feared, i.e., sexuality. Fear of the body was then corroborated by Graham's focus on controlling-male sexuality.

Graham, his diet, his theories, and the feminist response to these is more complex and revealing than we have traditionally espied. His claim as a moral reformer that meat caused undue pressure on male sexual organs has clouded the waters of historical reflection. His position implied that those concerned with eliminating meat from their diets might be unduly obsessed with sexual concerns. This equation, simplified to "not eating meat equals sexual hang-ups," has dictated the impressions of numerous historians for whom meat eating is an accepted and important aspect of their own lives. When we pull away the threads of distortion, an alternative feminist approach to the historic eschewing of meat, especially by women, becomes apparent. An emphasis on the influence of meat on male sexual organs may have appealed to women for reasons other than puritanism and moral control. Meat eating was for many yet another sign of capitulation to the control of others; vegetarianism was an enaction of self-identity and feminist consciousness.

Controlling male sexuality in and of itself was not a misguided goal of earlier feminists, especially if it meant controlling female fertility. In the light of our current movements that focus on marital rape, pornography, and child sexual abuse, controlling male sexuality is a legitimate and essential aspect of any campaign to insure female wholeness. The odd and quirky aspect of this earlier position was its emphasis on meat as a cause of unnatural sexuality and its inclusion of masturbation within this category. This is what Graham claimed: "Improper diet" was one of the "causes of extensive and excessive self-pollution." The stimulating use of "high-seasoned food, rich dishes, the free use of flesh" would all undesirably "increase the concupiscent excitability and sensibility of the genital organs."[27] To Graham, the body was a closed energy system. As Carroll Smith-Rosenberg summarizes this viewpoint:

> Individuals possessed limited amounts of nervous and nutritional energy which the body appropriated to the different organs according to their importance in man's overall metabolism. Sexual excitation and orgasm, the moral reformers argued, disrupted this natural order, drawing blood and energy to the lowest and least necessary of man's organs—his genitals.[28]

In addition to considering meat to be a stimulant like alcohol, meat was thought to cause constipation, thus predisposing a man to masturbation.

Graham's anti-meat crusade must be placed in the context of the amount of meat being consumed in the United States. Meat eating was quantitatively different for Americans than it was for Europeans. As historian Daniel Boorstin proclaimed, "Americans would become the world's great meat eaters."[29] European visitors commented with amazement on the immense amount of meat that Americans consumed. Frances Trollope, the inquisitive author of *Domestic Manners of the Americans,* reported in the 1830s, "They consume an extraordinary quantity of bacon. Ham and beef-steaks appear morning, noon and night."[30] During this decade, 1830–39, per capita meat consumption has been conservatively estimated at 178 pounds annually.[31] Anthony Trollope was astonished to find Americans consuming at least twice the amount of beef as Englishmen. After watching someone make a pie crust with lard, a vegetarian complained in 1846, "One might as well preach against licentiousness to a Sodomite, as to denounce grease to an American, especially to a Yankee."[32] Dr. John Wilson, Southern physician, criticized the American consumption of pork, estimated to be three times that of Europe: "The United States of America might properly be called the great Hog-eating Confederacy, or the Republic of Porkdom."[33] Numerous letters back to relatives in the Old World proclaimed, "we eat meat three times a day."[34] One immigrant feared that if he told the truth about the amount of meat consumed his European relatives would not believe him; thus he deliberately understated the frequency with which he ate meat.

Nineteenth-century women saw vegetarianism as liberating them from cooking fatty foods and laboring over a hot stove. The Grimké sisters, feminists and abolitionists, were convinced that the vegetarian diet of

Sylvester Graham, which they adopted, "was the 'most conducive to health and besides . . . such an emancipation of woman from the toil of the kitchen.' "[35] Their biographer observes, "No doubt, in an age of heavy over-eating and over-drinking, when the better part of woman's life was apt to be spent in baking, cooking and serving huge meals, the Graham diet simplified housekeeping and was a nutritional improvement."[36] Since nineteenth-century American women were nursemaids to a dyspeptic age, in which fried foods and meat dominated the diet, they saw in vegetarianism a promise of health. Catherine Beecher, arbiter of women's roles in society, and her sister, Harriet Beecher Stowe, claimed that a reduction in the consumption of meat would "greatly reduce the amount of fevers, eruptions, headaches, bilious attacks, and many other ailments which are produced or aggravated by too gross a diet. . . . The popular notion, that meat is more nourishing than bread, is a great mistake. Good bread contains more nourishment than butcher's meat."[37]

Vegetarianism offered a release from the dual roles of cook and nursemaid by eliminating the meats and fried foods from the diet. In the *American Vegetarian and Health Journal* of 1853 Mrs. F. Gale argued that women must learn to heal themselves, and described how she cured her six children of smallpox without a doctor through vegetarianism. According to her, "Women are slaves to fashion—slaves to appetite—slaves to man—and more especially slaves to physicians."[38] Similarly, after World War II, when Great Britain was experiencing the continuation of wartime rationing, women looked for alternative foods that promised health on a meager diet. Reflecting on her mother's conversion to vegetarianism, one daughter writes: "our diet was to do with the desperate need, wrenched from restricted circumstances, to be in charge of the body. Food Reform promised an end to sickness if certain procedures were followed." And, of course, one could eat well and cheaply—a point that was not lost on nineteenth-century women reformers such as the Grimké sisters either.[39] Grahamism promised that vegetarianism would release women not only from domestic oppression but also from the tyranny of the medical profession, upon which they would no longer need to rely because of their good health. In addition, vegetarianism provided a form of female networking.

The language used by women concerning their decision to be vegetarians reverberates with feminist meaning: the Grimkés see themselves as "emancipated" by their change in diet; Mrs. Gale speaks as a liberator to those enslaved by the dominant culture. Anne Denton in an article on the "Rights of Women" published in the *American Vegetarian and Health Journal* in 1852, called upon women to develop their intellect, learn physiology, become vegetarians and leave behind bourgeois patterns of behavior: "Women should live for something higher and nobler than cannibal tastes, good appearance, costly furniture or fine equippage." Mary Gove Nichols, nineteenth-century feminist and vegetarian, wrote with her husband of the new woman they anticipated: She "would not be the drudge of isolate household, cooking pork and other edibles for a gluttonous man." Instead, "she understands Water-Cure well; she is a good physician and a good nurse; she lives purely and simply on a vegetable diet; and is a water drinker." They conclude: "Many such women are growing amongst us."[40]

Besides the enticement of improved health, reduced cooking time and emancipation, many claimed that vegetarianism offered easier parturition. This appeal to an experience that was exclusively female, and often feared, proved sufficiently attractive to convert many women of childbearing age. Alice Stockham in her *Tokology: A Book for Every Woman,* which recommended a vegetarian diet for pregnant women, included testimonials from women who had experienced easy childbirths by following her advice.[41] Stockham's vegetarian appeal is ratified by the numerous advertisements for the book that appeared in the *Vegetarian Magazine* at that time. In a book edited by Virginia Woolf's good friend, Margaret Llewelyn Davies, *Maternity: Letters from Working-Women,* one letter writer described her choice of a vegetarian diet since "this produces a cleaner, healthier child."[42]

With these specific female-identified reasons for the appeal of vegetarianism in mind, let us consider the arguments about the connection between vegetarianism and the control of male sexuality. Since meat was thought to cause undue pressure on the male genitalia as well as being viewed as a stimulating food, these ideas could be appropriated into a female position that sought to control male sexuality. The absence of meat was promoted as a form of bringing about male abstinence. In a world of imperfect birth control in which women were the bearers of countless children, Grahamism offered a promise of liberation and implied that the control of sexuality could be placed in women's hands. Not only did many vegetarian leaders endorse birth control and abortion; some also advocated that women had a right to enjoy sex.[43] Thus we find on the one hand vegetarianism evoked as the cure for uncontrollable male sexuality and on the other hand vegetarianism as the chosen diet of utopian communities that practiced modified forms of free love.[44] Historian Susan Cayleff observes that "In nineteenth-century America, meatless diet was a legitimate social and moral issue."[45] As such it spoke directly to women about their social standing and appealed to them for legitimate social and moral reasons.

A Meat Phobia?

> Sometimes teenagers latch onto philosophies that involve a radical departure from the dietary customs of the rest of the family. *Vegetarian diets* are especially popular these days among idealistic youngsters who wish to save the world from starvation, or who think it's wrong to eat animals, or who want to avoid the "poisons" they believe exist in animal food. There's nothing wrong with a vegetarian diet.
>
> —Jane Brody[46]

> *Flesh* and *Blood* is too near akin to the *Animal Life* in man, to be a proper Food for him; 'tis like the marrying of Brothers and Sisters.
>
> —Thomas Tryon, 1683[47]

According to *The American Heritage Dictionary of the English Language,* a "phobia" is "a persistent, abnormal, or illogical fear of a specific thing or situation." If one finds meat disgusting, horrifying, unsettling, this personal emotional response may be seen as illogical and abnormal to the dominant society. After all, the dominant society has deemed meat acceptable and appetizing. Does vegetarianism, then, manifest a psychological problem with food? The attempt to squeeze the meaning of a response to food into the term "phobic" when it might be cultural, symbolic, or political demonstrates the labeling impulse of the dominant culture seeking to control interpretation. When refusal to eat meat is labeled phobic the dominant society is enacting distortion; it cannot grant positive status to objections to eating animals. When someone says that meat eating is disgusting, it is their psychological state historians or contemporary cultural interpreters seek to place in perspective. The perspective against which refusal to eat meat is judged is one that presumes meat eating is an appropriate activity. Thus the dominant perspective mutes the minority perspective, absorbing it within the dominant perspective by labeling it as individual and deviant.

The language of vegetarianism of the nineteenth century *sounds* phobic, but is it? Feminist and vegetarian Mary Gove Nichols describes a picnic of the 1840s: "There were stuffed hams, boiled, roast chickens, sausages, and mince pies, and other horrors composed of the corpses of animals."[48] In 1906, similar language can be found in the words of Josiah Oldfield: "And so at this moment the whole question of the dangers and the horrors and the unsavouriness of the meat-eating habit is prominently forward in men's minds."[49] What happens when otherwise undistinguished young women use the same terminology as these writers? I wish to examine a specific case in which a discussion of the refusal of meat by young women is shrouded in psychological terms that distort many of the issues raised by close examination of the eating of animals. It is a case study in historical distortion.

In *The Female Malady*, Elaine Showalter claims:

> Meat, the "roast beef of old England," was not only the traditional food of warriors and aggressors but also believed to be the fuel of anger and lust. Disgust with meat was a common phenomenon among Victorian girls; a carnivorous diet was associated with sexual precocity, especially with an abundant menstrual flow, and even with nymphomania.[50]

Showalter's source for this claim is an article by Joan Jacobs Brumberg about "chlorotic girls."[51] Chlorosis was a form of anemia. Common to these girls' responses to food was a disgust for meat. Brumberg reports that one contemporary studying the disease observed in 1897: "Almost all chlorotic girls are fond of biscuits, potatoes, etc. while they avoid meat on most occasions, and when they do eat meat, they prefer the burnt outside portion." One girl reported to her family doctor that "I can't bear meat." A medical guide observed that among chlorotics: "the appetite for animal food completely ceases."[52] These are physiological responses which numerous other people have observed their bodies making; but a psychological interpretation is applied to them. The implication we are left with is that the girls feared their sexuality and possible nymphomania. The source for the claims that "meat eating in excess was linked to adolescent insanity and to nymphomania" is an article on women and menstruation and nineteenth-century medicine.[53] *Their* source is an article from 1857, when the Graham model for sexuality and meat eating was widely popular. That these girls of the 1890s may have had an alternative perspective available—the perspective described above in which autonomous female identity was associated with vegetarianism—is not considered.[54]

Another viewpoint for considering disgust at the thought of meat is to recognize that the person expressing the disgust may have associated the form meat with the absent referent, the dead animal. The girls' objections to eating *meat* may be related to their dislike of the idea of eating *animals*. In fact, Blumberg provides evidence that this association had been made by some of the girls. "For many, meat eating was endured for its healing qualities but despised as a moral and aesthetic act."[55] As though writing in confirmation of the idea that girls might find meat unaesthetic, Lady Walb. Paget reported in 1893, "I have all my life thought that meat-eating was objectionable from the aesthetic point of view. Even as a child the fashion of handing around a huge *grosse pièce* on an enormous dish revolted my sense of beauty."[56] Blumberg continues: "Contemporary descriptions reveal that some young women may well have been phobic about meat eating because of its associations" and provides this quotation from a 1907 article:

> There is the common illustration which every one meets a thousand times in a lifetime, of the girl whose [functions need much fat but whose] stomach rebels at the very thought of fat meat. The mother tries persuasion and entreaty and threats and penalties. But nothing can overcome the artistic development in the girl's nature which makes her revolt at the bare idea of putting the fat piece of a dead animal between her lips.[57]

This article, written in response to an article by Dr. Josiah Oldfield, a vegetarian, is not concerned with chlorotic girls. It is reflecting on the issue Oldfield raises that "there is something in the very idea of eating a dead body which is repulsive to the artistic man and woman."[58] The writer of this article posits that the girls have an "artistic" response to eating dead animals. In fact, the article does not recommend that meat eating be enforced on the girls, but rather that they get their sources for fat from nonmeat items.[59] What this article most demonstrates is that "artistic men and women" and many girls restore the absent referent, they see themselves as eating dead animals rather than meat.

Is restoring the absent referent evidence of a meat phobia? Has the girl described in the above quotation overimagained anything? It appears that conflict in interpretation arises because some medical doctors and now historians assume that the meat being avoided is referent to the girls' experience of their bodies. Is the meat referring to their sexuality? or their own bodily bleeding? or have they restored the absent referent—the bodies of animals? Perhaps young girls did not eat meat because meat had a specific meaning in their own world *and* because they had overcome the structure of the absent referent. Indeed, what if dislike of meat was not limited to chlorotic girls? As the above article implies, many girls found meat unappetizing, but apparently the only times in general that their reactions were chronicled were when their other responses fit the culturally defined notion of "chlorotic girls." But then the question arises, "Could someone who has a psychological problem with food also have a legitimate objection to meat?"

Embodied Meanings

> "The doctor says she needs a good beating if she won't eat properly." You tried to say you couldn't stomach the welling blood the brains the private thinking tissues of the dead animal the pipes rivulets channels conduits and gulleys with their muscular veinous edges, tripe, brains and tongue. There were iron pails of sheeps' heads in the kitchen for boiling into broth. There were monthly pails of bloody white rags soaking. You had to eat everything that was put before you.
>
> —Denise Riley, "Waiting"[60]

Where does female meaning go in a patriarchal culture? If meanings have nowhere to go in terms of the verbal world, where do they go? Perhaps women's meaning is spoken in a different way at that point when they find themselves muted. Is it possible that food becomes the spoken language of dissent? Since women are the main preparers of food in Western culture and meat is defined as men's food, vegetarianism may carry meaning within a female language which seeks to escape its own mutedness. If "women tend to use speech to build upon rather than challenge the other's statements,"[61] then food choices can be a less confrontative initiation of challenge to another than breaking speech boundaries. Women may code their criticism of the prevailing world order in the choice of female-identified foods. In this case, women's bodies become the texts upon which they inscribed their dissent through vegetarianism. The adolescent girls whose refusal to eat meat is called phobic actually epitomize the situation of women whose meanings had nowhere to go; their inarticulateness became coded in food choices.

The work of scholars confirms the alliance between women and the symbolic meaning of food choices. Caroline Bynum's *Holy Feast and Holy Fast: The Religious Significance of Food to Medieval Women* offers some observations that are not exclusively restricted to interpretation of medieval women's experience. Bynum found that food acts as symbol for women more than for men: "Food practices and food symbols characterized women's experience more than men's." She concludes, "Food behaviors helped girls to gain control over self as well as over circumstance. Through fasting, women internalized as well as manipulated and escaped patriarchal familial and religious structures."[62] Brumberg suggests that food "was an integral part of individual identity. For women in particular, how one ate spoke to issues of basic character."[63]

If the body becomes a special focus for women's struggle for freedom then what is ingested is a logical initial locus for announcing one's independence. Refusing the male order in food, women practiced the theory of feminism through their bodies and their choice of vegetarianism.

There can be signs of uneasiness with the idea and fact of eating meat without this being a sign of personal or psychological problems. Gender roles, male dominance, and menstruation, to name just a few issues that arise from women's experience, are intertwined with our mythology of meat eating without even beginning to take into account the issue of the fate of animals. An alternative way of considering the girl's refusal of meat is this: they perceived meat as a symbol of male dominance—whose control over their lives would tighten as they reached adulthood—and thus they rejected not male eros but male power. This is not a totally illogical or ahistorical conclusion. There are many instances of the intersection of feminist and vegetarian insights that suggests an underlying, though generally unexpressed, feminist hostility to meat eating which these girls enacted. Consider Inez Irwin who recalls her childhood to explain the source for her radicalism:

> As I look back on those years, the mid-day Sunday dinner seemed in some curious way to symbolize everything that I hated and dreaded about the life of the middle-class woman. That plethoric meal—the huge roast, the blood pouring out of it as the man of the house carved; the many vegetables, all steaming; the heavy pudding. And when the meal was finished—the table a shambles that positively made me shudder—the smooth replete retreat of the men to their cushioned chairs, their Sunday papers, their vacuous nap, while the women removed all vestiges of the horror. Sunday-noon dinners! They set a scar upon my soul. I still shudder when I think of them. . . . Through all this spiritual turmoil there had been developing within me a desire to write. . . . When I look back on my fifty-odd years of life on this planet, I wonder what was the real inception of my desire to stand alone—fighting, ancestry, liberal influences; discussion-ridden youth? Perhaps it was those Sunday dinners![64]

Irwin is apparently writing about the time period of the late nineteenth century, when the adolescent girls refused their meat. Irwin's traditional Sunday dinner features a menu similar to that the adolescent girls would have encountered. Irwin is disconcerted by the following texts of meat: the bleeding, bloody roast; the male carver; the gorged men; women's role in removing the vestiges of the horror. Irwin's identification of the horror of Sunday dinners, which left a scar upon her soul, suggests that something is going on in the home which when confronted, thought about, responded to, sets one to shuddering. For a rebel, it may set one to writing; for adolescent girls it may set them to meat avoidance.

It may very well be that women's dislike for patriarchal culture makes meat unappetizing. What can be found in women's diaries and women's letters about food? To interpret the meaning of vegetarianism for women it must be set in the context of the male associations of meat eating and female associations with menstruation. Do women become vegetarian because they are more closely connected with blood? In the opposition between female blood versus animals' bleeding, we have a female constant versus a process that announces control and violence. In addition, our bodily experience of menstruation may differ, depending on whether meat is included in our diet or not. Barbara Seaman and Dr. Gideon Seaman write: "We suspect that there may be elements in meat which aggravate menstrual cramps as well as menopause complaints. In any case, both conditions are rarer in vegetarian societies, and American women who cut back on meat often report improvement."[65] How do we unravel the coded reactions to the women's or girls' experiences if we are not equipped to break the code or honor body-mediated knowledge?

Animals' bodies carry meanings. These meanings can be perceived even when they have been transformed into meat. Our bodies express meanings through food choices. The killing of animals for food is a feminist issue that feminists have failed to claim because of the charged atmosphere of food choices and the structure of the absent referent. Being in touch with the vegetarian body restores the absent referent and body-mediated knowledge.

chapter 9

For a Feminist-Vegetarian Critical Theory

> Papers omitted in vegetarian novel, use in feminist novel?
>
> —Agnes Ryan, note to herself

> As we talked of freedom and justice one day for all, we sat down to steaks. I am eating misery, I thought, as I took the first bite. And spit it out.
>
> —Alice Walker, "Am I Blue?"

> eat rice have faith in women
> what I dont know now
> I can still learn
>
> —Fran Winant, "Eat Rice Have Faith in Women"

Where does vegetarianism end and feminism begin, or feminism end and vegetarianism begin? None of these epigraphs indicates that the writer is changing subjects. Similarly, major moments in feminist history and major figures in women's literature conjoined feminism and vegetarianism in ways announcing continuity, not discontinuity.

Developing a feminist-vegetarian theory includes recognizing this continuity. Our meals either embody or negate feminist principles by the food choices they enact. Novelists and individuals inscribe profound feminist statements within a vegetarian context. Just as revulsion to meat eating acts as trope for feelings about male dominance, in women's novels and lives vegetarianism signals women's independence. An integral part of autonomous female identity may be vegetarianism; it is a rebellion against dominant culture whether or not it is stated to be a rebellion against male structures. It resists the structure of the absent referent, which renders both women and animals as objects.

Not only is animal defense the theory and vegetarianism the practice, but feminism is the theory and vegetarianism is part of the practice, a point this chapter will more fully develop. Meat eating is an integral part of male dominance; vegetarianism acts as a sign of dis-ease with patriarchal culture. I will describe a model for expressing this dis-ease which has three facets: the revelation of the nothingness of meat, the naming of relationships, and the rebuking of a patriarchal and meat-eating world. Lastly I provide ground rules for a feminist-vegetarian reading of history and literature.

Examining the material reality of a vegetarian life enlightens theory, past and present. What do we make of the fact that many notable feminists who have written since early modern times have either responded to animals' concerns or become interested in vegetarianism? In the seventeenth century, feminist writer Mary Astell cut back on her meat intake.[1] Katherine Philips and Margaret Cavendish discuss meat eating in their poetry as well as positing the Golden Age as vegetarian. As we learned in chapter 4, Aphra Behn, the eponymous heroine of our contemporary *Aphra* magazine, wrote a poem in praise of the writings of Thomas Tryon, whose seventeenth-century books on behalf of vegetarianism she said had influenced her to stop eating meat. Sarah Scott's *A Description of Millenium [sic] Hall* describes an animal sanctuary in which humans are not tyrants over animals, and uses Alexander Pope's words about Eden to reinforce the fact that the animals were protected from meat eating.[2] We know that Mary Wollstonecraft Shelley makes her Creature who is at odds with the world a vegetarian in *Frankenstein.*

We can follow the historic alliance of feminism and vegetarianism in utopian writings and societies, antivivisection activism, the temperance and suffrage movements, and twentieth century pacifism. Hydropathic institutes of the nineteenth century, which featured vegetarian regimens, were frequented by Susan B. Anthony, Elizabeth Cady Stanton, Sojourner Truth, and others. At a vegetarian banquet in 1853, the gathered guests lifted their alcohol-free glasses to toast: "Total Abstinence, Women's Rights, and Vegetarianism." In 1865, Dr. James Barry died. Dr. Barry was an army surgeon for more than forty four years, a vegetarian, and someone brought up by an ardent follower of Mary Wollstonecraft; it was discovered upon his death that Dr. Barry was a woman. Some who suspected all along that Dr. Barry was a woman referred to the vegetarian diet as one of the signs of her gender as well as her fondness for pets.[3]

Clara Barton, founder of the Red Cross, Matilda Joslyn Gage (an editor of *The History of Woman Suffrage* with Elizabeth Cady Stanton and Susan B. Anthony), and some leaders of the nineteenth-century dress reform movement were vegetarians. Feminist and vegetarian Alice Stockham was the American publisher of British socialist, anti-vivisectionist, and vegetarian Edward Carpenter.

In 1910, Canadian suffragists opened a vegetarian restaurant at their Toronto headquarters. The *Vegetarian Magazine* of the early twentieth century carried a column called "The Circle of Women's Enfranchisement." In the 1914 book, *Potpourri Mixed by Two,* two women exchange reflections on vegetarian cooking, women's suffrage, and other common concerns. Notable independent women of the twentieth century such as Louise Nevelson and Lou Andreas-Salome were vegetarians.[4] From all these examples arises a compelling revelation: There is a feminist-vegetarian literary and historical tradition. What is needed to espy it and interpret it?

Reconstructing the History of Feminism and Vegetarianism

> Why can't we be rounded out reformers? Why do we make one reform topic a hobby and forget all the others? Mercy, Prohibition, Vegetarianism, Woman's Suffrage and Peace would make Old Earth a paradise, and yet the majority advocate but one, if any, of these.
>
> —Flora T. Neff, Indiana State Superintendent of Mercy,
Women's Christian Temperance Union,
to the *Vegetarian Magazine,* 1907[5]

A feminist-vegetarian critical theory begins, as we have seen, with the perception that women and animals are similarly positioned in a patriarchal world, as objects rather than subjects. Men are instructed as to how they should behave toward women and animals in the Tenth Commandment. Since the fall of Man is attributed to a woman and an animal, the Brotherhood of Man excludes both women and animals. In reviewing Henry Salt's *Animal Rights* for *Shafts,* the British working-class, feminist, and vegetarian newspaper of the 1890s, Edith Ward argues that "the case of the animal is the case of the woman." She explained that the "similitude of position between women and the lower animals, although vastly different in degree, should insure from the former the most unflinching and powerful support to all movements for the amelioration of the conditions of animal existence. Is this the case?"[6] More recently, Brigid Brophy, vegetarian and feminist, observes: "In reality women in the western, industrialized world today are like the animals in a modern zoo. There are no bars. It appears that cages have been abolished. Yet in practice women are still kept in their place just as firmly as the animals are kept in their enclosures."[7] Or consider this declaration found in *The History of Woman Suffrage:* "Past civilization has not troubled either dumb creatures or women by consulting them in regard to their own affairs."[8] *Who Cares for the Animals?* the title of a history of 150 years of the Royal Society for the Prevention of Cruelty to Animals, provides an answer on its cover: women. Margaret Mead's description of her activist mother invokes two of her favorite causes in one paragraph: "Mother's vehemence was reserved for the causes she supported. . . . As a matter of principle she never wore furs; and feathers, except for ostrich plumes, were forbidden. Long before I had an idea what they were, I learned that aigrettes represented a murder of the innocents. There were types of people, too, for whom she had no use—anti-suffragettes."[9]

The patriarchal structure of the absent referent that renders women and animals absent as subjects, collapses referent points, and results in overlapping oppression, requires a combined challenge by feminism and vegetarianism. Yet, this oppression of women and animals, though unified by the structure of the absent referent, is experienced separately and differently by women and animals. Thus, it is an oppressive structure that, when perceived, is often perceived in fragments and attacked in fragmented ways, i.e., some women work for their liberation, other women and men challenge the oppression of animals.

A sign that the oppression is of one piece exists whenever patriarchal culture experiences its control over women to be threatened by the choice of a meatless diet. On the domestic level this can be seen when men use the pretext of the absence of meat in committing violence against women, as we saw in chapter 1. Additionally, a threatened worldview evidences the unity of this oppression when it concludes that arguments for women's rights will lead to arguments for animals' rights. In response to the woman suffrage movement of the nineteenth century one man retorted, "What will they be doing next, educating cows?" It is almost to be expected that the first challenge to Mary Wollstonecraft's *A Vindication of the Rights of Woman* was entitled *A Vindication of the Rights of Brutes.* Yet, the parody relied on one of the classic vegetarian texts: Porphyry's *On Abstinence from Animal Food.* Since the oppression of women and the other animals derives from one hierarchical structure, we can expect that at certain points in our history a few will have challenged the structure in a unified way; that is, we can expect to find the intersection of feminism and vegetarianism, the unifying of the arguments of Wollstonecraft and Porphyry. Thus Edith Ward in *Shafts* argues

> What, for example, could be more calculated to produce brutal wife-beaters than long practice of savage cruelty towards the other animals? And what, on the other hand, more likely to impress mankind with the necessity of justice for women than the awakening of the idea that justice was the right of even an ox or a sheep?[10]

Vegetarianism was one way that many people, especially women, expressed a connection with specific animals—those destined to become meat—by affirming "I care about these creatures. I will not eat them." Vegetarianism was one way to reject a male world that objectified both women and animals; women not only enunciated connections with animals but defined themselves as subjects with the right to act and make ethical decisions, and in doing so defined animals as subjects, not objects. Ethical vegetarianism became a symbolic as well as literal enaction of right relationships with animals.

Elemental aspects of feminism and vegetarianism intersect. While vegetarians posit a fall from grace, a Golden Age that was vegetarian, many feminists hearken to a similar time in which women's power was not restricted, a matriarchal period of human existence. When considered as a mythopoesis which motivates feminism, rather than as a historically validated period, its intersection with the Golden Age of vegetarianism is revealing. What, after all, were the great goddesses the great goddesses of? Grains and vegetables possess a long history of woman-association.

Earlier in this century, we can find an equation of matriarchal power with vegetarianism and patriarchal power with meat eating, an association that is an intimate part of current feminist mythmaking. In 1903, when Jane Harrison published *Prolegomena to the Study of Greek Religion,* she offered clues to the association of the worship of goddesses and vegetarianism. In her book we find Pausanias's report on his sacrifice to the goddess Demeter according to local custom: "I sacrificed no victim to the goddess, such being the custom of the people of the country. They bring instead as offerings the fruit of the vine and of other trees they cultivate, and honey-combs and wool." Harrison observes that this "was a service to content even Pythagoras." The ingredients of one of the women's festivals that Harrison describes would almost have satisfied Pythagoras's standards as well: "The materials of the women's feast are interesting. The diet prescribed is of cereals and of fish and possibly fowl, but clearly not of flesh. As such it is characteristic of the old Pelasgian population before the coming of the flesh-eating Achaeans."[11] She cannot be unequivocally claimed for the vegetarian side, this is true, but a further reference to Porphyry's *On Abstinence from Animal Food,* her suggestions of the invasion of flesh-eating male-god worshippers who overcame vegetarian goddess worshippers, may have offered a sense of historical or mythological perspective to feminist vegetarians of the time. Were they picked up on? We know that Harrison influenced Virginia Woolf. Were there others she influenced specifically because of their interest in vegetarianism? Whether or not Harrison was absorbed into feminist-vegetarian thought of her time, she has been assimilated by the current movement. (Recall the discussion of June Brindel's novel *Ariadne* in chapter 7.) Recent formulators of a matriarchal time period identify it as vegetarian as well.[12]

The recent history of feminism and vegetarianism also offers points of intersection. Both experienced a rebirth through books in the years after the French Revolution. Each considers a meeting held in the 1840s as very important: the 1847 Ramsgate meeting at which the term vegetarianism was either coined or ratified; the 1848 meeting at Seneca Falls in which American women's rights demands were outlined. According to certain historical analyses, each has been viewed as lapsing into obscurity; feminism after the achievement of suffrage in 1920, vegetarianism practically from the moment it began as a self-identified movement.

Reconstructing feminist-vegetarian history requires heightened attention to meanings hidden within statements about health and diet. For instance, in a book of oral interviews with surviving suffragists, we can discover a statement with clues that point to vegetarianism. Jessie Haver Butler in describing her childhood states: "But my mother was very smart. She had a great big health book with which she was thoroughly familiar. She was also a faddist, so it's natural that I've been somewhat of a faddist all my life. She had all the books of a man named Dr. Jackson, who started a whole new system of eating."[13] Clues that she is describing a vegetarian diet include her reference to the "faddishness" of her mother, as vegetarianism has been saddled with that label. Corroborating this is her reference to "a new system of eating." The final confirmation comes from her invocation of the name of Dr. Jackson. James Caleb Jackson ran a hydropathic health institute in Dansville, New York.

Jackson encouraged meatless diets. Ellen G. White who frequented Jackson's "Home on the Hillside" reported, "Dr. Jackson carries out his principles in regard to diet to the letter. He places no butter or salt upon his table, no meat or any kind of grease."[14] Clara Barton's "entire philosophy of living underwent a change in this environment" of Jackson's Home on the Hillside, so much so that she moved to Dansville and adopted vegetarianism.[15]

Jackson adhered to Sylvester Graham's principles concerning food. Graham, for instance, recommended that meals be no more frequent than every six hours and never before retiring. At Dansville there were only two meals a day: breakfast at eight and dinner at 2:30. Butler remarked that Jackson "had some strange ideas that didn't fit with farm life very well. One of them was there was to be no supper." Yet Butler's mother followed Jackson's recommendations to the letter, as Butler recalls the situation of the farm workers: "To go without supper until breakfast, from the dinner meal until breakfast, must have been a great strain."

Jackson's influence through his popular book, *How to Treat the Sick without Medicine,* reached all the way to Butler's mother in Colorado. Butler was right when she called it "a great big health book"—it was 537 pages long. A common measure prevails for healing the diseases he discusses in his book whether it be scald head, measles, inflammation of the eyes, insanity, diabetes, or alcoholism: omitting flesh foods. And there in Colorado, on a prairie farm, removed from conventions and the wide circle of support for these reforms in the East, in the midst of feeding the workhands, raising four children *and* stumping for suffrage, Jessie Haver Butler's mother felt it was important to find the time to learn about Dr. Jackson's ideas, own all of his books, and be so thoroughly familiar with one of them that her daughter knew about its recommendations for proper diet.

In fact, it may be because she was stumping for suffrage that she learned of Dr. Jackson. Jackson was a good friend of numerous suffragists. Amelia Bloomer lectured at Dansville. Elizabeth Cady Stanton retreated to Dansville for rest and restoration[16]; the residents of Dansville raised money for Susan B. Anthony's trial when she was charged with voting illegally in 1872. Jackson faithfully sent messages to suffrage conventions; tribute was paid to him during the memorial services of the 1896 convention.

Other suffrage workers adopted vegetarianism as well. The obituary of Jessica Henderson, suffragist and vegetarian, can be found in Agnes Ryan's papers. Gloria Steinem describes her vegetarian suffragist grandmother who continued to serve meat to her meat-eating and anti-feminist sons.[17] Socialist Anna Gvinter, imprisoned with other suffragists in 1917, wrote from jail that she did not eat meat.[18] The Canadian suffragists who opened a vegetarian restaurant in 1910 certainly thought that there would be customers for such a venture.

The confrontation at the 1907 meeting of the National American Woman Suffrage Association reveals the challenge of reconstructing feminist-vegetarian history. As I indicated in the last chapter, this confrontation was omitted from the official record, *The History of Woman*

Suffrage, yet it reveals the demand some were making at the time to unify reform issues. During an appeal for funds, Harriet Taylor Upton, the national treasurer, reported that she had been asked to promise not to wear the aigretted hat she had worn during the convention. To which she responded "Nobody who will eat a chicken or a cow or a fish has any right to say a word when anybody else kills a parrot or a fox or a seal. It's just as bad, one way or another, and I guess we have all eaten chickens!" It was at this point that the feminist vegetarian milliner interrupted the meeting, trembling with indignation and anger. "I must protest," she said, "against being included in such a sweeping statement. Nothing would persuade me to eat a chicken, or to connive at the horror of trapping innocent animals for their fur. It causes a thrill of horror to pass through me when I attend a woman's suffrage convention and see women with ghastly trophies of slaughter upon their persons." In her response, she countered the challenge of inconsistency that Upton invoked to deflect criticism.

The overlap of feminism and vegetarianism becomes more complex when considering temperance. The Women's Christian Temperance Union Department of Health and Hygiene was headed by Mrs. Ella Kellogg, a vegetarian. Hydropathists such as her husband, Dr. J. Kellogg, and Dr. Jackson held that the stimulating influence of meat contributed to alcoholism. Consequently vegetarianism was needed to cure alcoholism. Jackson exhorted: "I do not believe reformed inebriates, generally, can be kept sober after they are pronounced cured, if they are permitted to eat largely of flesh meats seasoned with the various spices in common use with our people."[19] How did this perspective influence, if it did, the activities of the WCTU? Both Frances Willard, WCTU President and her successor, Lillian Stevens, were vegetarians. When the World Temperance Organization met in London in 1895, their reception was a vegetarian one organized by the Women's Vegetarian Union.

What of feminist-vegetarian-lesbian (or homosocial) connections? Historically, homosocial relationships often included vegetarianism.[20] Thus, besides "The Historical Denial of Lesbianism," which Blanche Cook identifies, there is a historical denial of vegetarianism as it was shared within lesbian relationships. For instance, Cook notes that Anna Mary Well's *Miss Marks and Miss Woolley* denies the possibility of sexuality in the lives of these two women who had a forty-seven-year-long relationship. Because of this denial, Wells "inevitably diminishes the quality of their life together." Cook notes in addition, "The entire political dimension of their lives, the nature of their socialism, feminism, and internationalism remains unexplored."[21] Cook falls into the same trap as Wells—failing to recognize the importance and legitimacy of private behavior—because Cook omits vegetarianism in her listing of this couple's interests. When Jeanette Marks returned from Battle Creek sanitarium, operated by John Harvey Kellogg, Miss Woolley "ordered nuts, raisins, and whole-grain cereals from the S. S. Pierce Co. in Boston."[22]

Other close female friendships may have included a shared concern for vegetarianism. Mary Walker, feminist, dress reformer, Civil War hero, was a vegetarian. Was her "Adamless Eden," a retreat for women, vegetarian, as most people viewed the original Eden to be? Did feminist lawyer Belva Lockwood, who lived with Mary Walker for a while, try vegetarianism as a result? Did Clara Barton's close friendship with Harriet Austin, a hydropathic doctor and vegetarian at Dr. Jackson's institute influence her decision to live in Dansville and adopt vegetarianism? In 1893 Frances Willard met Lady Somerset, head of the British WCTU, and joined the Fabian Society and the London Vegetarian society. Was vegetarianism a part of her relationship with Lady Somerset, and did the homosocial world of British temperance and feminist workers accentuate vegetarianism in a way that attracted Willard? Were the Grimké sisters able to sustain their vegetarianism because they were two, not one, and had a built-in support of it?

If the woman of the past ate a vegetarian meal we need to ask:

- Where did she eat it? At the vegetarian restaurant run by suffragists at their headquarters in Toronto? The Wheatsheaf or the Orange Grove in London, John Maxwell's in Chicago, or Bernarr Macfadden's Physical Culture and Strength Food Restaurant in New York City?
- What were her resources? A vegetarian-feminist magazine like *Shafts?* Membership in the Millennium Guild? The *Vegetarian Magazine?* Vegetarian cookbooks? Dr. Jackson's great big health book?
- What was her context? Animal rights? A utopian society? The WCTU? The time-saving nature of vegetarianism?

Vegetarianism was an integral part of autonomous female identity. It was de facto a rebellion against a dominant culture regardless of whether it was claimed to be a rebellion. But many women did claim its rebellious aspects. Recall that Mary Alden Hopkins, writing in the 1920s, reported that at one point in her life she reacted "against all established institutions, like marriage, spanking, meat diet, prison, war, public schools and our form of government."[23]

The Vegetarian Quest

> May 1, 1922:
> Should like to talk diet with you both—but I hereby warn you—that all vegetarians but me place vegetarian diet all out of proportion—(it is 100% of life's aims—meat is 100% of mistakes—no causes operating on the human frame but diet.) I deny the "foul aspersion." There are some causes in the universe beside meat and vegetarianism.
>
> December 31, 1936:
> But as to propaganda and agitation—I always choose feminism first. I'd like a chance to argue with you on that point.
>
> February 5, 1941:
> But beware of the almost universal bigotry of vegetarians that meat is the biggest or only devil—
>
> —Alice Park, feminist, pacifist, vegetarian,
> author of "The Circle of Women's Enfranchisement"
> in *The Vegetarian Magazine,*
> letters to Agnes Ryan and Henry Bailey Stevens[24]

Carol Christ in *Diving Deep and Surfacing* describes a typology for women's spiritual quest.[25] In adopting vegetarianism, certain patterns I call "the vegetarian quest" are evident. It consists of three parts: an awakening in which the revelation of the nothingness of meat occurs, naming the relationships one sees with animals, and rebuking a meat-eating world.

The first step in the vegetarian quest is experiencing *the revelation of the nothingness of meat* as an item of food. The nothingness of meat arises because one sees that it came from something, or rather someone, and it has been made into no-thing, no-body. The revelation involves recognizing the structure of the absent referent. The revelation can also be catalyzed when meat has been divested of any positive qualities with which it is usually associated. After the awakening to meat's nothingness one sees that its sumptuousness derives from the disguises of sauces, gravies, marinades, and cooking, that its protein offerings are not unique nor irreplaceable. In experiencing the nothingness of meat, one realizes that one is not eating food but dead bodies. Thus, George Sand stopped eating red meat for two weeks after a grisly battle left human corpses rotting within view of her window.[26] Many writers describe an epiphanal experience that locks them into movement away from meat. It is a moment of realization in which they say, "What am I doing eating meat?" Barbara Cook ascribes her "*awakening* to love" and animal rights activism to a time when she held a small calf in her arms, who "seemed the symbol of every new creature ever brought into the world." But she learned that this symbol often became veal. Thus, the nothingness of meat was revealed to her: "For months afterward I cried when I thought of the calf. I cried when I saw milk-fed veal on a menu. The piece of pale flesh wrapped neatly in cellophane in the supermarket would never again be faceless masses."[27]

Agnes Ryan's unpublished autobiography discusses her vegetarianism in a chapter called "I Meet a New Force." Her recollections of this event provide an excellent case study for describing the revelation of the nothingness of meat. When she began to prepare some meat, she realized that it was rotten.

> The chops were spoiled. They had been frozen. The warmth of the room was thawing them out. I was horrified. It was a long time since I had known that smell. A terrible and devastating flood of thoughts began to pour in on me. Something true in my life was fighting for release. It is amazing what a lifetime can race through the mind in a half minute.[28]

Memories, reactions, revulsions, reflections are triggered by the putrid meat: "Had I ever in my life been able to eat meat at all if I allowed myself to think of the living creature which had been deprived of life?"

She considers meat from the view of a New Woman who has bifurcated the world at large: "I knew that men were not supposed to mind killing. Weren't men usually the butchers, the soldiers, the hangmen?" She confides to her husband, "I had never been able to swallow a bite of meat or fish in all my life—if I remembered where the stuff came from, *how* it came! I told him of the violence, the horror, the degradation that flesh-eating involves." Ryan reports that she had never heard of vegetarians, but, "I thought of all the girls and women who loathed the handling of meat as I had done, and who saw no way out, believing that flesh food was necessary for bodily health and strength." Then she hears the president of the Millennium Guild, Emarel Freshel, speak out against meat eating and her reaction is given a new context: "Here was a new type of woman: here was a new spiritual force at work in the universe. . . . She clearly stressed the idea that wars will never be overcome until the belief that it is justifiable to take life, to kill—*when expedient,*—is eradicated from human consciousness." According to Ryan's reconstruction of this event, the revelation of meat eating provides a context for considering the role expectations for men and women in Western culture. Through exposure to a female role model, Freshel, she finds a context for interpreting the nothingness of meat in a warring world. Her revelation was undergirded by connections between feminism, vegetarianism, and pacifism.

Ryan's story of this event conflicts with that of her husband's, Henry Bailey Stevens. Stevens states that he was skeptical of vegetarianism at first; Ryan portrays him as being receptive to the idea. Stevens says that they had purchased fresh meat; Ryan says they were frozen. Ryan describes her meeting with Freshel as coincidental and endows it with providential meaning, "What power it was that brought me as by accident to the meeting of the Millennium Guild the very week of our awakening I do not know." But Stevens quotes Ryan as saying, "I've just learned there's a woman giving lectures on vegetarianism."[29] Because Ryan syncretizes her most relevant positions against meat into this event, I am not convinced that the sequence and intensity of her reactions are as she reported. However, in her eyes, this moment was of such consequence that reflecting back on it she saw within it the originating point for all the major positions she held for the next forty years. That she placed them at the point in her life when she became a vegetarian confirms the revelatory experience of the nothingness of meat.

Experiencing the nothingness of meat can amount to a conversion experience, a turning away from meat eating accompanied by active proselytizing. The zealous loyalty to vegetarianism that characterizes many converts concerned feminist-vegetarian Alice Park, as we see in the epigraphs to this section. Vegetarianism, she argued to Ryan and Stevens, has a context, a context of feminism.

The revelation of the nothingness of meat may be less dramatic or less elaborately reconstructed as that which we have examined in depth. Yet whatever its trigger—and there are endless catalysts, such as association with an animal who was then butchered, a recall of the eyes of an animal, connecting meat with human corpses, seeing a slaughterhouse, reading another's views—it brings about a detachment from the desire to eat meat.

Experiencing the nothingness of meat does not automatically result in vegetarianism: it requires a context and an interpretation. Thus, the second step in the vegetarian quest is *naming the relationships*. These relationships include: the connection between meat on the table and a living animal; between ourselves and the other animals; between our ethics and our diet; and the recognition of the needless violence of meat eating. The interpretation moves from the nothingness of meat to the conviction that killing animals is wrong. It may include the realization of a continuity between war and meat eating within a patriarchal world as Freshel showed Ryan. Revulsion toward human corpses can erupt into refusal of animal corpses, as happened with George Sand. Identifying women's fate with that of animals appears in the naming stage as well. Women identify their own nothingness with that of the nothingness of animals when they talk of being treated like pieces of meat. As we saw in chapter 7, when Marge Piercy describes an epiphanal moment in the life of Beth in her novel *Small Changes,* she links the double-edged nothingness. Beth was a "trapped animal eating a dead animal."[30] It would be illuminating to know how many women became vegetarians because of the analogies they perceived between the treatment of animals and the treatment of women under patriarchy.

One aspect of naming the relationships is reclaiming appropriate words for meat, words which do not rely on euphemisms, distortions, mis-naming. By re-naming words about meat, vegetarians re-define meat and offer a vision of how human beings should see themselves in relationship to animals.

The vegetarian quest often becomes more intense over time. In 1905 May Wright Sewall wrote: "I grow to be a more and more enthusiastic vegetarian all the time."[31] As one of the participants on the Ford Peace Ship a decade later, her enthusiasm was not limited solely to vegetarianism. Henry Bailey Stevens's vegetarian conversion prompted a book, which thirty years later named relationships, those of vegetarianism, goddess worship, and pacifism, *The Recovery of Culture.*[32]

Rebuking a meat-eating world is the final stage in the vegetarian quest. By its enaction vegetarianism rebukes a meat-eating society because it proves that an alternative to meat eating exists and that it works. In the Western world, vegetarians in great numbers are living free of heart attacks, hypertension, and cancer. The practice of vegetarianism seems to confirm the claims of a vegetarian body. But many vegetarians do not rest with the proof of the healthfulness of the vegetarian body. They seek to change the meat-eating world. Thus, though Gloria Steinem tells of her vegetarian feminist grandmother who served meat to her family, individual vegetarians often sought to alter meat-eating habits. We learn of vegetarian, pacifist, and feminist Charlotte Despard who did not serve meat meals to the poor. Agnes Ryan planned a "Vegetarian Pocket Monthly," a small, easy-to-carry manual, which would provide interested people with hints and thoughts on vegetarianism.

Vegetarianism does more than rebuke a *meat-eating* society; it rebukes a *patriarchal* society, since as we have seen meat eating is associated with male power. Colonialist British (male) Beefeaters are not viewed positively if you do not approve of eating beef, male control, or colonialism.

Indeed, male dominance hedges no words in exclaiming against vegetarianism because of a suspected anti-male bias. In seeing the nothingness of meat, we strip it of its phallocentric meaning, and deny it any symbolic, patriarchal meaning that requires an absent referent. Stevens's *The Recovery of Culture* simultaneously rebuked male dominance and meat eating.

The results of rebuking a meat-eating patriarchal world should not be minimized simply because of its perceived personal nature. Meat boycotts after World War II and in the 1970s were accomplished by individuals doing something together. In agreeing on what they would not purchase at grocery stores they forced the reduction of animals slaughtered for food. Though they were not motivated by ethical vegetarianism but by an attempt to gain consumer control, the effect they had was the same as if everyone became a vegetarian and individually acted according to that position. Indeed, it is of interest that women were more likely to observe the boycott than their husbands were.

Acknowledging the existence of the vegetarian quest helps place individual women's actions within a context that can make sense of their decisions. From this context sensitive readings of novels and women's lives arise. The model of the vegetarian quest provides opportunities for interpretation rather than distortion.

Vegetarian Meaning and Literary Criticism

> May the fairies be vegetarian!
>
> —Judy Grahn, *The Queen of Swords*[33]

What does contemporary women's fiction make of meat eating? There are times when the normative objectification of animals as edible bodies is displaced, eroded, disturbed, times when the texts of meat are overcome by feminist texts.

Vegetarianism is an act of the imagination. It reflects an ability to imagine alternatives to the texts of meat. Literary critics need to be alert to the ways in which vegetarianism appears in women's novels. As identified in chapter 5, vegetarianism appears in fiction through allusion to previous vegetarian words; in characters in novels who recall historic vegetarians; through direct quotations from earlier vegetarian texts; and through language that identifies the functioning of the structure of the absent referent. When Barbara Christian tells us that Alice Walker's novel *Meridian* echoes the title of "Jean Toomer's prophetic poem about America,

The Blue Meridian," we may be led to ask, is the vegetarianism of Meridian's best friend in the novel an echo of Jean Toomer's vegetarianism?[34]

We can find in women's writings descriptions of the vegetarian quest, meat as trope of women's oppression, and the figuring of women's autonomy through their adoption of vegetarianism. The implications of the inconsistencies of Pamela Smith in Ann Beattie's *Chilly Scenes of Winter* may be explained by the connection between autonomous female activity and vegetarianism. Pamela is a vegetarian who eats chicken, a lesbian who sleeps with men. Does the former activity figure the loss of autonomy accomplished by the latter?[35]

In feminist writings, vegetarian issues can be found at the intersection of politics and spirituality; in fiction, this intersection is expressed through the politics of mythmaking. Many examples of women's fiction which figure vegetarian issues do so in the context of new mythmaking. In the process of creating ourselves anew within a meaningful cosmology that reflects feminist values, vegetarianism appears. Thus, we see that those who control the stories, control memory and the future. This is an aspect of Aileen La Tourette's *Cry Wolf*.[36] In the stories her narrator tells, feminist political consciousness incorporates animals and connections with the nonhuman world. Relationship with animals is embedded within a larger radical vision that examines women and the feminine look, God the Father, and anti-nuclear activity.

Feminist mythmaking that includes vegetarianism can be found as well in Judy Grahn's *The Queen of Swords*, which features vegetarian fairies who reclaim the "beaten flesh" of Inanna, who had been beaten into a piece of meat. When writers call attention to story telling they indicate that mythmaking is a shared process in which the reader engages too. They offer a process of liberation for the readers from the grip of authoritarian authors as well as from the texts of meat.

Jeanette Winterson's *Oranges Are Not the Only Fruit* reveals the necessity of mythmaking in expressing the painful Bildungsroman of a young woman whose call to be an Evangelical preacher is cut short by the discovery of her lesbianism. The spiritual and psychic turmoil that erupts as she is banished from her home and her church is traced through a mythology of the power of a wizard. A wanderer who is vegetarian must disentangle herself from the hold the wizard has upon her. The wizard's power is demonstrated by his familiarity with one of her favorite meals: aduki bean stew. The autonomy that is declared by her vegetarianism is threatened by the wizard's claim to vegetarianism as well. In the parallel stories of her banishment from the church and the myth that tells of the control of the wizard, the hero must decide between allegiance, tradition, and meaning on the one hand, and maintaining the integrity of her own being on the other.[37]

Alice Thomas Ellis's *The Birds of the Air* features the role of mythmaking in providing meaning to loss and resurrection. Mary is a woman mourning the death of her son Robin. She is at her mother's home for Christmas. She imagines the story of an ancient feast that featured the reanimation of dead birds. The centerpiece for the ancient feast was a swan; within the swan "were concealed other birds, each containing one smaller. And at the very centre of all, where once had been the swan's liver, was a wren's egg, boiled." Just as the master of the feast raised his knife to begin carving, the feast is interrupted by the appearance of a bedraggled stranger. One person assumes he is a holy person who lives "on nuts and berries and the roots that only such people know of." She asks him to tell a story but he decides to show them a story instead. The wren's egg rolls out of the swan, cracks open, and from it staggers a wren chick. The swan heaves and out came "a scorched, plucked, mutilated, part-melted coot." The sauce is restored to the cows from whom it had been taken, they "lowed with astonishment as their udders filled instantly with warm milk faintly onion-flavoured." All foods were restored to their natural state: almonds to almond trees; onions entombed in the earth; currants returned to grapes; honey back to the comb; flour to wheat. Birds wandered forth from the belly of the swan: a pigeon, a hen, a duck, a heron, a widgeon, a bustard, a crane. Finally, the swan discards the trappings of quince, gingerbread, and thyme and rises to the rafters. Mary is called back from her "day-dreaming," as her mother refers to it, by the smell of burnt flesh. " 'Something's caught,' she said, wishing the turkey could unlatch the oven door, free itself [*sic*] like four-and-twenty blackbirds, rise like the phoenix and go and gobble in the garden, leaving the flesh-eaters to drink snow and eat chrysanthemums." But she cannot because the birds of the air are all dead: the Christmas turkey, the swan, the son, Robin.[38]

In this mythmaking, the function of the absent referent is clarified through the idea of reanimated birds; birds who escape the fate of being meat. A bird's body is less transformed by meat eating than that of cows or pigs or lambs. As one Pythagorean commented in 1825:

> in a bird . . . you have the perfect frame before you that once contained a breathing life,—the wings with which it [*sic*] used to fly, the legs for hopping or perching on a tree, and the parts for eating and singing with—the head and the bill. Therefore, in eating a bird, you have the image before you of a once-living creature, and know that you are destroying it, with its functions.[39]

The resemblance between the live and dead bird challenges the structure of the absent referent because the living bird's body continues to be a referent even in death. It is not absent until consumed. As a result, one aspect of contemporary women's fiction is the image of the dead bird.

If the vegetarian quest identifies the nothingness of meat, in feminist novels the image of dead birds reveals the *some-oneness* of living beings. Signs of revelation of the connectedness of life, especially the role of birds in triggering the recognition, can be found in the writings of many women. Recall the numerous instances in which the issue of consumption or killing of birds has recurred in this book: the literal chickenmeat in the movie *The Birds;* the two-year-old who asks her philosopher father why they are eating a turkey, who surely wanted to live; the uneaten pheasant, dead of a heart attack; the confrontation at the National American Woman Suffrage Association in 1907 over aigretted hats and eating chicken; the hundreds of birds killed in *The Shooting Party.* With these examples in mind, let us consider first a few historic writings that establish some of the issues that appear when we confront the image of dead birds. The presence of birds, especially chickens, clarifies the functioning of the absent referent in erasing animals' lives.

Mary Church Terrell, one of the founders of the National Association for the Advancement of Colored People, suffragist, and author of *A Colored Woman in a White World,* had to abandon an attempt to raise chickens because she could not contemplate the idea of eating them. She sold them instead, and recalled that day: "While I was catching them and tying their feet I was weeping inwardly. They are my feathered children. I raised them."[40] Beth Brant recalls her grandfather, who upon deciding to raise chickens for eggs and poultry gave them Mohawk names such as Atyo, which means brother-in-law. "But when it came time to kill the first hen, Grandpa couldn't do it. Said it was killing one of the family. And didn't Atyo look at him with those eyes, just like brother-in-law, and beg not to have its [*sic*] head chopped off?"[41]

Because of her closeness to peacocks, Flannery O'Connor encountered the meaning of the absent referent in dreams about them. "Lately I have had a recurrent dream," she wrote. "I am five years old and a peacock. A photographer has been sent from New York and a long table is laid in celebration. The meal is to be an exceptional one: myself. I scream 'Help! Help!' and awaken."[42]

Colette introduces us to the image of the dead bird, the dead, consumable—but will it be consumed?—bird:

> Vial looked at them and so did I. Good indeed! A little rosy blood remained in the broken joints of the plucked and mutilated chickens,

and you could see the shape of the wings, and the young scales covering the little legs that had only this morning enjoyed running and scratching. Why not cook a child, too? My tirade petered out and Vial said not a word. I sighed as I beat my sharp, unctuous sauce, but soon the aroma of the delicate flesh, dripping on the charcoal, would give me a yawning hunger. I think I may soon give up eating the flesh of animals; but not to-day.[43]

In Margaret Atwood's *Cat's Eye,* the narrator recognizes the similarity between a turkey and a baby. She looks at "the turkey, which resembles a trussed, headless baby. It has thrown off its disguise as a meal and has revealed itself to me for what it is, a large dead bird."[44] She restores the absent referent. In Atwood's *Surfacing* a dead heron represents purposeless killing and prompts thoughts about other senseless deaths. A dead bird figures in Alice Ellis's more recent work, *Unexplained Laughter.* Within a story in which the problem of muteness is acutely represented—we are introduced to characters who cannot speak, will not speak, and cannot avoid speaking—the question of what to do with a road-killed pheasant arises. Lydia has invited a vegetarian, Betty, on holiday with her to her Welsh cottage. Betty's vegetarianism, motivated by concerns about health and cruelty, yet continuously compromised by steak-and-kidney pies or sausages, carries less figurative importance than the role of the dead pheasant in focusing issues of flesh eating. The evening of a funeral, a friend arrives with the dead pheasant. Lydia decides to hang her in the kitchen for a week to allow for seasoning. Betty proposes burying her, "and Lydia did see what she meant, for human death was attended with such ritual and dispatch that for an instant it seemed cruelly perverse to deny something similar to this helpless creature."[45] But Lydia quickly changes her mind and proposes burying the bones after the bird has been consumed.

Anne Tyler's *The Clock Winder* exposes the functioning of the structure of the absent referent through the issue of consuming a turkey. One of the chapters is framed by the necessity for Elizabeth, who has been absorbed into the Emerson household as handyman, to kill a turkey for Thanksgiving. "Elizabeth stood by her window, flattening the rolled sleeves of her paint-shirt and wondering what she would do if it took more than one chop to kill the turkey. Or could she just refuse to do it at all? Say that she had turned vegetarian?"[46] Though she does not wish to kill a live turkey for Thanksgiving, she has no difficulty going to a supermarket and buying a dead turkey. The difference between killing a living turkey and buying a dead turkey is found in the structure of the absent referent.

The *might-have-beenness* of vegetarianism echoes in other Tyler novels so that the question arises, is "the vegetarian who is *not*" a talisman in her novels? Vegetarianism is something in the past or potentially in the future, but not in the present. For instance, *The Accidental Tourist* refers to a restaurant that might become vegetarian; in *If Morning Ever Comes,* the thinness of Ben Joe is attributed to a relapse into what had been his discarded vegetarianism; in *The Tin Can Tree,* Janie Rose, a young child tragically killed in an accident was a vegetarian.[47]

Can it be that literary consciousness is paradigmatic for vegetarian consciousness? A phenomenology of vegetarianism recapitulates the phenomenology of writing: of seizing language, of identifying gaps and silences. This vegetarian phenomenology includes identification with animals or animals' fate; questions of articulation, of when to speak up or accept silence; of control of food choices; and of challenging to patriarchal myths that approve of meat eating. As opposed to the brokenness and violence characteristic of the fall into patriarchal culture, vegetarianism in women's writings signifies a different way of relating to the world. We are told that there is something metaphorically instructive about our relationship to animals. Feminist use of story telling often conveys the importance of this metaphorical relationship. This story telling suggests that as we consider the power for nuclear annihilation or for interpersonal cruelty based on rigid social mores, vegetarianism may point to a reordering of the patriarchal moral order.

For a Feminist-Vegetarian Reading of the Vegetarian Body

> To be a feminist, one has first to become one. . . . Feminists are not aware of different things than other people; they are aware of the same things differently. Feminist consciousness, it might be ventured, turns a "fact" into a "contradiction."
>
> —Sandra Lee Bartky[48]

We cannot tell the truth about women's lives if we do not take seriously those dietary choices which were at odds with dominant culture. Vegetarianism spoke to women. They would not have adopted it, maintained it, proselytized for it, if vegetarianism were not a positive influence on their lives. This is a historical fact that needs to be accepted and then responded to by scholars studying women's lives and texts.

Vegetarian women's activism and their writings have been absorbed into the literary and historical feminist canon without noticing that they are saying and doing something different when it comes to meat eating. The numerous individual feminists who became vegetarians—from the Grimké sisters to Frances Willard, Clara Barton, Annie Besant, Matilda Joslyn Gage, May Wright Sewall, and Mary Walker—evidence a pattern of challenging patriarchal culture not only because it rendered women absent but also because it rendered animals absent. As women expressed and explored their own subjectivity, animals were released from the object category in which patriarchal culture had placed them. Consequently women writers such as Maxine Kumin, Alice Walker, Brigid Brophy, and Maureen Duffy actively articulate animal rights positions. In this same vein we ask, what has been the literary effect on Alexis DeVeaux, poet, playwright, and novelist, who acknowledges that along with having her first play produced, winning the Black Creation Literary Contest, and witnessing the immensity of poverty in Haiti, giving up meat was one of the seven transformative turning points in her career and life?[49]

Clearly, the reasons vegetarianism spoke to women and how they responded to it require close examination. What did feminist-vegetarians see themselves as doing? What compromises were they willing to accept? Feeding meat to a family like Gloria Steinem's vegetarian grandmother? Was it necessary for her to suppress feelings of disgust at the serving of meat? How do people live with the consequences of their dietary choices? How many authors and activists were vegetarians or included vegetarianism in their writings? What sort of vegetarian-feminist network existed? And what did meat-eating feminists think of it? We know, for instance, that Susan B. Anthony rushed to devour a steak in New York City after two days with some vegetarians.

Many historians and literary critics may metaphorically rush to devour a steak because meat eating makes sense within our dominant culture. But what is needed in developing a feminist-vegetarian critical theory is sensitivity to literary and historical meanings that differ from traditional interpretations. Any activity that counters prevailing custom requires innovation, persistence, and motivation.

In *Surfacing,* Margaret Atwood offers this observation about eating animals: "The animals die that we may live, they are substitute people. . . . And we eat them, out of cans or otherwise; we are eaters of death, dead Christ-flesh resurrecting inside us, granting us life."[50] Vegetarian activities counter patriarchal consumption and challenge the consumption of death. Feminist-vegetarian activity declares that an alternative worldview exists, one which celebrates life rather than consuming death; one which does not rely on resurrected animals but empowered people.

Epilogue:

Destabilizing Patriarchal Consumption

> The eating of animal flesh, an easy matter of course for most people unless made complex by ritual warnings, may yet turn out to be a problem of psycho-social evolution when humankind comes to review and reassess the inner and outer consequences of having assumed the life of an armed hunter, and all the practical and emotional dead ends into which this has led us. Only then will it be possible to separate the superstitious, neurotic and faddish aspects of vegetarianism from its possible ethical persuasiveness.
>
> —Erik H. Erikson, *Gandhi's Truth*

Beneath the equivocations and the hedges that cloak his criticism of meat, Erik Erikson, in the above passage acknowledges that vegetarianism has ethical meaning; its meaning is connected with the implications of killing animals, the consequences of which are experienced internally and externally. Like many meat eaters, Erikson perceives that vegetarianism is burdened by numerous associations, the superstitious, the neurotic, and the faddish; he fails to admit that so is meat eating. The eating of animal flesh is burdened by superstitions regarding our needs for animal protein and the equation of meat with strength; neurotic aspects of meat eating are revealed in the reactions of meat eaters to the threat of vegetarianism. Erikson's statement, though acknowledging the troubling dimension of killing animals for food, which has equipped our culture to be armed hunters even when this is no longer necessary, exemplifies the fact that one cannot be an objective viewer of one's own meat eating. Thus he raises questions about the texts of meat while staying firmly committed to them.

Because of the dominant discourse which approves of meat eating, we are forced to take the knowledge that we are consuming dead animals and accept it, ignore it, neutralize it, repress it. What are the costs of this? What are the implications of repressing facts about the absent referent whose death enables meat eating?

For women in patriarchal culture, additional concerns arise as well. For we have been swallowed *and* we are the swallowers. We are the consumers *and* the consumed. We are the ones whose stomachs do not listen—having no ears—and we are the ones who seek to be heard from within the stomach that has no ears.

Eating animals acts as mirror and representation of patriarchal values. Meat eating is the re-inscription of male power at every meal. The patriarchal gaze sees not the fragmented flesh of dead animals but appetizing food. If our appetites re-inscribe patriarchy, our actions regarding eating animals will either reify or challenge this received culture. If meat is a symbol of male dominance then the presence of meat proclaims the disempowering of women.

Many cultural commentators have observed that the rituals that attend the consumption of animals in nontechnological societies occur because meat eating represents patricide. What is consumed is the father. The men are said to resolve their hostility toward their father through the killing of animals.[1] The dead animal represents the father whose power has been usurped by the sons, yet, who, as ancestor forgives them. In this typology, the worst fears of a patriarchy—fathers being deposed by sons—are displaced through ritual and the killing of animals. Meat becomes a metaphor for the resolution of the tension between father and son for power; meat is viewed as male. The questions arises: do we ritually enact primal patricide whenever we sit down to a meal of meat?[2]

Though we are eating "father-food" we are not consuming the father. How can that which we eat be father when we rarely eat normal, adult male animals? The metaphor that whatever is killed becomes father screens the reality behind the metaphor. The reality is the structure of the absent referent. We are continuously eating mothers. The fact is that we proclaim and reinforce the triumph of male dominance by eating female-identified pieces of meat.

Kate Millet remarked that "every avenue of power" is male dominated. This includes the "power" we think we absorb from dead victims who are still bleeding. Meat is a "power-structured relationship" in which power is thought to transfer to the consumer.[3] The concept that meat gives physical strength derives from this symbolic power. Meat reflects back male power every time it is consumed. From symbolically defeated females flows the imagined power that is assimilated by the victor. Thus meat is both animalized *and* masculinized.

A reconceptualization of power has occurred. Power, mana, was imagined to exist in dead animals. Power would be absorbed through the consumption of the animal, and since fathers had power, the power being absorbed was considered to be the power of the father. We have been convinced to surrender part of our concept of power to the consumable, dead animal. We then think we absorb this power as we consume the dead. We are giving back to ourselves the power we think was in the victim.

How do we overthrow patriarchal power while eating its symbol? Autonomous, antipatriarchal being is clearly vegetarian. To destabilize patriarchal consumption we must interrupt patriarchal meals of meat.

Virginia Woolf seems to suggest that it is when thinking about women that we will forget the meat. Buried within the significant events of Woolf's *Jacob's Room* is a small interchange between mother and son. Betty Flanders, Woolf tells us, was thinking of

> responsibility and danger. She gripped Archer's hand. On she plodded up the hill.
>
> "What did I ask you to remember?" she said.
>
> "I don't know," said Archer.
>
> "Well, I don't know either," said Betty, humorously and simply, and who shall deny that this blankness of mind, when combined with profusion, mother wit, old wives' tales, haphazard ways, moments of astonishing daring, humour and sentimentality—who shall deny that in these respects every woman is nicer than any man?
>
> Well, Betty Flanders, to begin with.
>
> She had her hand upon the garden gate.
>
> "The meat!" she exclaimed, striking the latch down.
>
> She had forgotten the meat.[4]

But how, precisely, do we forget meat once our appetites are acclimated to her? The Yanomano of South America have two words for hunger: one word means that you have an empty stomach; the other word declares that you have a full stomach that craves meat. As the narrator in Colette's *Break of Day* discovered—despite seeing the reality of meat, the broken joints, the mutilations, imagining the life that only this morning enjoyed running and scratching, attempting to determine the difference between this and cooking a child, too—the aroma of the delicate flesh dripping on the charcoal gives one a yawning hunger, a hunger that begs that she forget her objections to meat.

The codes of the texts of meat must be broken down. They cannot be broken down while meat is present for it reifies all of the old codes. We must admit that there will be a destruction of the pleasure of meals as we now know it. But what awaits us is the discovery of the pleasure of vegan meals.

To forget the meat we begin by naming and claiming the absent referent, restoring to animals their individual beings. We must consider our own appetites and whether we wish to be dependent on them; we place the importance of acceding to these appetites within the symbolic patriarchal order that they will either accept or challenge.

One way by which we accept the eating of animal flesh is by creating a symbolic order, a cosmology, which reifies meat eating. Patriarchal values are expressed by appropriating images of animals' deaths into our symbolism. As Joseph Campbell describes this imagery:

> the paramount object of experience is the beast. Killed and slaughtered, it [*sic*] yields to people its [*sic*] flesh to become our substance, teeth to become our ornaments, hides for clothing and tents, sinews for ropes, bones for tools. The animal life is translated into human life entirely, through the medium of death, slaughter, and the arts of cooking, tanning, sewing.

The killed and slaughtered animal yields as well imagery of ferociousness, territorial imperative, armed hunting, aggressive behavior, the vitality and virility of meat eating. Carnivorous animals provide a paradigm for male behavior. Through symbolism based on killing animals, we encounter politically laden images of absorption, control, domain, and the necessity of violence. This message of male dominance is conveyed through meat eating—both in its symbolism and reality.

According to Campbell, the plant world, in contrast to the animal world, supplies "the food, clothing and shelter of people since time out of mind, but also our model of the wonder of life—in its cycle of growth and decay, blossom and seed, wherein death and life appear as transformations of a single, superordinated, indestructible force."[5] The plant world yields imagery of tending, nurturing, slow evolutionary change, harmony with the seasons. Political implications are derived from a sense of organic unity rather than disjunction; harvest rather than violence; living in harmony rather than having domain over. This is the challenge that the uniting of feminist and vegetarian insights offers: political symbolism based on an affirmation of a diet drawn from the plant world.

Deriving meaning from plant imagery, we can say we wilt if we eat flesh. We will feed on the grace of vegetables. Virginia de Araújo describes such a perspective, that of a friend, who takes the barrenness of a cupboard, filled only with "celery threads, chard stems, avocado skins," and creates a feast, a grace:

> & says, On this grace I feed, I wilt
> in spirit if I eat flesh, let the hogs,
> the rabbits live, the cows browse,
> the eggs hatch out chicks & peck seeds.[6]

The creation of vegetarian rituals that celebrate the grace of eating plants will contribute to destabilizing patriarchal consumption. In place of the ritual of the fatted calf for the return of the prodigal son, the celebration of the return of a daughter would be vegetarian. Maxine Hong Kingston suggests this in describing her welcome home: "My parents killed a chicken and steamed it whole, as if they were welcoming home a son, but I had gotten out of the habit of meat." She ate rice and vegetables instead.[7]

To destabilize patriarchal consumption, eat rice have faith in women. By doing so we release Metis, and all who have been swallowed, from the belly of Zeus; we restore wholeness to our fragmented relationships with each and the other animals. The questions before us is, which images of the universe, of power, of animals, of ourselves, will we represent in our food? Of that which has preceded us, what shall remain?

Eat Rice Have Faith in Women. Our dietary choices reflect and reinforce our cosmology, our politics. It is as though we could say, "Eating rice *is* faith in women."

On this grace may we all feed.

Notes

Epigraphs to the book: *The Letters of Virginia Woolf: Volume Two, 1912–1922,* ed. Nigel Nicolson and Joanne Trautman (New York and London: Harcourt Brace Jovanovich, 1976), p. 598; Audre Lorde, *Sister Outsider: Essays and Speeches* (Trumansburg, NY: The Crossing Press, 1984), p. 133; *Jonathan Swift: The Complete Poems,* ed. Pat Rogers (New Haven and London: Yale University Press, 1983), p. 207.

Preface

1. Quoted in Dudley Giehl, *Vegetarianism: A Way of Life* (New York: Harper & Row, 1979), p. 128.

2. This is my interpretation of the properties of a text enumerated in Thomas A. Sebeok, "Poetics in the Lion's Den: The Circus Act as a Text," *Modern Language Notes* 86, no. 6 (December 1971), p. 845.

3. From the Introduction by Blanche W. Cook, Clare Coss, Alice Kessler-Harris, Rosalind P. Petchesky, and Amy Swerdlow in *Women, History and Theory: The Essays of Joan Kelly* (Chicago: University of Chicago Press, 1984), p. xxiv.

4. See for instance Frances Moore Lappé's statement: "Virtually all traditional societies based their diets on protein complementarity; they used grain and legume combinations as their main source of protein and energy." Frances Moore Lappé, *Diet for a Small Planet: Tenth Anniversary Edition* (New York: Ballantine Books, 1982), p. 161. In 1965 Aaron M. Altschul reported that "the average person in the Far East eats about 50 grams of protein per day of which 39 grams are of vegetable origin whereas in Northern Europe the total eaten per day is about 95 grams of which 53 or so are of animal origin." Aaron M. Altschul, *Proteins: Their Chemistry and Politics* (New York: Basic Books, Inc., 1965), p. 13. Jane Brody quotes the American Dietetic Association in noting that "most of mankind for much of human history has subsided on near-vegetarian diets." *Jane Brody's Nutrition Book* (New York: W. W. Norton & Co., 1981), p. 438.

See also Thelma Barer-Stein, *You Eat What You Are: A Study of Canadian Ethnic Food Traditions* (Toronto: McClelland and Stewart, 1979).

Epigraphs to part 1: Robert B. Hinman and Robert B. Harris, *The Story of Meat* (Chicago: Swift & Co., 1939, 1942), p. 194; from *The Man of Pleasure's Pocket Book,* quoted in Ronald Pearsall, *The Worm in the Bud: The World of Victorian Sexuality* (Toronto: The Macmillan Co., 1969), p. 259.

Chapter 1: The Sexual Politics of Meat

Epigraph: H. R. Hays, *The Dangerous Sex: The Myth of Feminine Evil* (New York: Pocket Books, 1964), p. 37.

1. P. Thomas Ziegler, *The Meat We Eat* (Danville, IL: The Interstate Printers and Publishers, 1966), pp. 5, 1.

2. Frank Gerrard, *Meat Technology: A Practical Textbook for Student and Butcher* (London: Northwood Publications, Inc., 1945, 1977), p. 348.

3. Waverley Root and Richard de Rochemont, *Eating in America: A History* (New York: William Morrow, 1976), p. 279.

4. Lisa Leghorn and Mary Roodkowsky, *Who Really Starves: Women and World Hunger* (New York: Friendship Press, 1977), p. 21.

5. Lloyd Shearer, "Intelligence Report: Does Diet Determine Sex?", summarizing the conclusions of Dr. Joseph Stolkowski, *Parade* 27 June 1982, p. 7.

6. William S. Baring-Gould and Ceil Baring-Gould, *The Annotated Mother Goose* (New York: Bramhall House, 1962), p. 103.

7. Elizabeth Cady Stanton, *The Woman's Bible: Part I* (New York: European Publishing Co., 1898; Seattle: Coalition Task Force on Women and Religion, 1974), p. 91.

8. Frederick J. Simoons, *Eat Not This Flesh: Food Avoidances in the Old World* (Madison: University of Wisconsin, 1961, 1967), p. 12. The quotation in the following paragraph is found in Simoons, p. 73.

9. Bridget O'Laughlin, "Mediation of Contradiction: Why Mbum Women do not eat Chicken," *Woman, Culture, and Society,* ed. Michelle Zimbalist Rosaldo and Louise Lamphere (Stanford: Stanford University Press, 1974), p. 303.

10. Robert B. Hinman and Robert B. Harris, *The Story of Meat* (Chicago: Swift & Co., 1939, 1942), p. 191.

11. Sunset Books and Sunset Magazines, *Sunset Menu Cook Book* (Menlo Park, CA: Lane Magazine and Book Co., 1969), pp. 139, 140.

12. *Oriental Cookery* from ChunKing and Mazola Corn Oil.

13. Edward Smith, M.D., *Practical Dietary for Families, Schools and the Labouring Classes* (London: Walton and Maberly, 1864), p. 199.

14. Laura Oren, "The Welfare of Women in Laboring Families: England, 1860–1950," *Feminist Studies* 1, no. 3–4 (Winter-Spring 1973), p. 110, quoting B. S. Rowntree and May Kendall, *How the Labourer Lives: A Study of the Rural Labour Problem* (London: Thomas Nelson and Sons, 1913). The quotations in the following paragraph are from Oren, p. 110, quoting Rowntree and Maud Pember Reeves, *Round About a Pound a Week.*

15. Maud Pember Reeves, *Round About a Pound a Week* (G. Bell and Sons, 1913, London: Virago Press, 1979), pp. 144 and 97.

16. Cicely Hamilton, *Marriage as a Trade* (1909, London: The Women's Press, 1981), p. 75.

17. Todd L. Savitt, *Medicine and Slavery: The Diseases and Health Care of Blacks in Antebellum Virginia* (Urbana and Chicago: University of Illinois Press, 1978), p. 91.

18. Isaac Bashevis Singer, *Enemies: A Love Story* (New York: Farrar, Straus and Giroux, 1972), p. 257.

19. George M. Beard, M. D., *Sexual Neurasthenia [Nervous Exhaustion] Its Hygiene, Causes, Symptoms and Treatment with a Chapter on Diet for the Nervous* (New York: E. B. Treat & Co., 1898, New York: Arno Press, 1972). This and succeeding quotations are found on pp. 272–78.

20. Hinman and Harris, *The Story of Meat,* p. 1.

21. W. Arens, *The Man-Eating Myth: Anthropology and Anthropophagy* (New York: Oxford University Press, 1979).

22. Russell Baker, "Red Meat Decadence," *New York Times* 3 April 1973, p. 43.

23. Aaron M. Altschul, *Proteins: Their Chemistry and Politics* (New York: Basic Books, Inc., 1965), p. 101.

24. Reeves, p. 131.

25. Helen Hunscher and Marqueta Huyck, "Nutrition," in *Consumer Problems in Wartime,* ed. Kenneth Dameron (New York and London: McGraw-Hill, 1944), p. 414.

26. Irving Fisher, "The Influence of Flesh Eating on Endurance," *Yale Medical Journal* 13, no. 5 (March 1907), p. 207.

27. Quoted in "Red Meat: American Man's Last Symbol of Machismo," *National Observer* 10 July 1976, p. 13.

28. Marty Feldman, quoted in Rynn Berry, Jr., *The Vegetarians* (Brookline, MA: Autumn Press, 1979), p. 32.

29. *New York Times* 15 April 1973, p. 38.

30. She concludes, "and I wish he'd taken us with him." Carolyn Steedman, "Landscape for a Good Woman," in *Truth, Dare or Promise: Girls Growing Up in the Fifties,* ed. Liz Heron (London: Virago Press, 1985), p. 114.

31. Alice Walker, *The Temple of My Familiar* (San Diego, New York: Harcourt Brace Jovanovich, 1989), p. 50.

32. Richard E. Leakey and Roger Lewin, *People of the Lake: Mankind and Its Beginnings* (New York: Doubleday & Co., 1978, New York: Avon Books, 1979), pp. 210–11.

33. Peggy Sanday, *Female power and male dominance: On the origins of sexual inequality* (Cambridge and New York: Cambridge University Press, 1981), pp. 65, 66.

34. Sanday, p. 39.

35. Sandy Grady, "The Duke as Boring as Spinach," *Buffalo News* 26 March 1988.

36. From a catalog from Northern Sun Merchandising, 2916 E. Lake Street, Minneapolis, MN, 55406.

37. From Hegel's *Philosophy of Right,* para. 166, p. 263, quoted in Nancy Tuana, *The Less Noble Sex: Scientific, Religious, and Philosophical Conceptions of Woman's Nature.* Bloomington and London: Indiana University Press, 1994.

38. Mary Douglas, "Deciphering a Meal," in *Implicit meanings: Essays in anthropology* (London: Routledge & Kegan Paul, 1975), p. 273.

39. Marabel Morgan, *Marabel Morgan's Handbook for Kitchen Survival: The Total Woman Cookbook* (New Jersey: Fleming H. Revell Co., 1980), p. 13.

40. Mary McCarthy, *Birds of America* (New York: Harcourt Brace Jovanovich, 1965, New York: New American Library, 1972), pp. 167, 180, 183.

41. R. Emerson Dobash and Russell Dobash, *Violence Against Wives: A Case Against the Patriarchy* (New York: The Free Press, 1979), p. 100.

42. Erin Pizzey, *Scream Quietly or the Neighbours will Hear* (Hammondsworth, England: Penguin Books, 1974), p. 35.

43. James C. Whorton, " 'Tempest in a Flesh-Pot': The Formulation of a Physiological Rationale for Vegetarianism," *Journal of the History of Medicine and Allied Sciences* 32, no. 2 (April 1977), p. 122.

44. Editorial, *New York Times,* 17 August 1981.

Chapter 2: The Rape of Animals, the Butchering of Women

Epigraphs: John Berger, *About Looking* (New York: Pantheon, 1980), p. 5. Mary Gordon, *Final Payments* (New York: Random House, 1978), p. 119. Upton Sinclair, *The Jungle* (1906; New York: New American Library, 1973), p. 40.

1. *The Beast: The Magazine That Bites Back* 10 (Summer 1981), pp. 18–19.

2. Heidnik was convicted of two counts of first-degree murder, six counts of kidnapping, five counts of rape, four counts of aggravated assault and one count of involuntary deviate sexual intercourse.

3. Whereas feminist critics have examined the correspondences between the treatment by Western, scientific culture of women and nature in a generalized sense, (see, for instance, Carolyn Merchant's *The Death of Nature: Women, Ecology, and the Scientific Revolution* [New York: Harper & Row, 1980]) and even some of the specific alliances between animals and women (as is found in Susan Griffin's *Woman and Nature: The Roaring Inside Her* [New York: Harper & Row, 1978]), none has addressed explicitly the significance of the overlap in representations of women and animals who are butchered. However, feminist analysis of the metaphors for nature used by early modern scientists reveals the scientists' sexualized view of nature and hence of animals.

4. Teresa de Lauretis, *Alice Doesn't: Feminism, Semiotics, Cinema* (Bloomington: Indiana University Press, 1984), p. 141.

5. I am indebted to Margaret Homans's discussion of the absent referent in literature for this expanded explanation of the cultural function of the absent referent. See her *Bearing the Word: Language and Female Experience in Nineteenth-Century Women's Writing* (Chicago: University of Chicago Press, 1986), p. 4.

6. Kathy Barry, *Female Sexual Slavery* (Englewood Cliffs, NJ: Prentice Hall, 1979), p. 3.

7. Keith Thomas, *Man and the Natural World: A History of the Modern Sensibility* (New York: Pantheon, 1983), p. 44.

8. Marjorie Spiegel, *The Dreaded Comparison: Human and Animal Slavery* 2nd Edition. (New York: Mirror Books, 1989).

9. Vincent Harding, *There Is a River: The Black Struggle for Freedom in America* (New York: Harcourt Brace Jovanovich, 1981, New York: Vintage Books, 1983), p. 7. Harding's source is Peter H. Wood's *Black Majority: Negroes in Colonial South Carolina From 1670 through the Stono Rebellion* (New York: Alfred A. Knopf, 1974). Wood discusses the reasons that the Proprieters of the Carolina colony protested the enslavement of Indians. They did so not only because they feared "prompting hostilities with local tribes" but also because "they were anxious to protect their peaceful trade in deerskins, which provided the colony's first source of direct revenue to England. With the opening up of this lucrative Indian trade to more people in the 1690s, the European settlers themselves became increasingly willing to curtail their limited reliance upon native American labor." *Black Majority,* p. 39.

10. Dick Gregory, *The Shadow That Scares Me,* ed. James R. McGraw (Garden City, NY: Doubleday & Co., Inc., 1968), pp. 69–70.

11. See Carol J. Adams, "Bringing Peace Home: A Feminist Philosophical Perspective on the Abuse of Women, Children, and Pet Animals," in *Neither Man nor Beast: Feminism and the Defense of Animals.* (New York: Continuum Publishing Company, 1994), pp. 144–61.

12. See Carol J. Adams, "Woman-Battering and Harm to Animals," in *Animals and Women: Feminist Theoretical Explorations,* ed. Carol J. Adams and Josephine Donovan (Durham and London: Duke University Press, 1995).

13. Susan Glaspell, *A Jury of Her Peers* (London: Ernest Benn, Ltd., 1927).

14. R. Emerson Dobash and Russell Dobash, *Violence Against Wives: A Case Against the Patriarchy* (New York: The Free Press, Macmillan, 1979), p. 110.

15. Andrea Dworkin, *Pornography: Men Possessing Women* (New York: Perigee Books, 1981), p. 209; Gena Corea, *The Hidden Malpractice: How American Medicine Mistreats Women* (New York: William Morrow and Co., 1977, New York: Jove-Harcourt Brace Jovanovich Books, 1978), p. 129.

16. Linda Lovelace with Mike McGrady, *Ordeal* (New York: Citadel Press, 1980, Berkley Books, 1981), p. 96. Note that this is one woman looking at another as "meat."

17. Susan Griffin, *Rape: The Power of Consciousness* (San Francisco: Harper & Row, 1979), p. 39.

18. Ecofeminists, including Susan Griffin, discuss the matter/spirit dualism as it interacts with other major dualisms (including human/animal and male/female) that are associated with patriarchal culture. Val Plumwood, in *Feminism and the Mastery of Nature* (London and New York: Routledge, 1993), provides a profound discussion of these dualisms in her chapter "Dualism: The Logic of Colonisation." In the light of interconnected forms of violence, I extend Elizabeth Spelman's analysis of somatophobia (or hostility to the body) to include the way animals are always equated with their bodies (matter) and are not seen as having souls (spirit). See "Bringing Peace Home," p. 152.

19. Annette Kuhn remarks: "Representations are productive: photographs, far from merely reproducing a pre-existing world, constitute a highly coded discourse that, among other things, constructs whatever is in the image as object of consumption—consumption by looking, as well as often quite literally by purchase. It is no coincidence, therefore, that in many highly socially visible (and profitable) forms of photography women dominate the image. Where photography takes women as its subject matter, it also constructs 'woman' as a set of meanings which then enter cultural and economic circulation on their own account." (*The power of the image: Essays on representation and sexuality* [London: Routledge and Kegan Paul, 1985], p. 19.) Also see Kaja Silverman, *The Subject of Semiotics* (New York: Oxford University Press, 1983), especially her chapter on "Suture," pp. 194–236.

20. William Morris, ed., *The American Heritage Dictionary of the English Language* (Boston: American Heritage Publishing Co., Inc., and Houghton Mifflin Co., 1969), p. 734. The third edition corrects this and restores the absent referent.

21. William Hazlitt, *The Plain Speaker* (EL, n.d.), 173, quoted in Keith Thomas, *Man and the Natural World,* p. 300.

22. Robert Graves, *The Greek Myths: 1* (Baltimore: Penguin Books, 1955), p. 46. Original reference is found in Hesiod's *Theogony,* trans. Apostolos Athanassakis (Baltimore: Johns Hopkins University Press, 1983), lines 886–900.

23. From Leslie Friedman Goldstein's *The Constitutional Rights of Women: Cases in Law and Social Change* (New York and London: Longman, 1979), we learn of a curious coincidence of history: the legal affirmation of the location of slaughterhouses in a distinctly separate part of a community occurred simultaneously with the denial of women's protection under the Fourteenth Amendment. In 1873, *Bradwell v. State of Illinois,* the "first women's rights case" (p. 2), was argued before the Supreme Court. *Bradwell* challenged sex classification as a violation of the Fourteenth Amendment. (Myra Bradwell had been denied admission to the Illinois Bar because she was married.) Two weeks later, the *Slaughterhouse Cases* were argued, which brought a challenge by butchers to a Louisiana statute restricting the location of slaughterhouses. The statute's purpose was "to protect the general population from the unpleasant fumes, sounds, and other disturbances associated with the slaughtering of animals by limiting those activities to a single, narrowly circumscribed area of town." However, the statute de facto permitted a monopoly (pp. 2–3). Reversing the chronology in which the cases were heard, the Supreme Court issued its decision in the *Slaughterhouse Cases* first; it affirmed that zoning could limit the location of slaughterhouses. This first Fourteenth Amendment decision severely limited the potential sweep of the privileges and immunities clause. It appears to have been issued first so as to provide the legal framework that excluded women from protection under the Fourteenth Amendment, a position announced the next day in the *Bradwell* Case.

24. Coral Lansbury, *The Old Brown Dog: Women, Workers and Vivisection in Edwardian England* (Madison: University of Wisconsin, 1985), p. 177.

25. Richard Selzer, "How to Build a Slaughterhouse," *Taking the World in for Repairs* (New York: Morrow, 1986), p. 116.

26. Tillie Olsen, *Yonnondio: From the Thirties* (New York: Dell, 1974), pp. 133–35.

27. Plutarch, "Essay on Flesh Eating," in *The Ethics of Diet: A Catena of Authorities Deprecatory of the Practice of Flesh-Eating,* ed. Howard Williams (London, 1883), pp. 47–48.

28. "Violence—as distinct from power, force, or strength—always needs *implements.*" Hannah Arendt, *On Violence* (New York: Harcourt, Brace & World, 1970), p. 4.

29. Selzer, p. 120.

30. Selzer, p. 116.

31. Quotations in the following paragraph are from the slaughterhouse tour episode found in Upton Sinclair, *The Jungle* (1906, New York: New American Library), pp. 38–45.

32. Sinclair, p. 311.

33. Robert B. Downs, afterword to Sinclair, *The Jungle,* as cited above, p. 346. Toward the end of the novel, Sinclair does include a plug for vegetarianism when he has Dr. Schliemann state "[I]t has been proven that meat is unnecessary as a food; and meat is obviously more difficult to produce than vegetable food, less pleasant to prepare and handle, and more likely to be unclean" (p. 337).

34. Quoted by Downs in Sinclair, p. 349. Referring to Sinclair's offensive characterization of black laborers, Michael Brewster Folsom concludes, "Clearly Sinclair did not 'accidentally' hit his reader's stomach; he aimed straight at it." ("Upton Sinclair's Escape from *The Jungle:* The Narrative Strategy and Suppressed Conclusion of America's First Proleterian Novel," *Prospects* 4 [1979], p. 261.)

35. Bertolt Brecht, "Writing the Truth: Five Difficulties," in *Civil Liberties and the Arts: Selections "From Twice A Year, 1938–1948,"* ed. William Wasserstrom (Syracuse, NY: Syracuse University Press, 1964), p. 295.

36. Bertolt Brecht, *Saint Joan of the Stockyards,* trans. Frank Jones (Bloomington and London: Indiana University Press, 1969, Second Edition, 1971).

37. Henry Ford, *My Life and Work* (1922), p. 81, quoted in Allan Nevins, *Ford: The Times, The Man, The Company* (New York: Charles Scribner's Sons, 1954), pp. 471–72.

38. Robert B. Hinman and Robert B. Harris, *The Story of Meat* (Chicago: Swift & Co., 1939, 1942), pp. 64–65.

39. As James Barrett observes, "Historians have deprived the [meat]packers of their rightful title of mass-production pioneers, for it was not Henry Ford but Gustavus Swift and Philip Armour who developed the assembly-line technique that continues to symbolize the rationalized organization of work." (*Work and Community in the Jungle: Chicago's Packinghouse Workers, 1894–1922* [Urbana and Chicago: University of Illinois Press, 1987], p. 20.)

40. In "Structural Constraints on Learning: Butchers' Apprentices," Hannah Meara Marshall observes that being a meat-cutting apprentice can be "a boring and frustrating experience," suggesting that this double alienation continues over from slaughterhouse to meat departments. (*American Behavioral Scientist* 16, no. 1 [September/October 1972], p. 35.)

41. John Robbins, *Diet for a New America* (Walpole, NH: Stillpoint Publishing, 1987), p. 136.

42. "Up to this time one skilled worker had taken a little pile of materials and assembled one flywheel-magneto complete. The average employee in this section finished thirty-five to forty magnetos in a nine-hour day, averaging about twenty minutes to each assembly. Now the assembly was divided into twenty-nine operations performed by twenty-nine men spaced along a moving belt. At once the average assembly time was cut to thirteen minutes ten seconds." Concluding his discussion of the "moving line," Nevins observes "Thus was mass production born—the mass production that Ford gave its classic definition as the focusing of power, accuracy, speed, continuity, and other principles upon the manufacture of a standardized commodity in great quantities." Nevins, *Ford,* pp. 472, 476.

43. Harry Braverman, *Labor and Monopoly Capital: The Degradation of Work in the Twentieth Century* (New York and London: Monthly Review Press, 1974), pp. 148–49.

44. Ray Allen Billington, *Land of Savagery Land of Promise: The European Image of the American Frontier in the Nineteenth Century* (New York: W. W. Norton & Co., 1981), p. 235.

45. Lenore E. Walker, *The Battered Woman* (New York: Harper & Row, 1979), p. 120. The following quotation in this paragraph is from Walker, p. 5.

46. Philip Roth, *Portnoy's Complaint* (New York: Random House, 1969, New York: Bantam Books, 1970), p. 19.

47. These questions were raised by Carol Barash.

48. *PETA News,* 1, no. 8 (1986) People for the Ethical Treatment of Animals, p. 2. See also Gena Corea, *The Mother Machine: Reproductive Technologies from Artificial Insemination to Artificial Wombs* (New York: Harper & Row, 1985), pp. 12–13.

49. Samuel Butler, *Erewhon* (1872), Hammondsworth, England: Penguin Books, 1970), p. 230.

50. Marabel Morgan, "365 Ways to Fix Hamburger," *Total Joy* (New Jersey: Fleming H. Revell Co., 1971), p. 113.

51. G. J. Barker-Benfield, *The Horrors of the Half-Known Life: Male Attitudes Toward Women and Sexuality in Nineteenth-Century America* (New York: Harper and Row, 1976), p. 113.

52. Although it might be thought that animals killed according to Jewish and Islamic dietary laws are killed instantly and thus do not suffer, this assumption is wrong. Peter Singer reports: "Instead of being quickly knocked to the floor and killed almost as they hit the ground, animals being ritually slaughtered in the United States may be shackled around a rear leg, hoisted into the air, and then hung, fully conscious, upside down on the conveyor belt for between two and five minutes—and occasionally much longer if something goes wrong on the 'killing line'—before the slaughterer makes his cut." *Animal Liberation: A New Ethics for Our Treatment of Animals* 2nd Edition (New York: A New York Review

Book, 1990), p. 154. See also, Roberta Kalechofsky, "Shechitah—The Ritual Slaughter of Animals," which can be found at: <*www.micahbooks.com*>.

53. P. Thomas Zeigler, *The Meat We Eat* (Danville, IL: The Interstate Printers and Publishers, 1966), p. 10. Travers Moncure Evans and David Greene, *The Meat Book* (New York: Charles Scribner's Sons), p. 107.

54. These descriptions accompany illustrations in Ziegler, *The Meat We Eat,* pp. 40–44.

55. Milan Kundera, *The Book of Laughter and Forgetting* (New York: Alfred A. Knopf, 1980, New York: Penguin Books, 1985), p. 75.

56. Ronald Pearsall, *The Worm in the Bud: The World of Victorian Sexuality* (Toronto: The Macmillan Co., 1969), p. 308.

57. Judith R. Walkowitz, "Jack the Ripper and the Myth of Male Violence," *Feminist Studies* 8, no. 3 (1982), p. 550.

58. Quoted in Pearsall, p. 308.

59. Quoted in Walkowitz, p. 551.

60. Stephen Knight, *Jack the Ripper: The Final Solution* (London: Granada Publishing Limited, 1977), p. 59.

61. Pearsall, p. 307.

62. Quoted in Pearsall, p. 313.

63. Marge Piercy, "In the men's room(s)," *Circles on the Water* (New York: Alfred A. Knopf, Inc., 1982), p. 80.

64. Dworkin, *Pornography,* p. 67.

65. Phyllis Chesler, "Men and Pornography: Why They Use It," in *Take Back the Night: Women on Pornography,* ed. Laura Lederer (New York: William Morrow and Company, Inc. 1980), p. 155.

66. Dario Fo and Franca Rame, "A Woman Alone," *Female Parts: One Woman Plays,* adapted by Olwen Wywark, trans. Margaret Kunzle (London: Pluto Press, 1981), pp. 15–16.

67. Norma Benney, "All of One Flesh: The Rights of Animals," in *Reclaim the Earth: Women Speak out for Life on Earth,* ed. Léonie Caldecott and Stephanie Leland (London: The Women's Press, 1983) p. 148. Benney cites an uncredited photographic centerfold from *Zig Zag* no. 129 (August 1982).

68. Phyllis Trible's translation in *Texts of Terror: Literary-Feminist Readings of Biblical Narratives* (Philadelphia: Fortress Press, 1984), pp. 76–77. Trible concludes her commentary on this biblical story of violence by saying that we should "recognize the contemporaneity of the story. . . . Woman as object is still captured, betrayed, raped, tortured, murdered, dismembered, and scattered. To take

to heart this ancient story, then, is to confess its present reality." Her footnote refers to the brutal New Bedford gang rape of a woman.

69. Judges 19:29, Trible's translation, p. 80. Trible notes that the Hebrew verb "divide" used in this passage "is used elsewhere only for animals" (p. 90 note 51). Alice Thomas Ellis's *The Sin Eater* refers to this passage. One of the female characters "was back in Judges 19 and the dreadful country of the Benjamites, wondering wholly against her will how the Levite had jointed his concubine—with what affronted, legalistic skill he had made her into *twelve* pieces: one each for each of the tribes of Israel. . . . People didn't cut up naturally into *twelve* pieces. Eleven pieces was what people would cut up into. If the Levite had had a mind inclined to symmetry, and she was sure he had from what she knew of him, it would have annoyed him, the tiresome inability of the human body to fall into twelve even pieces." (London: Duckworth, 1977), p. 145.

70. Kate Millet, *Sexual Politics* (Garden City, NY: Doubleday & Co., 1970), p. 292.

71. Beverly LaBelle, "*Snuff*—The Ultimate in Woman-Hating," in Lederer, *Take Back the Night,* pp. 273–4. In reflecting on the shower murder scene in *Psycho,* Kaja Silverman observes: "When the stabbing begins, there is a cinematic cut with almost every thrust of the knife. The implied equation is too striking to ignore: the cinematic machine is lethal; it too murders and dissects." (*Subject of Semiotics,* p. 211.)

72. Simone de Beauvoir, *The Second Sex,* trans. and ed. H. M. Parshley (Hammondsworth, England: Penguin, 1972), p. 236; Mary Daly, *Gyn/Ecology: The Metaethics of Radical Feminism* (Boston: Beacon Press, 1978), p. 31. Andrea Dworkin, *Woman Hating* (New York: E. P. Dutton & Co., 1974), p. 63; Ti-Grace Atkinson, *Amazon Odyssey* (New York: Links Books, 1974), pp. 57–63; bell hooks, *Ain't I a Woman: black women and feminism* (Boston: South End Press, 1981), p. 112. Each of these feminist critics is commenting on a different aspect of patriarchal culture, and this list does not communicate the range of theoretical assumptions upon which their ideas build. What fascinates me is that each writer gravitates to metaphors of butchering or consumption.

73. Carol Barash suggested the phrase "butcher the metaphor" for the dependence in radical feminist theory on images of women's (and animals') violent dismemberment.

Chapter 3: Masked Violence, Muted Voices

Epigraph: Mary Daly, *Beyond God the Father: Toward a Philosophy of Women's Liberation* (Boston: Beacon Press, 1973), p. 8.

1. Beverly Wildung Harrison, "Sexism and the Language of Christian Ethics," in *Making the Connections: Essays in Feminist Social Ethics,* ed. Carol S. Robb (Boston: Beacon Press, 1985), p. 29.

2. Peter Singer, *Animal Liberation: A New Ethics for Our Treatment of Animals* (New York: A New York Review Book, 1975), p. 96.

3. Dale Spender, *Man Made Language* (London, Boston and Henley: Routledge & Kegan Paul, 1980), p. 145.

4. Spender, p. 183.

5. Reported in James Serpell, *In the Company of Animals: A Study of Human-Animal Relationships* (New York: Basil Blackwell, 1986), pp. 158–59.

6. M. R. L. Sharpe, [later Freshel] *The Golden Rule Cookbook: 600 Recipes for Meatless Dishes* (Cambridge, MA: The University Press, 1908), p. 18.

7. Except for the statistics on veal calves, chickens, and turkeys, all statistics are from People for the Ethical Treatment of Animals, "Living without Cruelty" (501 Front St., Norfolk, VA 23510). *Animal Place News* supplied the statistic of chickens and turkeys (Summer 1999 4, no. 2). These statistics provide no breakdown according to gender, race, or class.

8. T. H., "Pythagorean Objections against Animal Food," *London Magazine* (November 1825), p. 382.

9. J. Byrnes, "Raising Pigs by the Calendar at Maplewood Farm," *Hog Farm Management,* September 1976, p. 30, quoted in Jim Mason and Peter Singer, *Animal Factories* (New York: Crown Publishers, 1980), p. 1.

10. Colman McCarthy, "Sins of the Flesh," *Washington Post,* March 25, 1990.

11. Paul M. Postal, "Anaphoric Islands," in *Papers from the Fifth Regional Meeting of the Chicago Linguistic Society, April 18–19, 1969,* ed. Robert I. Binnick, Alice Davison, Georgia M. Green, Jerry L. Morgan (Chicago: Department of Linguistics, University of Chicago, 1969), p. 235.

12. Daly, p. 8.

13. Joseph Ritson, "A new Dictionary for the Orthography, Pronunciation, and Etymology, of the English Language," left in manuscript at his death, quoted in Bertrand H. Bronson, *Joseph Ritson: Scholar-at-Arms* volume 1 (Berkeley: University of California Press, 1938), p. 136.

14. Elsa Lanchester, *Herself* (New York: St. Martin's Press, 1983), p. 12.

15. Quoted in Cheris Kramarae and Paula A. Treichler, *A Feminist Dictionary* (Boston, London and Henley: Pandora Press, 1985), p. 33.

16. Geoffrey L. Rudd, *Why Kill for Food?* (Madras, India: The Indian Vegetarian Congress, 1973), p. 77; Peter Singer, *Animal Liberation,* p. xii; Bernard Shaw quoted in Dudley Giehl, *Vegetarianism: A Way of Life* (New York: Harper & Row, 1979), p. 137; *The Autobiography of Benjamin Franklin,* ed. Leonard W. Labaree, Ralph L. Ketcham, Helen Boatfield, and Helene Fineman (New Haven: Yale University Press, 1964), p. 87; Richard Holmes, *Shelley: The*

Pursuit (New York: E. P. Dutton and Co., 1975), p. 129. This may have been tongue-in-cheek, yet as she and Percy Shelley were attempting vegetarianism at this time, Harriet reveals the attitudes that they associated with vegetarianism.

17. These stickers are advertised in *PETA News* 1, no. 9 (Winter 1986).

18. Mary Daly with Jane Caputi, *Websters' First New Intergalactic Wickedary of the English Langauge* (Boston: Beacon Press, 1987), p. 257.

19. Daly, *Wickedary,* p. 250.

20. Simone Weil, *The Iliad, or the Poem of Force,* 1940, trans. Mary McCarthy (Wallingford, PA: Pendle Hill, 1956, 1970), p. 3.

21. Mary Rayner, *Garth Pig and the Ice Cream Lady* (New York: Atheneum, 1977), p. 5.

22. Richard Selzer, "How to Build a Slaughterhouse," *Taking the World in for Repairs* (New York: Morrow, 1986), p. 129.

23. André Joly, "Toward a Theory of Gender in Modern English," in *Studies in English Grammar,* ed. A. Joly and T. Fraser (Paris: Editions Universitaires, 1975), p. 267. The following quotations are from pp. 270, 271.

24. Mason and Singer, p. 5.

25. P. Thomas Ziegler, *The Meat We Eat* (Danville, IL: The Interstate Printers and Publishers, 1966), p. 23.

26. A. R. Miller, *Meat Hygiene* (Philadelphia: Lea & Febiger, 1951, 1958), p. 41.

27. Maureen Duffy, "Beast for Pleasure," in *Animals, Men and Morals: An Enquiry into the Maltreatment of Non-Humans,* ed. Stanley Godlovitch, Roslind Godlovitch, and John Harris (New York: Taplinger, 1972), p. 117.

28. Paul Shepard, *The Tender Carnivore and the Sacred Game* (New York: Charles Scribner's Sons, 1973), p. 172.

29. Kate Millet, *Sexual Politics* (Garden City, NY: Doubleday & Co., 1970), p. 292n.

30. Cited in E. P. Evans, *The Criminal Prosecution and Capital Punishment of Animals* (London: William Heinemann, New York: E. P. Dutton and Co., 1906), pp. 55–56.

31. Vladamir Estragon, *Waiting for Dessert* (New York: The Viking Press, 1982), p. 177. See also W. D. Snodgrass's "The Boy Made of Meat: A Poem for Children," which conveys the role of the dominant culture in enforcing meat eating, to the dismay of the protesting child. W. D. Snodgrass, *Selected Poems: 1957–1987* (New York: Soho Press, 1987), p. 71.

32. Interview with Dr. Alan Long in Rynn Berry, Jr., *The Vegetarians* (Brookline, MA: Autumn Press, 1979), pp. 102–3.

33. Cited in Giehl, *Vegetarianism: A Way of Life,* p. 204.

34. Personal communication from Kathy Epling, Garbersville, CA, April 18, 1986.

35. Spender, pp. 164, 229.

36. Lynn Meyer, *Paperback Thriller* (New York: Random House, 1975), pp. 4–5.

37. Elaine Showalter, "Feminist Criticism in the Wilderness," in *The New Feminist Criticism: Essays on Women, Literature, and Theory,* ed. Elaine Showalter (New York: Pantheon Books, 1985), p. 262.

38. Zora Neale Hurston, *Their Eyes Were Watching God* (1937, Greenwich, CT: A Fawcett Premier Book, 1965), p. 51.

39. Mary Helen Washington, *Invented Lives: Narratives of Black Women 1860–1960* (Garden City, NY: Doubleday & Co., 1987), p. 237.

40. Hurston, p. 16. Hurston may have known of encounters such as the one Mary Church Terrell described in *A Colored Woman in a White World:* Terrell while traveling in the South was not always recognized as black. " 'So far as the nigger is concerned,' one man told me, 'he is like a mule. He is a good animal, so long as you keep him broken.' 'But the colored soldiers rendered great service to the Allies during the World War,' I interjected. 'And so did the mule,' quickly retorted the speaker. 'There is no animal in the world that did better service than the mule during the war. The mule is just like the nigger. He will do the work if you will furnish the brain.' " (Washington, DC: Ransdell, Inc., 1940; New York: Arno Press, 1980), p. 325.

41. Lorraine Bethel, " 'This Infinity of Conscious Pain': Zora Neale Hurston and the Black Female Literary Tradition," in *All the Women are White, All the Blacks are Men, But Some of Us Are Brave. Black Women's Studies,* ed. Gloria T. Hull, Patricia Bell Scott, and Barbara Smith (Old Westbury, NY: The Feminist Press, 1982), p. 182.

42. Washington, p. 253, n. 15. Hurston may have chosen the mule as the representative of both the oppression of black women and of the other animals because she knew that the "word *mulatto* itself etymologically is derived from the word *mule* and echoes the debate Americans engaged in about whether blacks were of the same species as whites." Barbara Christian, *Black Women Novelists: The Development of a Tradition, 1892–1976* (Westport, CT and London: Greenwood Press, 1980), p. 16.

43. Hurston, p. 51.

44. This passage appears to follow the pattern Washington describes: "Passages which are supposed to represent Janie's interior consciousness begin by marking some internal change in Janie, then gradually or abruptly shift so that a male character takes Janie's place as the subject of the discourse; at the conclusion of these passages, ostensibly devoted to the revelation of Janie's interior life, the male voice predominates," pp. 243–44.

45. Benedict de Spinoza, *Ethic,* iv. prop. 37 (trans. W. Hale White, 4th ed. 1910, 209). Quoted in Keith Thomas, *Man and the Natural World: A History of the Modern Sensibility* (New York: Pantheon Book, 1983), p. 298.

46. Brigid Brophy, "In Pursuit of a Fantasy," in *Animals, Men, and Morals,* p. 130.

47. Audre Lorde, *Sister Outsider: Essays and Speeches* (Trumansburg, NY: The Crossing Press, 1984), p. 41.

48. Nancy F. Cott, *The Grounding of Modern Feminism* (New Haven and London: Yale University Press, 1987), p. 15.

49. Vic Sussman, *The Vegetarian Alternative: A Guide to a Healthful and Humane Diet* (Emmaus, PA: Rodale Press, 1978), p. 2.

50. Isabel Giberne Sieveking, *Memoir and Letters of Francis W. Newman* (London: K. Paul, Trench, Trubner & Co., 1909), p. 118.

51. Ellen G. White, Letter 72, *Counsels on Diet and Foods* (Takoma Park: Review and Herald Publishing Assoc., 1938, 1976), p. 396.

52. It has been argued that the placenta is another food produced by females while alive.

53. For the intersection between white racism and the failure to acknowledge the gynocentrism of many cultures see Paula Gunn Allen's *The Sacred Hoop: Recovering the Feminine in American Indian Tradition* (Boston: Beacon Press, 1986).

54. E. B. White, *Charlotte's Web* (New York: Harper & Row, 1952, 1973), pp. 78, 95.

55. Plutarch, "Of Eating of Flesh," in *Animal Rights and Human Obligations,* ed. Tom Regan and Peter Singer (Englewood Cliffs, NJ: Prentice-Hall, Inc., 1976), p. 111.

Chapter 4: The Word Made Flesh

Epigraphs: Ovid, *Metamorphoses,* trans. Rolfe Humphries (Bloomington and London: Indiana University Press, 1955, 1971), p. 367. *The Poems of Emily Dickinson,* ed. Thomas H. Johnson (Cambridge: The Belknap Press of Harvard University Press, 1951), poem 1651.

1. Teresa de Lauretis, *Alice Doesn't: Feminism, Semiotics, Cinema* (Bloomington: Indiana University Press, 1984) pp. 8–9.

2. Dudley Giehl, *Vegetarianism: A Way of Life* (New York: Harper & Row, 1979); Vic Sussman, *The Vegetarian Alternative: A Guide to a Healthful and Humane Diet* (Emmaus, PA: Rodale Press, 1978); Keith Akers, *A Vegetarian*

Sourcebook: The Nutrition, Ecology, and Ethics of a Natural Foods Diet (New York: G. P. Putnam's Sons, 1983).

3. Keith Thomas, *Man and the Natural World: A History of the Modern Sensibility* (New York: Pantheon, 1983), p. 297.

4. Aphra Behn, "On the Author of that excellent and learned Book, entitled, *The Way to Health, long Life and Happiness,*" in Thomas Tryon, *The Way to Make All People Rich; or, Wisdoms Call to Temperence and Frugality* . . . [sic] (London, 1685).

5. *The Autobiography of Benjamin Franklin,* ed. Leonard W. Labaree, Ralph L. Ketcham, Helen Boatfield, and Helene Fineman (New Haven: Yale University Press, 1964), p. 63.

6. Joseph Ritson, *An Essay on Abstinence from Animal Food as a Moral Duty* (London: Phillips, 1802), p. 201.

7. Bernard Mandeville, *The Fable of the Bees; or, Private Vices, Publick Benefits* (Oxford: Clarendon Press, 1911), Remark P, p. 173.

8. James Turner, *Reckoning with the Beast: Animals, Pain and Humanity in the Victorian Mind* (Baltimore and London: Johns Hopkins University Press, 1980), p. 18.

9. Bertrand H. Bronson, *Joseph Ritson: Scholar-at-Arms* vol. 1 (Berkeley: University of California Press, 1938), p. 34. To convey this he includes the entire Mandeville reference from Remark P in one of only two appendices to the biography, vol 2, pp. 743–48.

10. Quoted in Ritson, p. 225.

11. Frederick A. Pottle, *Shelley and Browning: A Myth and Some Facts* (Hamden, CT: Archon Books, 1965), p. 22.

12. Mohandas K. Gandhi, *An Autobiography: The Story of My Experiments with Truth* (1927, 1929, Boston: Beacon Press, 1956, 1972), p. 48.

13. Quoted in Brigid Brophy, "The Way of no Flesh," in *The Genius of Shaw,* ed. Michael Holroyd (New York: Holt Rinehart and Winston, 1979), p. 100.

14. Sheila Rowbotham, *Women, Resistance and Revolution: A History of Women and Revolution in the Modern World* (New York: Pantheon Books, 1972), p. 12.

15. Quoted in Brian Hill, "Vegetables and Distilled Water: William Lambe, M.D. (1765–1847)," *Practitioner* 194 (1965), p. 285.

16. William Cobbett, *Journal of a Year's Residence in the United States of America* (1819, Gloucester: Alan Sutton, 1983), p. 202.

17. Harriot K. Hunt, *Glances and Glimpses; or Fifty Years Social, Including Twenty Years Professional Life* (Boston: John P. Jewett and Co., 1856, New York: Source Book Press, 1970), p. 140.

18. John Oswald, *The Cry of Nature; or, an Appeal to Mercy and to Justice, on Behalf of the Persecuted Animals* (London, 1791), p. i.

19. *The Life of Thomas Holcroft Written by Himself Continued to the Time of His Death from his Diary Notes & Other Papers by William Hazlitt,* ed. Elbridge Colby (New York: Benjamin Blom, 1928, 1968, 1980), vol. 2, pp. 127, 129.

20. George Borrow, *Lavengro: The Scholar, the Gypsy, the Priest,* ed. George F. Whicher (New York: The MacMillan Company, 1927), p. 197.

21. Paraphrase of comments made by Susanne Kappeler.

22. This incident and the following one are reported in Bronson, who viewed them as either exaggerated or apocryphal stories, vol 1. p. 251, from J. G. Lockhart's *Life of Sir Walter Scott.*

23. de Lauretis, *Alice Doesn't,* p. 37.

24. Isabel Colegate, *The Shooting Party* (New York: The Viking Press, 1980, Avon Books, 1982), p. 94.

25. Alice B. Toklas, *The Alice B. Toklas Cook Book* (1954, Garden City, NY: Anchor Books, 1960), pp. 37–57.

26. Roland Barthes, "Introduction to the Structural Analysis of Narratives," *Image-Music-Text,* trans. Stephen Heath (New York: Hill and Wang, 1977), p. 79. Sexist language changed.

27. de Lauretis, p. 5.

Epigraph to part 2: Robert Graves, *The Greek Myths: Volume 1* (Middlesex, England and Baltimore, MD: Penguin Books, 1955, 1974), p. 46.

Chapter 5: Dismembered Texts, Dismembered Animals

Epigraph: Simone Weil, *The Need for Roots: Prelude to a Declaration of Duties toward Mankind* (New York: G. P. Putnam's Sons, 1952), pp. 224–25.

1. William Godwin, *Fleetwood or, The New Man of Feeling* (London, 1805, New York and London: Garland Publishing Inc., 1979), p. 177.

2. Bernard Shaw letter to Sidney Webb, October 18, 1898, in *Bernard Shaw: Collected Letters 1898–1910,* ed. Dan H. Laurence (New York: Dodd, Mead & Co., 1972), p. 67.

3. See for instance, Lillian S. Robinson, "Treason Our Text: Feminist Challenges to the Literary Canon," *Tulsa Studies in Women's Literature* (Spring 1983), pp. 83–98. The appearance of *The Norton Anthology of Literature by Women,* edited by Susan Gubar and Sandra Gilbert, by its attempts to re-member

women's texts implies the pre-existence of a dismembered canon. (New York and London: W. W. Norton and Co., 1985).

4. Barbara Smith, "Toward a Black Feminist Criticism," in *All the Women are White, All the Blacks are Men, But Some of Us Are Brave: Black Women's Studies,* ed. Gloria T. Hull, Patricia Bell Scott, and Barbara Smith (Old Westbury, NY: The Feminist Press, 1982), p. 161. See also Alice Walker, "*One* Child of One's Own: A Meaningful Digression within the Work(s)," in Walker, *In Search of Our Mother Gardens: Womanist Prose* (San Diego, New York: Harvest/Harcourt Brace Jovanovich, 1983), pp. 361–383. Deborah E. McDowell, "New Directions for Black Feminist Criticism," *Black American Literature Forum* (Winter 1980), pp. 153–59.

5. Elizabeth Robins, *Ancilla's Share* (1924, Westport, CT: Hyperion, 1976), pp. 94–95.

6. Lorraine Bethel, " 'This Infinity of Conscious Pain': Zora Neale Hurston and the Black Female Literary Tradition," in Hull, Scott and Smith, p. 177.

7. Caren Greenberg, "Reading Reading: Echo's Abduction of Language," in *Women and Language in Literature and Society,* ed. Sally McConnell-Ginet, Ruth Borker and Nelly Furman (New York: Praeger, 1980), p. 303. Further quotations are from pp. 306, 307.

8. H. S. V. Jones, "Joseph Ritson: A Romantic Antiquarian," *Sewanee Review Quarterly* 22, no. 3 (July 1914), p. 348.

9. *The Letters of Joseph Ritson, Esq. Edited chiefly from originals in the possession of his nephew. To which is prefixed a Memoir of the Author by Sir Harris Nicolas* (London: William Pickering, 1833), p. 38.

10. Bertrand H. Bronson, *Joseph Ritson: Scholar-at-Arms* (Berkeley: University of California Press, 1938), vol. 2, p. 608.

11. See definition of *anonymous* in Cheris Kramarae and Paula A. Treichler, *A Feminist Dictionary* (Boston: Pandora Press, 1985), p. 53.

12. For background on the colonialist influence on writers such as Ritson see *Critical Inquiry* 12 (1985), which includes articles by Patrick Brantlinger, "Victorians and Africans: The Genealogy of the Myth of the Dark Continent," (pp. 166–203) and Mary Louise Pratt, "Scratches on the Face of the Country; or, What Mr. Barrow Saw in the Land of the Bushmen," (pp. 119–43).

13. *Edinburgh Review* 2 (April 1803): pp. 128ff; *British Critic* 22 (November 1803): pp. 483–89. Quoted in Bronson, vol. 1, pp. 280, 296.

14. Sidney Lee, "Joseph Ritson," *Dictionary of National Biography Volume 16,* ed. Sir Leslie Stephen and Sir Sidney Lee (London: Oxford University Press), p. 1216.

15. Tom P. Cross, "Review of *Joseph Ritson, A Critical Biography* by Henry Alfred Burd," *Modern Philology* 17 (1919–1920), pp. 234, 233.

16. Annette B. Hopkins, "Ritson's *Life of King Arthur,*" *PMLA* 43 (March 1928), p. 251.

17. Cross, p. 233.

18. Included among these is "the literalization of a figure," when an extended metaphor becomes translated into an actual event; the reference to the figure of the Virgin Mary who was the Mother of the Word; the representation of women characters who translate language, carry messages or who act as amaneunses, which Homans sees as "the thematic presentation of women carrying or bearing language itself;" and times when the text recalls the language of other authors, especially men. Margaret Homans, *Bearing the Word: Language and Female Experience in Nineteenth-Century Women's Writing* (Chicago and London: University of Chicago Press, 1986), pp. 30–31.

19. See *Alastor,* line 101. *English Romantic Writers,* ed. David Perkins (New York: Harcourt, Brace and World, Inc., 1967), p. 961.

20. Mary Wollstonecraft Shelley, *Frankenstein; or, The Modern Prometheus: The 1818 Text,* ed. James Regier (Indianapolis: Bobbs-Merrill, 1974; Chicago: University of Chicago Press, 1982), p. 202.

21. Iris Murdoch, *The Good Apprentice* (New York and Hammondsworth: Penguin Books, 1987). See Laura Huxley on "The Cooking Meta Toy," in *Between Heaven and Earth: Recipes for Living and Loving* (New York: Farrar, Straus and Giroux, 1975), pp. 141–61.

22. Helen Yglesias, *The Saviors* (Boston: Houghton Mifflin Co., 1987), p. 301. See for instance Helen and Scott Nearing, *Living the Good Life: How to Live Sanely and Simply in a Troubled World* (New York: Shocken Books, 1954, 1970) and Helen Nearing, *Simple Food for the Good Life: An Alternative Cook Book* (New York: Dell Publishing Co., 1980).

23. Margaret Drabble, *The Ice Age* (New York and Scarborough, Ontario: New American Library, 1977), pp. 3–4.

24. Isabel Colegate, *The Shooting Party* (New York: The Viking Press, 1980, Avon Books, 1982), p. 30. Further substantive quotations are found on pp. 30, 111, 32.

25. Henry S. Salt, *The Creed of Kinship* (New York: E. P. Dutton and Co., 1935), p. viii.

26. Henry Salt, *Animals' Rights Considered in Relation to Social Progress* (1892, Clarks Summit, PA: Society for Animal Rights, Inc., 1980), p. 5.

27. Heywood Broun, "The Passing of Shaw's Mentor," *New Republic,* 98 (May 3, 1939), p. 376.

28. Henry Salt, *Seventy Years Among Savages* (London: George Allen and Unwin, 1921), p. 64.

29. Besides sharing similar reform impulses, the fictional character and historical figure are linked in their private lives as well because Colegate draws on information about Salt's marriage to describe Cardew's. Salt's wife, Kate, was the daughter of the Lower Master at Eton, the Reverend J. L. Joynes. She was an accomplished pianist and a feminist. (See George Hendrick, with the special assistance of John F. Pontin, *Henry Salt, Humanitarian Reformer and Man of Letters* [Urbana, Chicago, London: University of Illinois Press, 1977], p. 14.) Cardew's wife Ada is the headmaster's daughter, an accomplished pianist whose preferred cause was "Votes for Women." Salt and his wife set up housekeeping in a cottage near Tilford after leaving Eton; Cardew lives with his wife in a cottage in the Surrey hills. Edward Carpenter made frequent visits to Tilford to play duets with Kate Salt. Later, with Carpenter's urging, the Salts built a house near his residence in Millthorpe and they and Carpenter met daily. (Kate Salt was actually "hopelessly" in love with Carpenter. See Sheila Rowbotham and Jeffrey Weeks, *Socialism and the New Life: The Personal and Sexual Politics of Edward Carpenter and Havelock Ellis* [London: Pluto Press, 1977], pp. 77 and 97.) Cardew thinks about his friend, philosopher H. W. Brigginshaw, who often joins Ada in playing duets on the piano. Salt was close friends with Shaw and "wrote very often to Shaw." (Stephen Winsten, *Salt and His Circle* [London: Hutchinson and Co., Ltd., 1951], p. 126.) Cardew imagines what he shall put in a letter to Shaw. Kate was a lesbian. (She supposedly told her brother she was not interested in sex, or at least, we presume, heterosexual sex. Winsten, p. 71.) Ada preferred to keep "all that nonsense" [presumably sexual intercourse] "to a minimum." Cardew is similar to Salt only up until the time when the shooting party is said to have occurred, 1913; after this time, Cardew's life diverges from the pattern of Salt's.

30. Colegate, pp. 32-33.

Chapter 6: Frankenstein's Vegetarian Monster

Epigraph: John Oswald, *The Cry of Nature; or, An Appeal to Mercy and to Justice, on Behalf of the Persecuted Animals* (London, 1791), p. 44.

1. Mary Wollstonecraft Shelley, *Frankenstein or, The Modern Prometheus The 1818 Text,* ed. James Rieger (Indianapolis: Bobbs-Merrill, 1974, Chicago and London: University of Chicago Press, 1982), "Preface," p. x. Though I have chosen the 1818 version rather than the 1831 revision, according to Rieger's collation of the texts of 1818 and 1831 in Appendix B, Shelley left the inner circle of the Monster's narrative, where its vegetarianism is revealed, the least tampered section of the emended novel.

2. Like other feminist critics who have identified Frankenstein's Creature as female and thus avoid the use of the masculine pronoun, I will use "it" to refer to the Creature. See for instance U. C. Knoepflmacher "Thoughts on the Aggression of Daughters": "the Monster—purposely not called a 'he' in this discus-

sion—initially displays feminine qualities" and "beneath the contorted visage of Frankenstein's creature lurks a timorous yet determined female face." *The Endurance of Frankenstein,* ed. George Levine and U. C. Knoepflmacher (Berkeley and Los Angeles: University of California Press, 1979), pp. 106, 112.

3. Mary Midgley, *Animals and Why They Matter* (Athens: University of Georgia Press, 1984), pp. 22, 32.

4. Shelley, p. 142.

5. Henry Salt, *The Humanities of Diet: Some Reasonings and Rhymings* (Manchester: The Vegetarian Society, 1914).

6. John Frank Newton, *The Return to Nature; or, A Defence of the Vegetable Regimen* (London, 1811). Godwin may have known John Oswald as well, author of *The Cry of Nature; or an Appeal to Mercy and to Justice, on Behalf of the Persecuted Animals* (1791). Godwin was the acting editor for *The Political Herald, and Review* for which Oswald wrote. However, according to David Erdman, "Not only were the contributors' names omitted or disguised by pseudonyms, as was the general custom; apparently the major contributors were also kept unacquainted with each other." *Commerce des lumières: John Oswald and the British in Paris, 1790–1793* (Columbia: University of Missouri Press, 1986), p. 37. Erdman continues, "we must suppose that Oswald at this time was developing some acquaintances in publishing circles; possibly he and Godwin had met early on" (p. 42). For instance, Oswald and Mary Wollstonecraft shared the same publisher, Joseph Johnson.

7. James Turner, *Reckoning with the Beast: Animals, Pain, and Humanity in the Victorian Mind* (Baltimore: Johns Hopkins University Press, 1980), p. 19.

8. Keith Thomas, *Man and the Natural World: A History of the Modern Sensibility* (New York: Pantheon Books, 1983), p. 296.

9. Turner, p. 17.

10. Cited in Kenneth Neill Cameron, *The Young Shelley: Genesis of a Radical* (New York: Macmillan, 1950; Octagon Books, 1973), p. 378.

11. Joseph Ritson, *An Essay on Abstinence from Animal Food as a Moral Duty* (London: Phillips, 1802), p. 89. Percy Shelley, *A Vindication of Natural Diet,* in *The Complete Works of Percy Bysshe Shelley, Volume 6, Prose,* ed. Roger Ingpen and Walter E. Peck, (New York: Gordian Press, 1965), p. 11, (hereinafter called *Vindication*).

12. John Oswald stated the viewpoint this way: "When he considers the natural bias of the human heart to the side of mercy, and observes on all hands the barbarous governments of Europe giving way to a better system of things, he is inclined to hope that the day is beginning to approach when the growing sentiment of peace and good-will towards men will also embrace, in a wide circle of benevolence, the lower orders of life" (p. 11).

13. His most recent biographer calls him a "British military intellectual," commenting "the most sensational-biographical oddity being his combining a military career with a Pythagorean diet." David Erdman, *Commerce des lumières,* p. 3.

14. *Vindication,* p. 13.

15. As Keith Thomas notes: "Vegetarianism was also encouraged by Christian teaching, for all theologians agreed that man had not originally been carnivorous." *Man and the Natural World,* p. 289.

16. Thomas, p. 289, in *Minor Poets of the Caroline Period,* ed. George Saintsbury (Oxford, 1968), i. 558.

17. See Ritson, p. 55. Alexander Pope, Epistle III, "An Essay on Man," ll. 152–54, in *Poetry and Prose of Alexander Pope,* ed. Aubrey Williams (Boston: Houghton Mifflin Co., 1969), pp. 142–43.

18. *Paradise Lost,* Book 5, ll. 303–4, in *John Milton: Complete Poems and Major Prose,* ed. Merritt Y. Hughes (New York: The Bobbs-Merrill Co., Inc., 1957), p. 309.

19. Newton, p. 5.

20. See Sandra Gilbert and Susan Gubar, *The Madwoman in the Attic: The Woman Writer and the Nineteenth-Century Literary Imagination* (New Haven: Yale University Press, 1979), pp. 230, 234–46.

21. Quoted in Shelley, *Vindication,* p. 6 and cited as "Plin., *Nat. Hist.* lib. vii. sect. 57."

22. *Vindication,* p. 6.

23. Ovid, *Metamorphoses,* ed. Sir Samuel Garth, trans. John Dryden (London, 1720), Book 1, p. 8.

24. Madeleine A. Simons, "Rousseau's Natural Diet," *Romantic Review* 45 (1 Feb. 1954), pp. 18–28.

25. From the *Confessions,* 1, 72, quoted in Simons, p. 25. Mary Shelley reread the *Confessions* while transcribing *Frankenstein* in October 1817.

26. Shelley, p. 101.

27. Plato, *The Republic of Plato,* trans. Francis MacDonald Cornford (New York: Oxford University Press, 1966), Part 2, 373, pp. 60–61.

28. William Paley, *The Principles of Moral and Political Philosophy* (1785, New York and London: Garland Publishing Inc., 1978), p. 599.

29. Quoted in *The Ethics of Diet: A Catena of Authorities Deprecatory of the Practice of Flesh-Eating,* ed. Howard Williams (London, 1883), p. 241. This observation first appeared in the *Medical Journal* for July 27, 1811.

30. *Vindication,* p. 13.

31. Williams, p. 243.

32. Denise Riley, "Waiting," in *Truth, Dare or Promise: Girls Growing Up in the Fifties,* ed. Liz Heron (London: Virago Press, 1985), p. 239.

33. David Ketterer, *Frankenstein's Creation: The Book, the Monster and Human Reality* (University of Victoria: English Literary Studies, 1979), p. 15.

34. Shelley, p. 119.

35. Marc A. Rubenstein, " 'My Accursed Origin': The Search for the Mother in *Frankenstein,*" *Studies in Romanticism* 15 (Spring, 1976), p. 169.

36. Mary Wollstonecraft, *A Vindication of the Rights of Woman,* ed. Charles W. Hagelman, Jr. (1792; New York: W. W. Norton & Co., 1967), p. 32.

37. Shelley, p. 227, (Introduction to Third Edition).

38. Marcia Tillotson, " 'A Forced Solitude': Mary Shelley and the Creation of Frankenstein's Monster," in *The Female Gothic,* ed. by Juliann E. Fleenor, (Montreal and London: Eden Press, 1983), p. 168.

39. Carolyn Heilbrun and Catharine Stimpson, "Theories of Feminist Criticism: A Dialogue," in *Feminist Literary Criticism: Explorations in Theory,* ed. Josephine Donovan (Lexington: University Press of Kentucky, 1975), p. 68.

40. These have been described as strategies of negative politeness in Penelope Brown, "How and Why Are Women More Polite? Some Evidence from a Mayan Community," in *Women and Language in Literature and Society,* ed. Sally McConnell-Ginet, Ruth Borker, and Nelly Furman (New York: Praeger, 1980), p. 116.

Chapter 7: Feminism, the Great War, and Modern Vegetarianism

Epigraph: "Civilization? Culture?" notes for *Vegetarian Pocket Monthly.* Box 2, file no. 33, "Vegetarian Writings, circa 1952–3." All correspondence and unpublished manuscripts by Agnes Ryan cited in this chapter are in the Agnes Ryan Collection of the Arthur and Elizabeth Schlesinger Library on the History of Women in America, Radcliffe College, Cambridge, MA. Permission to publish material provided by The Schlesinger Library and the late Henry Bailey Stevens.

1. Mary Wollstonecraft Shelley, *Frankenstein or, The Modern Prometheus The 1818 Text,* ed. James Rieger (Indianapolis: Bobbs-Merrill, 1974, Chicago and London: University of Chicago Press, 1982), p. 142.

2. Edward Carpenter and George Barnefield, *The Psychology of the Poet Shelley* (London: George Allen & Unwin Ltd., 1925), p. 19.

3. C. Roland Marchand, *The American Peace Movement and Social Reform, 1898–1918* (Princeton: Princeton University Press, 1972), p. 202.

4. Olive Schreiner, *Woman and Labour* (1911, London, Virago, 1978), p. 176.

5. Virginia Woolf, *Three Guineas* (London: The Hogarth Press, 1938, 1968), pp. 13–14.

6. Agnes Ryan, "The Heart to Sing," unpublished autobiography, pp. 314–15.

7. Kohlberg is so struck by this that he cites this interchange in three of his lectures in Lawrence Kohlberg, *Essays on Moral Development, Volume I: The Philosophy of Moral Development* (New York: Harper & Row, 1981), pp. 14, 46, 143. James Sully's *Studies of Childhood* details a similar transition. He describes a four-year old who objected to his parents eating animals, to the killing of seals, and the hunting of stags. He wants the police to stop such activities and is informed that "They can't do that because people are allowed to kill them."

> C. (loudly and passionately). "Allowed, allowed? People are not allowed to take other people and kill them."
> M. "People think there is a difference between killing men and killing animals."

Sully refers to this time period as a time when the boy was wrestling "with the dreadful 'must,' which turns men into killers," and refers to the fact that at this time the boy has also learned to accept as positive the existence of soldiers. (James Sully, *Studies of Childhood* [New York and London: D. Appleton and Co., 1914], p. 475.)

Matthew Lipman's *Lisa,* a book to aid children in focused discussions of philosophical and ethical issues, begins at episode 1 with the question, "Can We Both Love Animals and Eat Them?" A debate about hunting is described. One side argues that killing people evolves from hunting; the other that killing people is different from killing animals. Lisa remarks, "Once we get in the habit of killing animals, we may find it hard to stop when it comes to people." (Matthew Lipman, *Lisa* [Upper Montclair, New Jersey: Institute for the Advancement of Philosophy for Children, 1983], pp. 1, 2.)

8. Walter de la Mare, "Dry August Burned," *The Complete Poems of Walter de la Mare* (New York: Alfred A. Knopf, 1970), p. 365.

9. Mary Alden Hopkins, "Why I Earn My Own Living," in *These Modern Women: Autobiographical Essays from the Twenties* (Originally published 1926–1927 in *The Nation*), ed. Elaine Showalter (Old Westbury, NY: The Feminist Press, 1978), p. 44.

10. Reported in Andro Linklater, *An Unhusbanded Life: Charlotte Despard, Suffragette, Socialist and Sinn Feiner* (London: Hutchinson, 1980), p. 179.

11. The four were Alice Park, Lucinda Chandler, May Wright Sewall, and Mary Alden Hopkins.

12. Eugene Christian, *Meatless and Wheatless Menus* (New York: Alfred A. Knopf, 1917), pp. 6–7.

13. Quincy Wright, *A Study of War,* Volume 1 (Chicago: University of Chicago Press, 1942), p. 134.

14. Edward Maitland, *Anna Kingsford: Her Life, Letters, Diary and Work* vol. 1 (London: Redway, 1896), p. 28.

15. Percy Shelley, *On the Vegetable System of Diet,* in *The Complete Works of Percy Bysshe Shelley,* Volume 6, ed. Roger Ingpen and Walter E. Peck (New York: Gordian Press, 1965), p. 343.

16. Quoted in Max Davis, *The Case for the Vegetarian Conscientious Objector* with a foreword by Scott Nearing (Brooklyn, NY: Tolstoy Peace Group, 1944), p. 13.

17. Douglas Goldring, *The Nineteen Twenties: A General Survey and some Personal Memories* (London: Nicholson and Watson, 1945; reprinted by Folcroft Library Editions, 1975), p. 140.

18. L. F. Easterbrook, "Alcohol and Meat," *Nineteenth Century and After 95* (February 1924), p. 306. One recent vegetarian, a true inheritor of this position, traced his abandonment of meat eating to viewing "posters that showed the devastation of people and property in Vietnam." In response he asked himself, "What am I doing eating meat? I'm just adding to the violence." The *New York Times,* interview with Frederick P. Salvucci, March 21, 1975, p. 33. Dick Gregory writes of the connection between vegetarianism and the nonviolent civil rights movement:

> Under the leadership of Dr. King I became totally committed to nonviolence, and I was convinced that nonviolence meant opposition to killing in any form. I felt the commandment "Thou shalt not kill" applied to human beings not only in their dealings with each other—war, lynching, assassination, murder and the like—but in their practice of killing animals for food or sport. Animals and humans suffer and die alike. Violence causes the same pain, the same spilling of blood, the same stench of death, the same arrogant, cruel and brutal taking of life.

Dick Gregory's Natural Diet for Folks Who Eat: Cookin' with Mother Nature ed. James R. McGraw (New York: Harper & Row, 1973), pp. 15–16.

19. Mary Midgley, *Animals and Why They Matter* (Athens: The University of Georgia Press, 1983), p. 15.

20. The more extensive appeal to English women to become vegetarians during World War II is detailed in Raynes Minns, *Bombers and Mash: The Domestic Front 1939–45* (London: Virago, 1980).

21. Mikkel Hindhede, "The Effect of Food Restriction During War on Mortality in Copenhagen." *Journal of the American Medical Society,* 74 No. 6 (February 7, 1920), p. 381. Similar studies after World War II confirmed a relationship between a drop in mortality and the rationing of food. Axel Strøm M.D. and R. Adelsten Jensen, M.D. "Mortality from Circulatory Diseases in Norway 1940–1945," *The Lancet* 260 (Jan. 2, 1951), pp. 126–29.

22. Mervyn G. Hardinge and Hulda Crooks, "Non-Flesh dietaries. 1. Historical Background," *Journal of the American Dietetic Association* 43 (December 1963), p. 548.

23. Quoted by Rynn Berry, Jr., *The Vegetarians* (Brookline, MA: Autumn Press, 1979), p. 44.

24. Henry Salt, *Seventy Years Among the Savages,* quoted in George Hendrick, with the special assistance of John F. Pontin, *Henry Salt: Humanitarian Reformer and Man of Letters* (Urbana, Chicago, London: University of Illinois Press, 1977), p. 84.

25. Agnes Ryan, "For the Church Door," March 1943, Box 2.

26. Amanda Cross, *The James Joyce Murders* (New York: Macmillan Co., 1967), p. 89.

27. See Paul Fussell's discussion of these works, *The Great War and Modern Memory* (London, Oxford, New York: Oxford University Press, 1975), p. 91.

28. Henry Salt, "Sport as a Training for War," in *Killing for Sport: Essays by Various Writers,* ed. Henry Salt (London: G. Bell and Sons, Ltd. for the Humanitarian League, 1914).

29. In Graves's *Good-bye to All That* (Jonathan Cape: 1929, Hammondsmith, UK.: Penguin Books, 1957) the first paragraph of the first chapter ends: "or Mr Eustace Miles the English real-tennis champion and vegetarian with his samples of exotic nuts, I knew all about them in my way" (p. 9). See also Fussell, *The Great War,* pp. 203–20.

30. In his introduction to *The Home,* William O'Neill maintains that Gilman "published very little after the war," and attributes this to the fact that "World War I, and the changes that accompanied it, destroyed the moral foundation of her career" (William O'Neill, Introduction to *The Home* by Charlotte Perkins Gilman [Urbana: University of Illinois Press, 1972], p. x.) In contrast, I would argue that the war confirmed her claim of the need to involve women and women's values in decision making, and that *Herland* and *His Religion and Hers* suggest in opposite ways, first positively and then negatively, the conclusion that violence was a result of male dominance. *His Religion and Hers: A Study of the Faith of Our Fathers and the Work of Our Mothers* (London: T. Fisher Unwin, 1924).

31. Isabel Colegate, *The Shooting Party* (New York: The Viking Press, 1980, New York: Avon Books, 1982), p. 131. Other quotations cited in this chapter are found on pp. 20, 102, 188.

32. See for instance Susan Schweik, "A Word No Man Can Say for Us: American Women Writers and the Second World War" (PhD dissertation, Yale University, 1984) which examines the phenomenon that, especially during wartime, women are to be the receivers of information, objects who read, not objectors who write; repositories of meaning, not originators of meaning.

33. I am indebted here to DuPlessis's analysis, in *Writing beyond the Ending,* of women writers' strategy for challenging traditional romance. See Rachel Blau DuPlessis, *Writing beyond the Ending: Narrative Strategies of Twentieth-Century Women Writers* (Bloomington: Indiana University Press, 1985).

34. Marge Piercy, *Small Changes* (Garden City: Doubleday and Co., 1972, Greenwich, Conn: A Fawcett Crest Book, 1973), p. 41. The succeeding quotations in this paragraph are found on pp. 42, 48.

35. These metaphors are mine and not Piercy's. I use them to suggest that from her epiphanal moment in her kitchen, Beth evolves a systematic, ongoing rejection of a male, meat-eating culture that can be best represented by using metaphors from the anti-war movement.

36. Margaret Atwood, *The Edible Woman* (Boston: Little Brown and Co., New York: Warner Books, 1969), p. 25. Further quotations in this chapter are found on pp. 155, 183, 279.

37. Atwood reports that the idea for this scene came as she was looking "at a confectioner's display window full of marzipan pigs. It may have been a Woolworth's window full of Mickey Mouse cakes, but in any case I'd been speculating for some time about symbolic cannibalism." This scene, both as she experienced it as an individual and inscribed it as a novelist, exemplifies the structure of the absent referent. She saw a Marzipan pig or Mouse cakes; she imagines an edible woman cake. This association demonstrates the interchangeability of the categories of animal and woman. In addition, the relationship between symbol (cake animal or cake woman) and reality (consumed animal or consumed woman) suggests the alliance between what is really consumed and what is figured as being consumed. See Margaret Atwood, "An Introduction to *The Edible Woman,*" in *Second Words: Selected Critical Prose* (Boston: Beacon Press, 1982), p. 369.

38. Letter to Freshel, October 14, 1936, Box 6, file no. 81.

39. Letter, March 23, 1937, Box 4, file no. 82.

40. "Who Can Fear Too Many Stars?", Box 3, file no. 35, p. 131.

41. Berry interview with Brophy in Berry, p. 88.

42. Henry Bailey Stevens, *The Recovery of Culture* (New York: Harper & Row, 1949), p. 105.

43. Brigid Brophy, "An Anecdote of the Golden Age [Homage to *Back to Methuselah*]," in *The Adventures of God in his Search for the Black Girl* (Boston: Little, Brown & Co., 1968), p. 35.

44. See for instance, "The Rights of Animals" and "Women" in Brophy, *Don't Never Forget: Collected Views and Reviews* (New York: Holt, Rinehart and Winston, 1966), pp. 15–21, 38–44; *Hackenfeller's Ape* (London: Allison and Busby, 1953, 1979); and "In Pursuit of Fantasy," in *Animals, Men, and Morals: An Enquiry into the Maltreatment of Non-Humans,* ed. Stanley Godlovitch, Roslind Godlovitch, and John Harris (London: Gollancz, and New York: Taplinger, 1972).

45. June Rachuy Brindel, *Ariadne: A Novel of Ancient Crete* (New York: St. Martin's Press, 1980), p. 76.

46. June Rachuy Brindel, *Phaedra: A Novel of Ancient Athens* (New York: St. Martin's Press, 1985).

47. It could be argued that Shelley's *Queen Mab* is the first feminist, vegetarian, pacifist utopia.

48. Charlotte Perkins Gilman, *Herland* (New York: Pantheon Books, 1979), p. 27. First serialized in the *Forerunner* 6 (1915).

49. As I summarize this position in chapter 6, Socrates tells Glaucon that meat production necessitates large amounts of pasture. Resultingly, it will require cutting "off a slice of our neighbours' territory; and if they too are not content with necessaries, but give themselves up to getting unlimited wealth, they will want a slice of ours." Thus Socrates pronounces, "So the next thing will be, Glaucon, that we shall be at war." Plato, *The Republic of Plato,* trans. Francis MacDonald Cornford, (New York and London: Oxford University Press, 1966), 2. 373, p. 61. See also Frances Moore Lappé, *Diet for a Small Planet: Tenth Anniversary Edition* (New York: Ballantine Books, 1971, 1982), pp. 67–74.

50. Dorothy Bryant, *The Kin of Ata are Waiting for You* (1971, Berkeley: Moon Books, 1976), originally titled *The Comforter,* p. 159.

51. DuPlessis, p. 113.

52. Lucio P. Ruotolo, *The Interrupted Moment: A View of Virginia Woolf's Novels* (Stanford: Stanford University Press, 1986), p. 16.

53. Midgley, *Animals and Why They Matter,* p. 27.

54. Dale Spender points out that "98 per cent of interruptions in mixed sex conversation were made by males." She continues, "Interruption is a mechanism by which (a) males can prevent females from talking, and (b) they can gain the floor for themselves; it is therefore a mechanism by which they engineer female silence." If women are not supposed to interrupt men in public, yet the presence of a vegetarian, especially at dinners, will call attention to the vegetarian and cause an interruption or disruption, then women have found a way of dislodging the conversation without being seen as verbally aggressive. Dale Spender, *Man Made Language* (London: Routledge & Kegan Paul, 1980), pp. 43–44.

55. In a similar vein, Lucio P. Ruotolo argues that finding meaning in interruption is important when considering the novels of Virginia Woolf. Ruotolo argues for the creative, positive nature of interruption because of the new direction it provokes, the new space it creates. "Those who allow the often-random intrusion of others to reshape their lives emerge at times heroically. Those who voice distaste for interruption fall back, invariably it seems, into self-supporting insularity." *The Interrupted Moment,* p. 2.

56. War images in this sentence remind us that the patterns of war have been adopted in the style and content of discourse.

57. Isadora Duncan, *My Life* (New York: Liveright, 1927, 1955), p. 309.

58. Emarel Freshel and others ascribe to Shaw a poem entitled "Living Graves," which begins:

> We are the living graves of murdered beasts,
> Slaughtered to satisfy our appetites.

As Janet Barkas reports: "It continues in a similarly violent vein to condemn animal slaughter as well as war. However, there are no references to this work in any of Shaw's manuscripts, notebooks, correspondence, or diaries. That it was created by Shaw as an adventure in rhyming is possible but improbable." Janet Barkas, *The Vegetable Passion: A History of the Vegetarian State of Mind* (New York: Charles Scribner's Sons, 1975) p. 89.

59. Mary McCarthy, *Birds of America* (New York: Harcourt Brace Jovanovich, 1965, New York: New American Library, 1972), p. 166. Further quotations are from pp. 171, 172, 183.

60. Colegate, *The Shooting Party,* p. 92.

61. Spender, *Man Made Language,* pp. 82–83.

62. Mary Daly, *Beyond God the Father: Toward a Philosophy of Women's Liberation* (Boston: Beacon Press, 1973), p. 56.

63. See DuPlessis, p. 115.

64. DuPlessis, p. 107.

65. Jean Bethke Elshtain makes an observation about this fact as she concludes her preface to *Women and War.* "In thinking and sometimes dreaming about war over the past few years; in reading war stories and watching war movies; in composing portions of chapters on walks as well as on my word processor, I have gained a heightened awareness of the fleeting preciousness of life, including the lives we humans share with the other creatures with whom we have yet to learn to live in decency." Jean Bethke Elshtain, *Women and War* (New York: Basic Books, Inc., 1987), p. xiv.

Epigraphs to part 3: Ruth Bordin, *Frances Willard: A Biography* (Chapel Hill and London: University of North Carolina Press, 1986), p. 122. Fran Winant,

"Eat Rice Have Faith in Women," in Winant, *Dyke Jacket: Poems and Songs* (New York: Violet Press, 1980).

Chapter 8: The Distortion of the Vegetarian Body

1. Beverly Harrison, "The Power of Anger in the Work of Love: Christian Ethics for Women and Other Strangers," in *Making the Connections: Essays in Feminist Social Ethics,* ed. Carol S. Robb (Boston: Beacon Press, 1985), p. 13.

2. *Vegetarian Magazine* 14, no. 5 (January 1911), p. 156.

3. Mary Wollstonecraft, *A Vindication of the Rights of Woman,* ed. Charles W. Hagelman, Jr. (1792, New York: W. W. Norton & Co., 1967), p. 42.

4. T. L. Cleave, G. D. Campbell, N. S. Painter, *Diabetes, Coronary Thrombosis, and the Saccharine Disease* 2nd ed. (Bristol, England: John Wright & Sons, 1969), p. 11.

5. Nancy Makepeace Tanner, *On Becoming Human: A Model of the Transition from Ape to Human and the Reconstruction of Early Human Social Life* (Cambridge and New York: Cambridge University Press, 1981), p. 187.

6. *Jane Brody's Nutrition Book* (New York: W. W. Norton & Co., 1981), p. 436.

7. Cleave et al., p. 11.

8. The health information in this paragraph is taken from chapter 3, "The World's Healthiest Diet," in Virginia and Mark Messina's *The Vegetarian Way* (New York: Crown, 1996). They provide a wealth of medical citations for anyone who wishes to access the research material directly. This research does not speak directly to the debate about anatomy; some people conclude that the protective benefits of a complete vegetarian diet confirm the anatomical arguments.

9. Sarah N. Cleghorn, *Threescore: The Autobiography of Sarah N. Cleghorn* (New York: H. Smith and R. Haas, 1936, reprint New York: Arno Press, 1980), p. 172.

10. Agnes Ryan, "The Cancer Bogy," pp. 6, 79. Letters and manuscripts of Agnes Ryan referred to in this chapter are all located in the Agnes Ryan Collection, Schlesinger Library, Radcliffe College.

11. "The Cancer Bogy," pp. 107, 108.

12. Anna Kingsford, *The Perfect Way in Diet* (London: Kegan Paul, 1892), p. 90.

13. Agnes Ryan to Alice Park, January 6, 1936, Box 5, file no. 62. Park sent her Kingsford's *The Perfect Way in Diet* and Maitland's two volume biography.

14. Edward Maitland, *Anna Kingsford: Her Life, Letters, Diary and Work vol. 2* (London: Redway, 1896), pp. 223–24.

15. Maria Loomis, *The Communitist* 1, no. 22 (April 9, 1845), p. 87.

16. Henry Salt, *The Logic of Vegetarianism* (London: Ideal Publishing, 1899), p. 106.

17. See Rynn Berry Jr.'s interview with Malcolm Muggeridge in *The Vegetarians* (Brookline, Mass: Autumn Press, 1979). "You see, my father was an early Fabian, and those people tended to be vegetarian." p. 93.

18. Colin Spencer accepts the claim that Hitler was a vegetarian (*The Heretic's Feast: A History of Vegetarianism* [Hanover and London: University Press of New England, 1996], pp. 304–9). However Roberta Kalechofsky and Rynn Berry provide compelling evidence that Hitler's "vegetarianism" was similar to that of many omnivores today who call themselves vegetarians although they have only eliminated "red meat" from their diet. Hitler continued to eat squab, sausage, and liver dumplings. Hitler's "vegetarianism" was part of a Nazi public-relations campaign to portray him as ascetic and "pure." But when Hitler came to power, vegetarian societies were declared illegal. (See Roberta Kalechofsky, "Hitler's Vegetarianism," *<www.micahbooks.com>;* Rynn Berry, Jr., "Hitler and Vegetarianism," in *The Way of Compassion,* ed. Martin Rowe [New York: Stealth Technologies, 1999], pp. 83–85.) Hitler was against smoking and implemented antismoking policies but as with vegetarianism, this need not mean that antismoking activism is now somehow suspect. In my current book project, *Living among Meat Eaters,* I further examine the dynamic that impels people to protect their own meat eating by clinging to the idea of Hitler's "vegetarianism."

19. See Robert Proctor, *Racial Hygiene: Medicine under the Nazis* (Cambridge, MA and London: Harvard University Press, 1988), p. 228.

20. Bernard Shaw, *Complete Plays with Prefaces: Vol. 1* (New York: Dodd, Mead & Co., 1962), p. 455.

21. Pat Parker, "To a Vegetarian Friend," *Womanslaughter* (Oakland, CA: Diana Press, 1978), p. 14.

22. See Mary Keyes Burgess, *Soul to Soul: A Soul Food Vegetarian Cookbook* (Santa Barbara, CA: Woodbridge Publishing Co., 1976) and *Dick Gregory's Natural Diet for Folks Who Eat: Cookin' with Mother Nature,* ed. James R. McGraw with Alvenia M. Fulton (New York: Harper & Row), 1973.

23. Reported in *The Vegetarian Magazine* 10, no. 11 (March 1907), p. 16.

24. Keith E. Melder, "Abigail Kelley Foster," *Notable American Women 1607–1950,* vol. 1, ed. Edward T. James and Janet James (Cambridge, MA: The Belknap Press of Harvard University Press, 1971), p. 649.

25. Carroll Smith-Rosenberg, "Sex as Symbol in Victorian Purity: An Ethnohistorical Analysis of Jacksonian America," *Turning Points: Historical and Socio-*

logical Essays on the Family, ed. John Demos and Sarane Spence Boocock, *American Journal of Sociology* 84, Supplement (1978) (Chicago and London: University of Chicago Press, 1978), p. S213.

26. *Porphyry on Abstinence from Animal Food,* ed. Esmé Wynne-Tyson, trans. Thomas Taylor (n.p.: Centaur Press, 1965; Barnes & Noble), p. 53.

27. Sylvester Graham, *Lecture to Young Men on Chastity* 3rd ed. (Boston, 1834, 1837), pp. 152–53, 47. See also R. T. Trall, *Home Treatment for Sexual Abuses. A Practical Treatise* (New York: Fowlers and Wells, 1853). It was not solely the vegetarians who considered meat a stimulant; the orthodox did as well. As James Whorton reports: "This stimulating power of flesh was regarded by physicians as both its contribution and its danger to health: a certain degree of stimulation was required." (James Whorton, *Crusaders for fitness: the history of American health reformers* [Princeton: Princeton University Press, 1982], p. 78.)

28. Smith-Rosenberg, pp. S222–3.

29. Daniel J. Boorstin, *The Americans: The Democratic Experience* (New York: Random House, 1973), p. 5.

30. Frances Trollope, *Domestic Manners of the Americans* (1832, New York: Alfred A. Knopf, 1949), p. 297.

31. Richard Osborn Cummings, *The American and His Food: A History of Food Habits in the United States* 2nd ed. (Chicago: University of Chicago Press, 1941), p. 15.

32. Maria Loomis, *The Communitist* 2, no. 29 (March 5, 1846), p. 115.

33. Sam Bowers Hilliard, *Hog Meat and Hoecake: Food Supply in the Old South, 1840–1860* (Carbondale: Southern Illinois University Press, 1972), p. 42.

34. "The phrase 'we eat meat three times a day' was repeated in 'American Letter' after 'American Letter,' that crossed the Atlantic." Ray Allen Billington, *Land of Savagery, Land of Promise: The European Image of the American Frontier* (New York: W. W. Norton & Co., 1981), p. 233.

35. Gerda Lerner, *The Grimké Sisters from South Carolina: Pioneers for Woman's Rights and Abolition* (New York: Schocken Books, 1971), p. 253.

36. Lerner, p. 253.

37. Catherine Beecher and Harriet Beecher Stowe, *The American Woman's Home or Principles of Domestic Science* (New York: J. B. Ford and Co., 1869; reprint New York: Arno Press and The New York Times, 1971), pp. 132–33.

38. F. Gale, *American Vegetarian and Health Journal* 3, no. 5 (May 1853), p. 100.

39. Carolyn Steedman, "Landscape for a Good Woman," in *Truth, Dare or Promise: Girls Growing Up in the Fifties,* ed. Liz Heron (London: Virago Press, 1985), p. 115. See also Lerner, p. 253.

40. Thomas L. Nichols and Mary Gove Nichols, *Marriage: Its History, Character and Results: Its Sanctities and Its Profanities; Its Science and Its Facts* (New York: T. L. Nichols, 1854), pp. 212, 214.

41. Alice Stockham, *Tokology: A Book for Every Woman* (New York: Fenno and Co., 1911).

42. Letter no. 151. "Systematic Preparation," in *Maternity: Letters from Working-Women,* ed. Margaret Llewelyn Davies (London: G. Bell and Sons, 1915, reprint, New York: W. W. Norton & Co., 1978), p. 178.

43. Vegetarian and moral reformer Lucinda Chandler held a moderate free-love position. See as well Susan Cayleff's discussion of the beliefs of Dr. Trall in *Wash and Be Healed: The Water-Cure Movement and Women's Health* (Philadelphia: Temple University Press, 1987), pp. 56–58.

44. In fact, historian Stephen Nissenbaum in *Sex, Diet and Debility in Jacksonian America: Sylvester Graham and Health Reform* (Westport, CT: Greenwood Press, 1980) argues that Graham's theories are quite similar to those of free-love advocate Percy Shelley. "Like Graham, Shelley was profoundly suspicious of the emergent capitalist order and the threat it posed to traditional social values. Like Graham, too, he associated the new order with physical as well as moral decay. Finally, both Shelley and Graham attributed both types of decay to the introduction of animal food into the human diet." p. 48.

45. Cayleff, *Wash and Be Healed,* p. 119.

46. Brody, p. 400.

47. Thomas Tryon, *The way to health, long life and happiness* (London, 1683), p. 396.

48. Mary Gove Nichols, *Mary Lyndon or, Revelations of a Life: An Autobiography* (New York: Stringer and Townsend, 1855), p. 180.

49. Josiah Oldfield, "The Dangers of Meat Eating," *Westminster Review* 166, no. 2 (August 1906), p. 195.

50. Elaine Showalter, *The Female Malady: Women, Madness, and English Culture, 1830–1980* (New York: Pantheon Books, 1985), p. 129.

51. Joan Jacobs Brumberg, "Chlorotic Girls, 1870–1920: A Historical Perspective on Female Adolescence," in *Women and Health in America,* ed. Judith Walzer Leavitt (Madison, WI: The University of Wisconsin Press, 1984), pp. 186–95. Blumberg continues her exploration of girls with a disease that involves the avoidance of foods, as well as their specific dislike of meat in *Fasting Girls: The Emergence of Anorexia Nervosa as a Modern Disease* (Cambridge and London: Harvard University Press, 1988).

52. Brumberg, "Chlorotic Girls," p. 191.

53. Brumberg, *Fasting Girls,* p. 176. Her essay on chlorotic girls includes a paraphrase of this sentence, p. 191. Blumberg's source is Vern Bullough and Martha Voght, "Women, Menstruation, and Nineteenth-Century Medicine," *Bulletin of the History of Medicine* 47 (1973), pp. 66–82.

54. The fact that *Fasting Girls* basically rehashes the same material on meat eating that "Chlorotic Girls" contained suggests that Blumberg failed to explore other sources with alternative viewpoints on meat eating. To ascertain the girls' point of view, one might wish to ignore the medical analysis and determine the cultural context. One glaring problem with Brumberg's interpretation of why girls would not want to eat meat involves comparative studies. She observes that the "last decades of the nineteenth century may be an important transitional period in the history of nutrition throughout the Western world" ("Chlorotic Girls," p. 195) and cites a study that in France "animal proteins accounted for only about 25 percent of the total protein intake until after 1880–90." But we know that meat consumption in the United States was at least twice that of European countries. One cannot generalize nutritional studies based on European experience to the United States. Blumberg in general appears unreceptive to vegetarianism (in a footnote she associates being a picky eater, a vegetarian, and the romance of undereating when discussing Byron and Shelley, *Fasting Girls,* p. 329, n. 60). Her opinions on meat eating demonstrate the ways in which even a careful scholar mutes that which the dominant viewpoint cannot incorporate.

55. *Fasting Girls,* p. 177.

56. Lady Walb. Paget, "Vegetable Diet," *Popular Science Monthly* 44 (1893), p. 94.

57. *Fasting Girls,* p. 177. That part of the quotation in brackets is in the 1906 article but was excluded from *Fasting Girls.*

58. "The Antagonism Between Sentiment and Physiology in Diet," *Current Literature* 42 (Feb. 1907), p. 222, responding to an article by Josiah Oldfield in *Chamber's Journal.*

59. As early as 1863, Dr. Edward Smith discusses the aversion of many children to fat on meat and makes recommendations for overcoming the refusal to eat this meat. Thus this aversion was not limited to chlorotic or anorexic girls. See Edward Smith, M.D., *Practical Dietary for Families, Schools, and the Labouring Classes* (London: Walton and Maberly, 1864), pp. 135–36.

60. Denise Riley, "Waiting," in Heron, p. 244.

61. Jessie Bernard, *The Female World* (New York: The Free Press, 1981), p. 381.

62. Caroline Walker Bynum, *Holy Feast and Holy Fast: The Religious Significance of Food to Medieval Women* (Berkeley and Los Angeles: University of California Press, 1987), pp. xiv, 298.

63. Brumberg, *Fasting Girls,* p. 178.

64. Inez Haynes Irwin, "The Making of a Militant," in *These Modern Women: Autobiographical Essays from the Twenties,* ed. Elaine Showalter (Old Westbury, NY: The Feminist Press, 1978), pp. 39, 40.

65. Barbara Seaman and Gideon Seaman, M.D., *Women and the Crisis in Sex Hormones* (New York: Rawson Associates Publishers, Inc., 1977), p. 142.

Chapter 9: For a Feminist-Vegetarian Critical Theory

Epigraphs: Agnes Ryan, note to herself. All quotations of Agnes Ryan are from manuscripts and letters found in the Agnes Ryan Collection, Schlesinger Library, Radcliffe College. Alice Walker, "Am I Blue?" *Ms.* July 1986, p. 30. Fran Winant, "Eat Rice Have Faith in Women," in Winant, *Dyke Jacket: Poems and Songs* (New York: Violet Press, 1980).

1. "Astell abstained from meat frequently—certainly more often than here fellow Londoners," according to her biographer Ruth Perry in *The Celebrated Mary Astell: An Early English Feminist* (Chicago and London: University of Chicago Press, 1986), p. 286.

2. Sarah Scott, *A Description of Millenium Hall* (London, 1762; New York and London: Garland Publishing Inc., 1974), p. 20.

3. Isobel Rae, *The Strange Story of Dr. James Barry: Army Surgeon, Inspector-General of Hospitals, Discovered on death to be a Woman* (London: Longmans, Green & Co., 1958), p. 93.

4. "Her personal needs had never been extravagant and were modest during her declining years. She no longer traveled, spent most of her time in her house, her garden or in solitary walks in the woods, and ate her frugal vegetarian meals alone in her room." H. F. Peters, *My Sister, My Spouse: A Biography of Lou Andreas-Salome* (New York: Norton & Co., 1962), p. 296.

5. Flora T. Neff, Letter to the Editor, *The Vegetarian Magazine* 10, no. 12 (April 1907), pp. 16–17.

6. *Shafts* 1, no. 3 (November 19, 1892).

7. Brigid Brophy, "Women," *Don't Never Forget: Collected Views and Reviews* (New York: Holt, Rinehart and Winston, 1966), p. 38.

8. Susan B. Anthony and Ida Husted Harper, ed. *The History of Woman Suffrage,* Vol. 4, 1883–1900 (Indianapolis: The Hollenbeck Press, 1902, New York: Arno Press and the New York Times, 1969), p. 245.

9. Margaret Mead, *Blackberry Winter: My Earlier Years* (New York: William Morrow & Co., New York: Touchstone Books, 1972), p. 25.

10. *Shafts* 1, no. 3 (November 19, 1892), p. 41. It is worth noting that Annie Besant, whose husband beat her, went on to become an ardent anti-vivisectionist and vegetarian.

11. Jane Ellen Harrison, *Prolegomena to the Study of Greek Religion* (Cambridge University Press, 1903, 1922, New York: Arno Press, 1975), pp. 94, 149.

12. See Elizabeth Gould Davis, *The First Sex* (New York: G. P. Putnam's Sons, 1971, Baltimore, MD: Penguin Books, 1972) and Evelyn Reed, *Women's Evolution: from matriarchal clan to patriarchal family* (New York: Pathfinder Press, Inc., 1975).

13. Interview with Jessie Haver Butler in Sherna Gluck, ed., *From Parlor to Prison: Five American Suffragists Talk about Their Lives: An Oral History* (New York: Vintage Books, 1976), p. 65.

14. Excerpt from White's letter to Bro. and Sister Lockwood, September 14, 1864 in Ronald L. Numbers, *Prophetess of Health: A Study of Ellen G. White* (New York: Harper & Row, 1976), p. 203. According to Numbers, White frequented Jackson's institute until she received messages while in trance, which adhered closely to Jackson's principles, and began to invoke a vegetarian diet as divinely ordained for Seventh Day Adventists.

15. Ishbel Ross, *Angel of the Battlefield* (New York: Harper & Brothers, 1956), p. 128.

16. "As late in the fall I had a bad cold and a general feeling of depression, I decided to go to the Dansville Sanatorium. . . . I was there six weeks and tried all the rubbings, pinchings, steamings, the Swedish movements of the arms, hands, legs, feet; dieting, massage, electricity, and soon felt like a new being." *Elizabeth Cady Stanton as Revealed in Her Letters, Diary and Reminiscences,* vol. 1, ed. Theodore Stanton and Harriot Stanton Blatch (1922, New York: Arno Press Reprint, 1969), p. 322.

17. Gloria Steinem, *Outrageous Acts and Everyday Rebellions* (New York: Holt, Rinehart and Winston, 1983, reprint New York: New American Library, 1986), p. 163.

18. See Doris Stevens, *Jailed for Freedom: The Story of the Militant American Suffragist Movement* (New York: Boni and Liveright, 1920, reprint New York: Shocken Books, 1976), p. 148.

19. James C. Jackson, *How to Treat the Sick without Medicine* (Dansville, NY: Austin, Jackson & Co., 1870), p. 235.

20. In an interesting twist on this connection, Malcolm Muggeridge suggests that Samuel Butler attacks vegetarianism in *Erewhon* to compensate for his own homosexuality. Interview with Malcolm Muggeridge in Rynn Berry, Jr., *The Vegetarians* (Brookline, MA: Autumn Press, 1979), p. 94.

21. Blanche Cook, "The Historical Denial of Lesbianism," *Radical History Review* 20 (1979), p. 63.

22. Anna Mary Wells, *Miss Marks and Miss Woolley* (Boston: Houghton Mifflin Co., 1978), p. 107. Regarding vegetarianism in their relationship see also

Susan E. Cayleff, *Wash and Be Healed: The Water-Cure Movement and Women's Health* (Philadelphia: Temple University Press, 1987), p. 153.

23. Mary Alden Hopkins, "Why I Earn My Own Living," in *These Modern Women: Autobiographical Essays from the Twenties,* ed. Elaine Showalter (Old Westbury: The Feminist Press, 1978), p. 44.

24. Alice Park to Agnes Ryan and Henry Bailey Stevens, Agnes Ryan Collection, May 1, 1922, December 31, 1936, and February 5, 1941. Box 5, file nos. 62, 66.

25. Carol Christ, *Diving Deep and Surfacing: Women Writers on Spiritual Quest* (Boston: Beacon Press, 1980, 1986).

26. Curtis Cate, *George Sand: A Biography* (Boston: Houghton Mifflin Co., 1975), p. 204.

27. Barbara Cook, "The Awakening," The *Animals' Agenda* 5, no. 8 (November 1985), pp. 30–31.

28. Agnes Ryan, "The Heart to Sing, an Autobiography," unpublished manuscript, Agnes Ryan Collection, p. 309. Further quotations are from pp. 311–16.

29. "Some Reminiscences of Henry Bailey Stevens," *Vegetarian World* 4 (1975), p. 6. That Stevens so vividly recalls an experience 58 years after the fact confirms it as a revelatory one for both of them, even if the details conflict.

30. Marge Piercy, *Small Changes* (Greenwich, CT: Fawcett Crest Book, 1972), p. 41.

31. *Vegetarian Magazine* 9, no. 10 (August 1905), p. 174.

32. See my discussion of Stevens's *The Recovery of Culture* in chapter 7.

33. Judy Grahn, *The Queen of Swords* (Boston: Beacon Press, 1987), p. 78.

34. Barbara Christian, *Black Women Novelists: The Development of a Tradition, 1892–1976* (Westport, CT: Greenwood Press, 1980), p. 207. Alice Walker, *Meridian* (New York: Harcourt Brace Jovanovich, 1976, New York: Washington Square Press, 1977). David Levering Lewis in *When Harlem Was in Vogue* refers to Toomer's vegetarianism (New York: Alfred A. Knopf, 1981, New York: Vintage Books, 1982), p. 63.

35. Ann Beattie, *Chilly Scenes of Winter* (Garden City, NY: Doubleday & Co., 1976).

36. Aileen La Tourette, *Cry Wolf* (London: Virago Press, 1986).

37. Jeanette Winterson, *Oranges are not the Only Fruit* (New York: The Atlantic Monthly Press, 1985, 1987).

38. Alice Thomas Ellis, *The Birds of the Air* (New York: The Viking Press, 1981), pp. 90–98.

39. T. H., "Pythagorean Objections Against Animal Food," *London Magazine* (November 1825), p. 382.

40. Cited in Dorothy Sterling, *Black Foremothers: Three Lives* (Old Westbury, NY: The Feminist Press, New York: McGraw-Hill Book Company, 1979), p. 151. Consider Alice Walker's description of a similar insight: "One day, I was walking across the road with my daughter and my companion. It was raining and we were trying to get home. I looked down and there was this chicken with her little babies. They were trying to get home too. It was one of those times feminists refer to as a 'click.' Well, this was one of those human animal-to-nonhuman animal clicks, where it just seemed so clear to me how one we are. I was a mother. She was a mother." Ellen Bring, "Moving towards Coexistence: An Interview with Alice Walker," *Animals' Agenda* 8, no. 3 (April 1988), pp. 8–9.

41. Beth Brant, (Degonwadonti) *Mohawk Trail* (Ithaca, NY: Firebrand Books, 1985), p. 27. They did eat the chickenmeat when the chickens died of natural causes.

42. Flannery O'Connor, "The King of the Birds," in *Mystery and Manners: Occasional Prose,* ed. Sally and Robert Fitzgerald (New York: Farrar, Straus & Giroux, 1957, 1970), p. 20.

43. Colette, *Break of Day* (New York: Farrar, Strauss and Giroux, Inc., 1961, New York: Ballantine Books, 1983), pp. 28–29. A similar experience accounts for Cloris Leachman's vegetarianism. In an interview she was asked, "I've read that you had a revelation while you were rinsing a chicken under the faucet: it suddenly occurred to you that what you were doing wasn't very different from bathing a baby." Leachman replied, "I had a new born baby, and it was exactly the same experience, yes." Interview with Cloris Leachman in Rynn Berry, Jr., *The Vegetarians,* p. 17.

44. Margaret Atwood, *Cat's Eye* (New York: Doubleday, 1989), pp. 138–39.

45. Alice Ellis, *Unexplained Laughter* (London: Duckworth, 1985), p. 76.

46. Anne Tyler, *The Clock Winder* (New York: Alfred Knopf, 1972), p. 35.

47. Anne Tyler, *The Accidental Tourist* (1985, New York: Berkley Books, 1986); *If Morning Ever Comes* (1964, New York: Berkley Books, 1986); *The Tin Can Tree* (1965, New York: Berkley Books, 1986).

48. Sandra Lee Bartky, "Toward a Phenomenology of Feminist Consciousness," in *Feminism and Philosophy,* ed. by Mary Vetterling-Braggin, Frederick A. Elliston, and Jane English, (Totowa, New Jersey: Littlefield, Adams & Co.), pp. 22, 26.

49. Referred to in the introduction to Alexis DeVeaux, "The Riddles of Egypt Brownstone," in *Midnight Birds: Stories of Contemporary Black Women Writers,* ed. Mary Helen Washington (Garden City, NY: Anchor Books, 1980), p. 16.

50. Margaret Atwood, *Surfacing* (New York: Simon and Schuster, New York: Popular Library, 1972), p. 165.

Epilogue

Epigraph: Erik H. Erikson, *Gandhi's Truth: On the Origins of Militant Nonviolence* (New York: W. W. Norton & Co. Inc., 1969), p. 142. (Sexist language has been changed.)

1. See for instance Joseph Campbell's use of Géza Róheim's statement that "whatever is killed becomes father" to explain "the rites of the paleolithic hunters in connection with the killing and eating of their totem beasts." Joseph Campbell, *The Masks of God: Volume I Primitive Mythology* (New York: The Viking Press, 1959, New York: Penguin Books, 1978), pp. 77, 129.

2. This is a paraphrase of a question posed by Rynn Berry, Jr., in his book *The Vegetarians* (Brookline, MA: Autumn Press, 1979), p. 83.

3. Kate Millet, *Sexual Politics* (Garden City, NY: Doubleday & Co., 1979' pp. 25, 23.

4. Virginia Woolf, *Jacob's Room* (Hogarth Press, 1922, Hammondsworth, England: Penguin Books, 1971), p. 9.

5. Campbell, *The Masks of God,* pp. 129, 137. Sexist language has been changed.

6. Virginia de Araújo, "The Friend . . ." *Sinister Wisdom* no. 20 (1982), p. 17.

7. Maxine Hong Kingston, *The Woman Warrior: Memoirs of a Girlhood among Ghosts* (New York: Alfred A. Knopf, 1977), p. 34.

Select Bibliography

This bibliography lists a few references that had a formative influence on my writing of the first edition of *The Sexual Politics of Meat.* Some of these references do not appear in the text; conversely, some references that can be found in the endnotes do not appear here. My use of specific material written by Agnes Ryan, feminist-vegetarian foremother, is detailed in the endnotes. Her writings—letters, novels, poems, "The Cancer Bogy," and notes for the *Vegetarian Pocket Monthly*—are in the Agnes Ryan Collection, Arthur and Elizabeth Schlesinger Library on the History of Women in America, Radcliffe College, Cambridge. To highlight writings that have appeared subsequent to the publication of the first edition, I have created a Tenth Anniversary Bibliography (see pages 259–60).

Vegetarian Writings

Akers, Keith. *A Vegetarian Sourcebook: The Nutrition, Ecology and Ethics of a Natural Foods Diet.* New York: G. P. Putnam's Sons, 1983.

Axon, William E. A. *Shelley's Vegetarianism.* Read at a Meeting of the Shelley Society, November 12, 1891. Reprint. New York: Haskell House Publishers Ltd., 1971.

Barkas, Janet. *The Vegetable Passion: A History of the Vegetarian State of Mind.* New York: Charles Scribner's Sons, 1975.

Berry, Rynn, Jr. *The Vegetarians.* Brookline, Mass.: Autumn Press, 1979.

Bloodroot Collective. *The Political Palate: A Feminist Vegetarian Cookbook.* Bridgeport, Connecticut: Sanguinaria Publishing, 1980.

———. *The Second Seasonal Political Palate: A Feminist Vegetarian Cookbook.* Bridgeport, Connecticut: Sanguinaria Publishing, 1984.

Braunstein, Mark Matthew. *Radical Vegetarianism: A Dialectic of Diet and Ethics.* Los Angeles: Panjandrum Books, 1981.

Burgess, Mary Keyes. *Soul to Soul: A Soul Food Vegetarian Cookbook.* Santa Barbara: Woodbridge Publishing Company, 1976.

Davis, Max. *The Case for the Vegetarian Conscientious Objector* with a Foreword by Scott Nearing. Brooklyn, New York: Tolstoy Peace Group, 1944.

Dombrowski, Daniel A. *The Philosophy of Vegetarianism.* Amherst: The University of Massachusetts Press, 1984.

Dyer, Judith. *Vegetarianism: An Annotated Bibliography*. Metuchen, New Jersey and London: Scarecrow Press, 1982.

Easterbrook, L. F. "Alcohol and Meat." *Nineteenth Century and After*. 95 (February 1924), pp. 306–14.

Giehl, Dudley. *Vegetarianism: A Way of Life*. New York: Harper & Row, 1979.

Gregory, Dick. *Dick Gregory's Natural Diet for Folks Who Eat: Cookin' with Mother Nature*. Edited by James R. McGraw. New York: Harper & Row, 1973.

T. H. "Pythagorean Objections against Animal Food." *London Magazine*. (November 1825), pp. 380–83.

Kingsford, Anna. *The Perfect Way in Diet: A Treatise Advocating a Return to the Natural and Ancient Food of Our Race*. London: Kegan Paul, 1892.

Lappé, Frances Moore. *Diet for a Small Planet: Tenth Anniversary Edition*. New York: Ballantine Books, 1982.

Newton, John Frank. *The Return to Nature; or, A Defence of the Vegetable Regimen*. London, 1811.

Oldfield, Josiah. "The Dangers of Meat Eating." *Westminster Review*. 166, no. 2 (August 1906), pp. 195–200.

Oswald, John. *The Cry of Nature; or, An Appeal to Mercy and to Justice, on Behalf of the Persecuted Animals*. London, 1791.

Paget, Lady Walb. "Vegetable Diet." *Popular Science Monthly*. 44 (1893), pp. 94–102.

Phillips, Sir Richard. *Golden Rules of Social Philosophy; or, a New System of Practical Ethics*. London, 1826.

Ritson, Joseph. *An Essay on Abstinence from Animal Food as a Moral Duty*. London: Phillips, 1802.

Robbins, John. *Diet for a New America*. Walpole, New Hampshire: Stillpoint Publishing, 1987.

Rudd, G. L. *Why Kill for Food?* 1956. Madras, India: The Indian Vegetarian Congress, 1973.

Salt, Henry S. *The Creed of Kinship*. New York: E. P. Dutton and Co., 1935.

———. *The Humanities of Diet: Some Reasonings and Rhymings*. Manchester: The Vegetarian Society, 1914.

———. *The Logic of Vegetarianism*. London: Ideal Publishing, 1899.

Sharpe, M. R. L. [later Freshel]. *The Golden Rule Cookbook: Six Hundred Recipes for Meatless Dishes*. Cambridge, Mass.: The University Press, 1908.

Shelley, Percy. *A Vindication of Natural Diet* and *On the Vegetable System of Diet*. In *The Complete Works of Percy Bysshe Shelley, Volume VI, Prose*. Edited by Roger Ingpen and Walter E. Peck. New York: Gordian Press, 1965.

Stevens, Henry Bailey. *The Recovery of Culture*. New York: Harper & Row, 1949.

Stockham, Alice. *Tokology: A Book for Every Woman*. New York: Fenno and Co., 1911.

Sussman, Vic. *The Vegetarian Alternative: A Guide to a Healthful and Humane Diet*. Emmaus, Pennsylvania: Rodale Press, 1978.

Tryon, Thomas. *The way to health, long life and happiness.* London, 1683.
Williams, Howard, ed. *The Ethics of Diet: a Catena of Authorities Deprecatory of the Practice of Flesh-Eating.* London: Pitman and Heywood, 1883.
Wynne-Tyson, Esmé, ed. *Porphyry on Abstinence from Animal Food.* Translated by Thomas Taylor. Centaur Press, Barnes & Noble, 1965.

Animal Concerns and Animal Defense

Amory, Cleveland. *Man Kind? Our Incredible War on Wildlife.* New York: Harper & Row, 1974.
Brophy, Brigid. "The Rights of Animals" in Brophy, *Don't Never Forget: Collected Views and Reviews.* New York: Holt, Rinehart and Winston, 1966, pp. 15–21.
Collard, Andrée with Joyce Contrucci. *Rape of the Wild: Man's Violence against Animals and the Earth.* London: The Women's Press, 1988.
Dombrowski, Daniel A. *Hartshorne and the Metaphysics of Animal Rights.* Albany: State University of New York Press, 1988.
Evans, E. P. *The Criminal Prosecution and Capital Punishment of Animals.* London: William Heinemann. New York: E. P. Dutton and Co., 1906.
Godlovitch, Stanley, Roslind Godlovitch, and John Harris, eds. *Animals, Men and Morals: An Enquiry into the Maltreatment of Non-Humans.* New York: Taplinger, 1972.
Linzey, Andrew. *Christianity and the Rights of Animals.* New York: Crossroad, 1987.
Mason, Jim and Peter Singer. *Animal Factories.* New York: Crown Publishers, Inc., 1980.
Midgley, Mary. *Animals and Why They Matter.* Athens: University of Georgia Press, 1983.
Regan, Tom. *The Case for Animal Rights.* Berkeley, Los Angeles: University of California Press, 1983.
Regan, Tom and Peter Singer. *Animal Rights and Human Obligations.* Englewood Cliffs, New Jersey: Prentice-Hall, Inc., 1976.
Salt, Henry. *Animals' Rights Considered in Relation to Social Progress.* 1892. Reprint. Clarks Summit, Pennsylvania: Society for Animal Rights, Inc., 1980.
———. "Sport as a Training for War." In *Killing for Sport: Essays by Various Writers.* Edited by Henry Salt. London: G. Bell and Sons, Ltd. for the Humanitarian League, 1914.
Serpell, James. *In the Company of Animals: A Study of Human-Animal Relationships.* New York: Basil Blackwell, 1986.
Singer, Peter. *Animal Liberation: A New Ethics for Our Treatment of Animals.* New York: A New York Review Book, 1975.
Spiegel, Marjorie. *The Dreaded Comparison: Human and Animal Slavery.* Philadelphia: New Society Publishers, 1988.
[Taylor, Thomas.] *A Vindication of the Rights of Brutes.* London: Jeffery, 1792.
Walker, Alice. "Am I Blue?" *Ms.*, July 1986.

Feminist Writings

Allen, Paula Gunn. *The Sacred Hoop: Recovering the Feminine in American Indian Tradition.* Boston: Beacon Press, 1986.

Atkinson, Ti-Grace. *Amazon Odyssey.* New York: Links Books, 1974.

Benney, Norma. "All of One Flesh: The Rights of Animals." In *Reclaim the Earth: Women speak out for Life on Earth.* Edited by Léonie Caldecott and Stephanie Leland. London: The Women's Press, 1983.

Bernard, Jessie. *The Female World.* New York: The Free Press, 1981.

Cannon, Katie G. *Black Womanist Ethics.* Atlanta: Scholars Press, 1988.

Corea, Gena. *The Hidden Malpractice: How American Medicine Mistreats Women.* New York: William Morrow and Co., 1977, Jove-Harcourt Brace Jovanovich, 1978.

———. *The Mother Machine: Reproductive Technologies from Artificial Insemination to Artificial Wombs.* New York: Harper & Row, 1985.

Daly, Mary. *Beyond God the Father: Toward a Philosophy of Women's Liberation.* Boston: Beacon Press, 1973.

———. *Gyn/Ecology: The Metaethics of Radical Feminism.* Boston: Beacon Press, 1978.

———. In cahoots with Jane Caputi. *Webster's First New Intergalactic Wickedary of the English Language.* Boston: Beacon Press, 1987.

de Beauvoir, Simone. *The Second Sex.* Translated and edited by H. M. Parshley. Jonathan Cape, 1953. Hammondsworth England: Penguin, 1972.

de Lauretis, Teresa. *Alice Doesn't: Feminism, Semiotics, Cinema.* Bloomington: Indiana University Press, 1984.

Dworkin, Andrea. *Pornography: Men Possessing Women.* New York: Perigee Books, 1981.

———. *Woman Hating.* New York: E. P. Dutton, 1974.

Elshtain, Jean Bethke. *Women and War.* New York: Basic Books, Inc., 1987.

Gilman, Charlotte Perkins. *His Religion and Hers: A Study of the Faith of Our Fathers and the Work of Our Mothers.* London: T. Fisher Unwin, 1924.

Grahn, Judy. *Another Mother Tongue: Gay Words, Gay World.* Boston: Beacon Press, 1984.

Griffin, Susan. *Woman and Nature: The Roaring Inside Her.* New York: Harper & Row, 1978.

Hamilton, Cicely. *Marriage as a Trade.* 1909. Reprint. London: The Women's Press, 1981.

Harrison, Beverly. *Making the Connections: Essays in Feminist Social Ethics.* Edited by Carol S. Robb. Boston: Beacon Press, 1985.

hooks, bell. *Ain't I a Woman: black women and feminism.* Boston: South End Press, 1981.

Kelly, Joan. *Women, History and Theory: The Essays of Joan Kelly.* Chicago: The University of Chicago Press, 1984.

Kramarae, Cheris and Paula A. Treichler. *A Feminist Dictionary.* Boston, London and Henley: Pandora Press, 1985.

Kuhn, Annette. *The power of the image: Essays on representation and sexuality.* London: Routledge & Kegan Paul, 1985.

Leghorn, Lisa and Mary Roodkowsky. *Who Really Starves? Women and World Hunger.* New York: Friendship Press, 1977.

Lorde, Audre. *Sister Outsider: Essays and Speeches.* Trumansburg, New York: The Crossing Press, 1984.

———. *Zami: A New Spelling of My Name.* Watertown: Persephone Press, 1982.

Merchant, Carolyn. *The Death of Nature: Women, Ecology, and the Scientific Revolution.* New York: Harper & Row, 1980.

Millet, Kate. *Sexual Politics.* Garden City: Doubleday & Co., 1970.

Morega, Cheríe. *Loving in the War Years; lo que nunca pasó por sus labios.* Boston: South End Press, 1983.

——— and Gloria Anzaldúa, eds. *This Bridge Called My Back: Writings By Radical Women of Color.* Watertown: Persephone Press, 1981.

Rosaldo, Michelle Zimbalist and Louise Lamphere. *Woman, Culture, and Society.* Stanford: Stanford University Press, 1974.

Sanday, Peggy. *Female power and male dominance: On the origins of sexual inequality.* Cambridge and New York: Cambridge University Press, 1981.

Schreiner, Olive. *Woman and Labour.* T. Fisher Unwin, 1911. Reprint. London: Virago, 1978.

Silverman, Kaja. *The Subject of Semiotics.* New York: Oxford University Press, 1983.

Smith, Barbara, ed. *Home Girls: A Black Feminist Anthology.* New York: Kitchen Table: Women of Color Press, 1983.

Spender, Dale. *Man Made Language.* London, Boston and Henley: Routledge & Kegan Paul, 1980.

Steinem, Gloria. *Outrageous Acts and Everyday Rebellions.* New York: Holt, Rinehart and Winston, 1983. New American Library, 1986.

Vetterling-Braggin, Mary, Frederick A. Elliston, and Jane English, eds. *Feminism and Philosophy.* Totowa, New Jersey: Littlefield, Adams & Co., 1982.

Wollstonecraft, Mary. *A Vindication of the Rights of Woman.* Edited by Charles W. Hagelman, Jr. 1792. New York: W. W. Norton & Co., 1967.

Woolf, Virginia. *Three Guineas.* London: The Hogarth Press, 1938, 1968.

Sexual and Domestic Violence

Barry, Kathy. *Female Sexual Slavery.* Englewood Cliffs: Prentice Hall, 1979.

Dobash, R. Emerson and Russell Dobash. *Violence Against Wives: A Case Against the Patriarchy.* New York: The Free Press, 1979.

Griffin, Susan. *Rape: The Power of Consciousness.* New York: Harper & Row, 1979.

Lederer, Laura, ed. *Take Back the Night: Women on Pornography.* New York: William Morrow and Company, Inc. 1980.

Lovelace, Linda, with Mike McGrady. *Ordeal.* Citadel Press, 1980. New York: Berkley Books, 1980.

Pizzey, Erin. *Scream Quietly or the Neighbours will Hear.* Hammondsworth, England: Penguin Books, 1974.

Walker, Lenore. *The Battered Woman.* New York: Harper & Row, 1979.

Literary Criticism

Atwood, Margaret. "An Introduction to *The Edible Woman.*" In *Second Words.* Boston: Beacon Press, 1982.

Barthes, Roland. "Introduction to the Structural Analysis of Narratives." In *Image, Music, Text.* Translated by Stephen Heath. New York: Hill and Wang, 1977.

Bethel, Lorraine. " 'This Infinity of Conscious Pain': Zora Neale Hurston and the Black Female Literary Tradition." In *All the Women are White, All the Blacks are Men, But Some of Us Are Brave. Black Women's Studies.* Edited by Gloria T. Hull, Patricia Bell Scott, and Barbara Smith. Old Westbury, New York: The Feminist Press, 1982.

Brophy, Brigid. "The Way of no Flesh." In *The Genius of Shaw.* Edited by Michael Holroyd. New York: Holt, Rinehart and Winston, 1979.

Cantor, Paul. *Creature and Creator: Myth-making and English Romanticism.* Cambridge: Cambridge University Press, 1981.

Carpenter, Edward and George Barnefield. *The Psychology of the Poet Shelley.* London: George Allen & Unwin Ltd., 1925.

Christ, Carol. *Diving Deep and Surfacing: Women Writers on Spiritual Quest.* Revised Edition. Boston: Beacon Press, 1986.

Christian, Barbara. *Black Women Novelists: The Development of a Tradition, 1892–1976.* Westport, Connecticut and London: Greenwood Press, 1980.

DuPlessis, Rachel Blau. *Writing beyond the Ending: Narrative Strategies of Twentieth-Century Women Writers.* Bloomington: Indiana University Press, 1985.

Fairchild, Hoxie. *The Noble Savage: A Study in Romantic Naturalism.* Columbia University Press, 1928. New York: Russell and Russell, 1961.

Folsom, Michael Brewster. "Upton Sinclair's Escape from *The Jungle:* The Narrative Strategy and Suppressed Conclusion of America's First Proletarian Novel." *Prospects.* 4 (1979), pp. 237–66.

Fussell, Paul. *The Great War and Modern Memory.* London, Oxford, New York: Oxford University Press, 1975.

Gates, Henry Louis, Jr. *The Signifying Monkey: A Theory of Afro-American Literary Criticism.* New York and Oxford: Oxford University Press, 1988.

Gilbert, Sandra and Susan Gubar. *The Madwoman in the Attic: The Woman Writer and the Nineteenth-Century Literary Imagination.* New Haven: Yale University Press, 1979.

Greenberg, Caren. "Reading Reading: Echo's Abduction of Language." In *Women and Language in Literature and Society.* Edited by Sally McConnell-Ginet, Ruth Borker and Nelly Furman. New York: Praeger, 1980.

Heilbrun, Carolyn and Catharine Stimpson, "Theories of Feminist Criticism: A Dialogue." In *Feminist Literary Criticism: Explorations in Theory.* Edited by Josephine Donovan. Lexington: University Press of Kentucky, 1975.

Homans, Margaret. *Bearing the Word: Language and Female Experience in Nineteenth-Century Women's Writing.* Chicago: University of Chicago, 1986.

Joly André. "Toward a Theory of Gender in Modern English." In *Studies in English Grammar.* Edited by A. Joly and T. Fraser. Paris: Editions Universitaires.

Levine, George and U. C. Knoepflmacher, eds. *The Endurance of Frankenstein.* Berkeley and Los Angeles: University of California Press, 1979.

McDowell, Deborah E. "New Directions for Black Feminist Criticism." *Black American Literature Forum.* (Winter 1980), pp. 153–59.

Mellor, Anne. *Mary Shelley: Her Life, Her Fiction, Her Monsters.* New York and London: Methuen, 1988.

Moers, Ellen. *Literary Women: The Great Writers.* Garden City, New York: Anchor Books, 1977.

Pryse, Marjorie. *Conjuring: Black Women, Fiction and Literary Tradition.* Bloomington: Indiana University Press, 1985.

Rohrlich, Ruby and Elaine Hoffman Baruch. *Women in Search of Utopia: Mavericks and Mythmakers.* New York: Shocken Books, 1984.

Rubenstein, Marc A. " 'My Accursed Origin': The Search for the Mother in *Frankenstein.*" *Studies in Romanticism.* 15 (Spring 1976), pp. 165–94.

Ruotolo, Lucio P. *The Interrupted Moment: A View of Virginia Woolf's Novels.* Stanford: Stanford University Press, 1986.

Said, Edward. *The World, the Text, and the Critic.* Cambridge: Harvard University Press, 1983.

Sebeok, Thomas A. "Poetics in the Lion's Den: The Circus Act as a Text." *Modern Language Notes.* 86, no. 6 (December 1971), pp. 845–57.

Showalter, Elaine. "Feminist Criticism in the Wilderness." In *The New Feminist Criticism: Essays on Women, Literature, and Theory.* Edited by Elaine Showalter. New York: Pantheon Books, 1985.

Simons, Madeleine A. "Rousseau's Natural Diet." *Romantic Review.* 45 (February 1954), pp. 18–28.

Smith, Barbara. "Towards a Black Feminist Criticism." In *All the Women are White, All the Blacks Are Men, but Some of Us Are Brave: Black Women's Studies.* Edited by Gloria T. Hull, Patricia Bell Scott, and Barbara Smith. Old Westbury, New York: The Feminist Press, 1982.

Smith, Carl S. *Chicago and the American Literary Imagination: 1880–1920.* Chicago: University of Chicago, 1984.

Tillotson, Marcia. " 'A Forced Solitude': Mary Shelley and the Creation of Frankenstein's Monster." In *The Female Gothic.* Edited by Juliann E. Fleenor. Montreal and London: Eden Press, 1983.

Trible, Phyllis. *Texts of Terror: Literary-Feminist Readings of Biblical Narratives.* Philadelphia: Fortress Press, 1984.

Veeder, William. *Mary Shelley and Frankenstein: The Fate of Androgyny.* Chicago: University of Chicago, 1986.

Walker, Alice. "*One* Child of One's Own: A Meaningful Digression within the Work(s)." In *In Search of Our Mothers' Gardens: Womanist Prose.* San Diego, New York: Harvest/Harcourt Brace Jovanovich, 1983.

Washington, Mary Helen. *Invented Lives: Narratives of Black Women 1860–1960.* Garden City: Doubleday & Co., 1987.

History, Autobiography, Biography

Barker-Benfield, G. J. *The Horrors of the Half-Known Life: Male Attitudes Toward Women and Sexuality in Nineteenth-Century America.* New York: Harper & Row, 1976.

Barrett, James. *Work and Community in the Jungle: Chicago's Packinghouse Workers, 1894–1922.* Urbana and Chicago: University of Illinois, 1987.

Beard, George M. *Sexual Neurasthenia [Nervous Exhaustion] Its Hygiene, Causes, Symptoms and Treatment with a Chapter on Diet for the Nervous.* New York: E. B. Treat & Co., 1898. Reprint. New York: Arno Press, 1972.

Beecher, Catherine and Harriet Beecher Stowe. *American Woman's Home; or, Principles of Domestic Science.* New York: J. B. Ford and Co., 1869. Reprint. New York: Arno Press and the *New York Times,* 1971.

Bennett, Betty T., ed. *The Letters of Mary Wollstonecraft Shelley.* Baltimore: Johns Hopkins University Press, 1980.

Billington, Ray Allen. *Land of Savagery Land of Promise: The European Image of the American Frontier in the Nineteenth Century.* New York: W. W. Norton & Co., 1981.

Bordin, Ruth. *Frances Willard: A Biography.* Chapel Hill and London: University of North Carolina Press, 1986.

Borrow, George. *Lavengro: The Scholar, the Gypsy, the Priest.* Edited with an introduction by George F. Whicher. New York: The MacMillan Company, 1927.

Bronson, Bertrand H. *Joseph Ritson: Scholar-at-Arms.* Berkeley: University of California Press, 1938.

Brumberg, Joan Jacobs. "Chlorotic Girls, 1870–1920: A Historical Perspective on Female Adolescence." In *Women and Health in America.* Edited by Judith Walzer Leavitt. Madison: The University of Wisconsin Press, 1984.

———. *Fasting Girls: The Emergence of Anorexia Nervosa as a Modern Disease.* Cambridge and London: Harvard University Press, 1988.

Burnett, John. *Plenty and Want: A social history of diet in England from 1815 to the present day.* 1966. London: Scolar Press, 1979.

Bynum, Caroline. *Holy Feast and Holy Fast: The Religious Significance of Food to Medieval Women.* Berkeley and Los Angeles: University of California Press, 1987.

Cameron, Kenneth Neill. *The Young Shelley: Genesis of a Radical.* Macmillan, 1950. New York: Octagon Books, 1973.

Cayleff, Susan E. *Wash and Be Healed: The Water-Cure Movement and Women's Health.* Philadelphia: Temple University Press, 1987.

Cleghorn, Sarah N. *Threescore: The Autobiography of Sarah N. Cleghorn.* New York: H. Smith and R. Haas, 1936. Reprint. New York: Arno Press, 1980.

Colby, Elbridge, ed. *The Life of Thomas Holcroft, Written by Himself Continued to the Time of His Death from his Diary Notes and Other Papers by William Hazlitt.* 1925. New York: Benjamin Blom, 1980.

Cott, Nancy. *The Grounding of Modern Feminism.* New Haven: Yale University Press, 1987.

Cummings, Richard Osborn. *The American and His Food: A History of Food Habits in the United States.* Second Edition. Chicago: University of Chicago Press, 1941.

Davies, Margaret Llewelyn, ed. *Maternity: Letters from Working-Women.* G. Bell & Sons, 1915. Reprint. New York: W. W. Norton & Co., 1978.

Duncan, Isadora. *My Life.* New York: Liveright, 1927, 1955.

Earhart, Mary. *Frances Willard: From Prayers to Politics.* Chicago: University of Chicago, 1944.

Erdman, David. *Commerce des lumières: John Oswald and the British in Paris 1790–1793.* Columbia: University of Missouri Press, 1986.

Erikson, Erik H. *Gandhi's Truth: On the Origins of Militant Nonviolence.* New York: W. W. Norton & Co., Inc., 1969.

French, R. D. *Antivivisection and Medical Science in Victorian Society.* Princeton: Princeton University Press, 1975.

Gluck, Sherna, ed. *From Parlor to Prison: Five American Suffragists Talk About Their Lives: An Oral History.* New York: Vintage Books, 1976.

Goldring, Douglas. *The Nineteen Twenties: A General Survey and some Personal Memories.* London: Nicholson and Watson, 1945. Reprint. Folcroft Library Editions, 1975.

Graham, Sylvester. *Lecture to Young Men on Chastity.* Third Edition. Boston, 1834, 1837.

Graves, Robert. *Good-bye to All That.* Hammondsmith, UK: Penguin Books, 1957.

Harding, Vincent. *There is a River: The Black Struggle for Freedom in America.* New York: Harcourt Brace Jovanovich, 1981; Vintage Books, 1983.

Hendrick, George. With the special assistance of John F. Pontin. *Henry Salt, Humanitarian Reformer and Man of Letters.* Urbana, Chicago, London: University of Illinois Press, 1977.

Heron, Liz, ed. *Truth, Dare, or Promise: Girls Growing Up in the Fifties.* London: Virago Press, 1985.

Hilliard, Sam Bowers. *Hog Meat and Hoecake: Food Supply in the Old South, 1840–1860.* Carbondale: Southern Illinois University Press, 1972.

Hogg, Thomas Jefferson. *The Life of Percy Shelley.* 1906. Reprint. London: George Routledge and Sons, Ltd.

Holmes, Richard. *Shelley: The Pursuit.* New York: E. P. Dutton and Co., 1975.

Hopkins, Mary Alden. "Why I Earn My Own Living." In *These Modern Women: Autobiographical Essays from the Twenties.* Edited by Elaine Showalter. Originally published 1926–27 in *The Nation.* Old Westbury, New York: The Feminist Press, 1978.

Hunt, Harriot Kezia. *Glances and Glimpses; or Fifty Years Social, Including Twenty Years Professional Life.* Boston: John P. Jewett and Co., 1856. Reprint. New York: Source Book Press, 1970.

Jones, Frederick L., ed. *Mary Shelley's Journal.* Norman, Oklahoma: University of Oklahoma Press, 1947.

Labaree, Leonard W., Ralph L. Ketcham, Helen Boatfield, and Helene Fineman, eds., *The Autobiography of Benjamin Franklin.* New Haven: Yale University Press, 1964.

Lanchester, Elsa. *Herself.* New York: St. Martin's Press, 1983.

Lansbury, Coral. *The Old Brown Dog: Women, Workers and Vivisection in Edwardian England.* Madison: The University of Wisconsin Press, 1985.

Lerner, Gerda. *The Grimké Sisters from South Carolina: Pioneers for Woman's Rights and Abolition.* New York: Schocken Books, 1971.

———. *The Majority Finds Its Past: Placing Women in History.* New York and Oxford: Oxford University Press, 1979.

Lewis, David Levering. *When Harlem Was in Vogue.* New York: Alfred A. Knopf, 1981. Vintage Books, 1982.

Linklater, Andro. *An Unhusbanded Life: Charlotte Despard, Suffragette, Socialist and Sinn Feiner.* London: Hutchinson, 1980.

Lorde, Audre. *The Cancer Journals.* Argyle, New York: Spinsters, Ink, 1980.

Marchand, C. Roland. *The American Peace Movement and Social Reform, 1898–1918.* Princeton: Princeton University Press, 1972.

Maitland, Edward. *Anna Kingsford: Her Life, Letters, Diary and Work.* London: Redway, 1896.

Marable, Manning. *How Capitalism Underdeveloped Black America.* Boston: South End Press, 1983.

Mead, Margaret. *Blackberry Winter: My Earlier Years.* New York: Touchstone Books, 1972.

Nevins, Allan. *Ford: The Times, The Man, The Company.* New York: Charles Scribner's Sons, 1954.

Nichols, Thomas L. and Mary Gove Nichols. *Marriage: Its History, Character and Results; Its Sanctities and Its Profanities; Its Science and Its Facts.* New York: T. L. Nichols, 1854.

Nicolas, Sir Harris. *The Letters of Joseph Ritson, Esq. Edited chiefly from originals in the possession of his nephew. To which is prefixed a Memoir of the Author by Sir Harris Nicolas.* London: William Pickering, 1833.

Nissenbaum, Stephen. *Sex, Diet, and Debility in Jacksonian America: Sylvester Graham and Health Reform.* Westport, Connecticut: Greenwood Press, 1980.

Numbers, Ronald L. *Prophetess of Health: A Study of Ellen G. White.* New York: Harper & Row, 1976.

Oren, Laura. "The Welfare of Women in Laboring Families: England, 1860–1950." *Feminist Studies* 1, no. 3–4. (Winter-Spring, 1973), pp. 107–25.

Pearsall, Ronald. *The Worm in the Bud: The World of Victorian Sexuality.* Toronto: The Macmillan Company, 1969.

Peters, H. F. *My Sister, My Spouse: A Biography of Lou Andreas-Salome.* New York: Norton & Co., 1962.

Perry, Ruth. *The Celebrated Mary Astell: An Early English Feminist.* Chicago and London: The University of Chicago Press, 1986.

Proctor, Robert. *Racial Hygiene: Medicine under the Nazis.* Cambridge and London: Harvard University Press, 1988.

Rae, Isobel. *The Strange Story of Dr. James Barry: Army Surgeon, Inspector-General of Hospitals, Discovered on Death to Be a Woman.* London: Longmans, Green & Co., 1958.

Reeves, Maud Pemer. *Round About a Pound a Week*. G. Bell & Sons, 1913. Reprint. London: Virago Press, 1979.

Ross, Ishbel. *Angel of the Battlefield*. New York: Harper & Brothers, 1956.

Rowbotham, Sheila and Jeffrey Weeks. *Socialism and the New Life: The Personal and Sexual Politics of Edward Carpenter and Havelock Ellis*. London: Pluto Press, 1977.

Ryan, Agnes. "The Heart to Sing." unpublished autobiography.

Salt, Henry Stephens. *Percy Bysshe Shelley: Poet and Pioneer*. 1896. Reprint. Port Washington, New York: Kennikat Press, Inc., 1968.

———. *Seventy Years Among Savages*. London: George Allen and Unwin, 1921.

Savitt, Todd L. *Medicine and Slavery: The Diseases and Health Care of Blacks in Antebellum Virginia*. Urbana and Chicago: University of Illinois Press, 1978.

Showalter, Elaine. *The Female Malady: Women, Madness, and English Culture, 1830–1980*. New York: Pantheon Books, 1985.

Sieveking, Isabel Giberne. *Memoir and Letters of Francis W. Newman*. London: K. Paul, Trench, Trubner & Co., 1909.

Smith-Rosenberg, Carroll. *Disorderly Conduct: Visions of Gender in Victorian America*. New York and Oxford: Oxford University Press, 1985, 1986.

———. "Sex as Symbol in Victorian Purity: An Ethnohistorical Analysis of Jacksonian America." In *Turning Points: Historical and Sociological Essays on the Family*. Edited by John Demos and Sarane Spence Boocock. Chicago and London: The University of Chicago Press, 1978.

Spruill, Julia Cherry. *Women's Life and Work in the Southern Colonies*. 1938. Reprint. New York: W. W. Norton and Co., 1972.

Stanton, Elizabeth Cady. *Elizabeth Cady Stanton as Revealed in Her Letters, Diary and Reminiscences*. Edited by Theodore Stanton and Harriot Stanton Blatch. 1922. Reprint. New York: Arno Press, 1969.

Sterling, Dorothy. *Black Foremothers: Three Lives*. Old Westbury, New York: The Feminist Press, 1979.

Stevens, Doris. *Jailed for Freedom: The Story of the Militant American Suffragist Movement*. New York: Boni and Liveright, 1920. Reprint. New York: Shocken Books, 1976.

Sunstein, Emily W. *Mary Shelley: Romance and Reality*. Boston, Toronto, London: Little, Brown and Co., 1989.

Sward, Keith. *The Legend of Henry Ford*. New York: Russell and Russell, 1948.

Terrell, Mary Church. *A Colored Woman in a White World*. Washington, D.C.: Ransdell, Inc. 1940. Reprint. New York: Arno Press, 1980.

Thomas, Keith. *Man and the Natural World: A History of the Modern Sensibility*. New York: Pantheon, 1983.

Trall, R. T. *Home-Treatment for Sexual Abuses. A Practical Treatise*. New York: Fowler and Wells, 1853.

Trollope, Frances. *Domestic Manners of the Americans*. 1832. New York: Alfred A. Knopf, 1949.

Turner, James. *Reckoning with the Beast: Animals, Pain and Humanity in the Victorian Mind*. Baltimore and London: Johns Hopkins University Press, 1980.

Wells, Anna Mary. *Miss Marks and Miss Woolley.* Boston: Houghton Mifflin Co., 1978.

Whorton, James C. *Crusaders for Fitness: The History of American Health Reformers.* Princeton: Princeton University Press, 1982.

———. " 'Tempest in a Flesh-Pot': The Formulation of a Physiological Rationale for Vegetarianism." *Journal of the History of Medicine and Allied Sciences.* 32, no. 2 (April 1977), pp. 115–39.

Winsten, Stephen. *Salt and His Circle.* London: Hutchinson and Co., Ltd., 1951.

Fiction, Poetry, Drama

Atwood, Margaret. *Cat's Eye.* New York: Doubleday, 1989.

———. *The Edible Woman.* Boston: Little, Brown and Co., New York: Warner Books, 1969.

———. *Surfacing.* New York: Simon and Schuster, Popular Library, 1972.

Beattie, Ann. *Chilly Scenes of Winter.* Garden City, New York: Doubleday & Co., 1976.

Behn, Aphra. "On the Author of that excellent and learned Book, entituled, *The Way to Health, long Life and Happiness.*" In Thomas Tryon, *The Way to Make All People Rich; or, Wisdoms Call to Temperance and Frugality. . . .* London, 1685.

Brant, Beth. (Degonwadonti). *Mohawk Trail.* Ithaca, New York: Firebrand Books, 1985.

Brecht, Bertolt. *Saint Joan of the Stockyards.* Translated by Frank Jones. Second Edition. Bloomington and London: Indiana University Press, 1971.

Brindel, June Rachuy. *Ariadne: A Novel of Ancient Crete.* New York: St. Martin's Press, 1980.

———. *Phaedra: A Novel of Ancient Athens.* New York: St. Martin's Press, 1985.

Broner, E. M. *A Weave of Women.* New York: Holt, Rinehart and Winston, 1978.

Brophy, Brigid. "An Anecdote of the Golden Age [Homage to *Back to Methuselah*]." In *The Adventures of God in his Search for the Black Girl.* Boston: Little, Brown & Co., 1968.

———. *Hackenfeller's Ape.* London: Allison and Busby, 1953, 1979.

Bryant, Dorothy. *The Kin of Ata are Waiting for You.* 1971. Berkeley: Moon Books, 1976. Originally entitled *The Comforter.*

Butler, Samuel. *Erewhon.* 1872. Hammondsworth, England: Penguin Books, 1970.

Colegate, Isabel. *The Shooting Party.* New York: The Viking Press, 1980; Avon Books, 1982.

Colette. *Break of Day.* New York: Farrar, Straus and Giroux, Inc., 1961; Ballantine Books, 1983.

Cross, Amanda. *The James Joyce Murders.* New York: Macmillan Co., 1967.

de Araújo, Virginia. "The Friend . . . ," *Sinister Wisdom.* no. 20 (1982), 17.

Drabble, Margaret. *The Ice Age*. New York: Alfred A. Knopf; New York and Scarborough, Ontario: New American Library, 1977.
Ellis, Alice T. *The Birds of the Air*. New York: The Viking Press, 1980.
———. *The Sin Eater*. London: Duckworth, 1977.
———. *The 27th Kingdom*. London: Duckworth, 1982.
———. *Unexplained Laughter*. London: Duckworth, 1985.
Fo, Dario and Franca Rame. *Female Parts: One Woman Plays*. Adapted by Olwen Wywark. Translated by Margaret Kunzle. London: Pluto Press, 1981.
Fraser, Antonia. *Your Royal Hostage*. New York: Atheneum, 1988.
Gilman, Charlotte Perkins. *Herland*. New York: Pantheon Books, 1979. First serialized in the *Forerunner* 6 (1915).
Glaspell, Susan. *A Jury of Her Peers*. London: Ernest Benn, Ltd., 1927.
Gordon, Mary. *Final Payments*. New York: Random House, 1978.
Grahn, Judy. *The Queen of Swords*. Boston: Beacon Press, 1987.
Hurston, Zora Neale. *Their Eyes Were Watching God*. 1937. Greenwich, Connecticut: A Fawcett Premier Book, 1965.
Jordan, June. *Passion: New Poems, 1977–1980*. Boston: Beacon Press, 1980.
Kingston, Maxine Hong. *The Woman Warrior: Memoirs of a Girlhood Among Ghosts*. New York: Alfred A. Knopf, 1977.
Kundera, Milan. *The Book of Laughter and Forgetting*. New York: Alfred A. Knopf. 1979; Penguin Books, 1985.
LaTourette, Aileen. *Cry Wolf*. London: Virago Press, 1986.
Lorde, Audre. *The Black Unicorn*. New York: W. W. Norton & Co., 1978.
Mackey, Mary. *McCarthy's List*. London: Pan Books Limited, 1981.
McCarthy, Mary. *Birds of America*. New York: Harcourt, Brace Jovanovich, 1965; New American Library, 1965.
Meyer, Lynn. *Paperback Thriller*. New York: Random House, 1975.
Murdoch, Iris. *The Good Apprentice*. New York and Hammondsworth: Penguin Books, 1987.
Nichols, Mary Gove. *Mary Lyndon or, Revelations of a Life: An Autobiography*. New York: Stringer and Townsend, 1855.
Olsen, Tillie. *Yonnondio: From the Thirties*. New York: Dell, 1974.
Parker, Pat. "To a Vegetarian Friend," *Womanslaughter*. Oakland, California: Diana Press, 1978.
Piercy, Marge. *Small Changes*. Garden City, New York: Doubleday and Co., 1972; Greenwich, Connecticut: A Fawcett Crest Book, 1973.
Roth, Philip, *Portnoy's Complaint*. New York: Random House, 1967.
Ryan, Agnes. "Who Can Fear Too Many Stars?" unpublished novel.
Scott, Sarah. *A Description of Millenium Hall*. London, 1762. Reprint. New York and London: Garland Publishing Inc., 1974.
Shelley, Mary Wollstonecraft. *Frankenstein or, The Modern Prometheus: The 1818 Text*. Edited by James Rieger. Indianapolis: Bobbs-Merrill, 1974: Chicago and London: University of Chicago Press, 1982.
Sinclair, Upton. *The Jungle*. 1906. New York: New American Library, 1973.
Singer, Isaac Bashevis. *Enemies: A Love Story*. New York: Farrar, Straus and Giroux, 1972.

Singer, Rochelle. *The Demeter Flower.* New York: St. Martin's Press, 1980.
Snodgrass, W. D. *Selected Poems: 1957–1987.* New York: Soho Press, 1987.
Tyler, Anne. *The Accidental Tourist.* 1985. New York: Berkley Books, 1986.
———. *If Morning Ever Comes.* 1964. New York: Berkley Books, 1986.
———. *The Tin Can Tree.* 1965. New York: Berkley Books, 1986.
———. *The Clock Winder.* New York: Alfred A. Knopf, 1972.
Walker, Alice. *Meridian.* New York: Harcourt Brace Jovanovich, 1976; Washington Square Press, 1977.
———. *The Temple of My Familiar.* San Diego, New York: Harcourt Brace Jovanovich, 1989.
Washington, Mary Helen, ed. *Midnight Birds: Stories of Contemporary Black Women Writers.* Garden City, New York: Doubleday and Co., 1980.
Winant, Fran. "Eat Rice Have Faith in Women," In Winant, *Dyke Jacket: Poems and Songs.* New York: Violet Press, 1980.
Winterson, Jeanette. *Oranges are not the Only Fruit.* 1985. New York: The Atlantic Monthly Press, 1987.
Woolf, Virginia. *Jacob's Room.* Hogarth Press, 1922. Hammondsworth, England: Penguin Books, 1971.
Yglesias, Helen. *The Saviors.* Boston: Houghton Mifflin Co., 1987.

Medical and Nutritional Writings

Brody, Jane. *Jane Brody's Nutrition Book.* New York: W. W. Norton, 1981.
Burkitt, D. P. "The Protective Value of Plant Fibre Against Many Modern Western Diseases." *Qualitas Plantarum—Plant Foods for Human Nutrition.* 29, nos. 1–2 (July 6, 1979), pp. 39–48.
Christian, Eugene. *Meatless and Wheatless Menus.* New York: Alfred A. Knopf, 1917.
Cleave, T. L., G. D. Campbell, N. S. Painter. *Diabetes, Coronary Thrombosis, and the Saccharine Disease.* Second Edition. Bristol, England: John Wright and Sons, 1969.
Drummond, Jack. *Nutritional Requirements of Man in the Light of Wartime Experience.* London, 1948.
Fisher, Irving. "The Influence of Flesh Eating on Endurance." *Yale Medical Journal.* 13, no. 5 (March 1907), pp. 205–21.
Hardinge, Mervyn G. and Hulda Crooks. "Non-Flesh Dietaries. 1. Historical Background." *Journal of the American Dietetic Association.* 43 (December 1963), pp. 545–49.
Hindhede, Mikkel. "The Effect of Food Restriction During War on Mortality in Copenhagen." *Journal of the American Medical Society.* 74, no. 6 (February 7, 1920), pp. 381–82.
Jackson, James C. *How to Treat the Sick without Medicine.* Dansville, New York: Austin, Jackson & Co., 1870.
Messina, Virginia and Mark. *The Vegetarian Way: Total Health for You and Your Family.* New York: Crown, 1996.

National Research Council. *Diet, Nutrition, and Cancer.* Washington, D. C.: National Academy Press, 1982.

Ryan, Agnes. "The Cancer Bogy," unpublished manuscript.

Seaman, Barbara and Gideon Seaman, M.D., *Women and the Crisis in Sex Hormones.* New York: Rawson Associates Publishers Inc., 1977.

Smith, Edward. *Practical Dietary for Families, Schools, and the Labouring Classes.* London: Walton and Maberly, 1864.

Strøm, Axel and R. Adelsten Jensen, "Mortality from Circulatory Diseases in Norway 1940–1945," *The Lancet.* 260 (January 2, 1951), pp. 126–29.

Other

Arendt, Hannah. *On Violence.* New York: Harcourt, Brace and World, 1970.

Arens, W. *The Man-Eating Myth: Anthropology and Anthropophagy.* New York: Oxford University Press, 1979.

Barer-Stein, Thelma. *You Eat What You Are: A Study of Canadian Ethnic Food Traditions.* Toronto: McClelland and Stewart, 1979.

Berger, John. *About Looking.* New York: Pantheon, 1980.

Braverman, Harry. *Labor and Monopoly Capital: The Degradation of Work in the Twentieth Century.* New York and London: Monthly Review Press, 1974.

Campbell, Joseph. *The Masks of God: Primitive Mythology, Volume 1.* New York: Penguin Books, 1959, 1978.

Douglas, Mary. "Deciphering a Meal." In *Implicit meanings: Essays in anthropology.* London: Routledge & Kegan Paul, 1975.

Gregory, Dick. *The Shadow That Scares Me.* Edited James R. McGraw. Garden City, New York: Doubleday and Co., Inc., 1968.

Estragon, Vladimir. [Geoffrey Stokes] *Waiting for Dessert.* New York: The Viking Press, 1982.

Evans, Travers Moncure and David Greene, *The Meat Book.* New York: Charles Scribner's Sons.

Hinman, Robert B. and Robert B. Harris, *The Story of Meat.* Chicago: Swift & Co., 1939, 1942.

Kohlberg, Lawrence. *Essays on Moral Development. Volume 1. The Philosophy of Moral Development.* New York: Harper & Row, 1981.

Leakey, Richard E. and Roger Lewin. *People of the Lake: Mankind and Its Beginnings.* New York: Doubleday & Co., 1978; Avon Books, 1979.

Miller, A. R. *Meat Hygiene.* Philadelphia: Lea and Febiger, 1951, 1958.

Postal, Paul M. "Anaphoric Islands." In *Papers from the Fifth Regional Meeting of the Chicago Linguistic Society.* Edited by Robert I. Binnick, Alice Davison, Georgia M. Green, Jerry L. Morgan. Chicago: Department of Linguistics, University of Chicago, 1969.

Selzer, Richard. "How to Build a Slaughterhouse." In *Taking the World in for Repairs.* New York: Morrow, 1986.

Shepard, Paul. *The Tender Carnivore and the Sacred Game.* New York: Charles Scribner's Sons, 1973.

Simoons, Frederick J. *Eat Not This Flesh: Food Avoidances in the Old World.* Madison: University of Wisconsin, 1961, 1967.

Tanner, Nancy Makepeace. *On Becoming Human: A Model of the Transition from Ape to Human and the Reconstruction of Early Human Social Life.* Cambridge and New York: Cambridge University Press, 1981.

Weil, Simone. *The Iliad, or the Poem of Force.* 1940. Translated by Mary McCarthy. Wallingford, Pennsylvania: Pendle Hill, 1956, 1970.

Ziegler, P. Thomas. *The Meat We Eat.* Danville, Illinois: The Interstate Printers and Publishers, Inc., 1962, 1966.

Tenth Anniversary Bibliography

Abbott, Jennifer, director, photographer, and editor. *A Cow at My Table.* Flying Eye Productions. 90 minutes. Color. 1998. (Contact: Flying Eye Productions, Denman Place Postal Outlet, PO Box 47053, Vancouver, BC, Canada, V6G 3E1; <*jawasin@portal.ca*>).

Adams, Carol J. " 'Mad Cow' Disease and the Animal Industrial Complex: An Ecofeminist Analysis," *Organization and Environment,* vol. 10, no. 1 (March 1997): 26–51.

———. *Neither Man nor Beast: Feminism and the Defense of Animals.* New York: Continuum, 1994.

———, ed. *Ecofeminism and the Sacred* New York: Continuum, 1993.

——— and Josephine Donovan, eds. *Animals and Women: Feminist Theoretical Explorations,* Durham: Duke University Press, 1995.

American Dietetic Association. 1993. "Position of the American Dietetic Association: Vegetarian Diets." *Journal of the American Dietetic Association.* 93 (11): 1317–19.

Birke, Linda. *Feminism, Animals and Science: The Naming of the Shrew.* Buckingham, England and Philadelphia: Open University Press, 1994.

Bloodroot Collective, *The Perennial Political Palate: The Third Feminist Vegetarian Cookbook.* Bridgeport, Connecticut: Sanguinaria Publishing, 1993.

Coe, Sue. *Dead Meat.* New York and London: Four Walls Eight Windows, 1995.

Consolidated. *Friendly Fascism.* Nettwerk. I.R.S. Records, 3939 Lankdershim Blvd., Universal City, California 91604.

Cox, Peter. *The New Why You Don't Need Meat.* London: Bloomsbury, 1992.

Daly, Mary. *Quintessence . . . Realizing the Archaic Future: A Radical Elemental Feminist Manifesto.* Boston: Beacon Press, 1998.

Davis, Karen. *Poisoned Chickens, Poisoned Eggs: An Inside Look at the Modern Poultry Industry.* Summerton, Tennessee: The Book Publishing Company, 1996.

Donovan, Josephine and Carol J. Adams, eds. *Beyond Animal Rights: A Feminist Caring Ethic for the Treatment of Animals.* New York: Continuum, 1996.

Dunayer, Joan. *Animal Equality: Language and Liberation.* Cheltenham, England: New Clarion, forthcoming.

Fano, Alex. *Lethal Laws: Animal Testing, Human Health and Environmental Policy.* London and New York: Zed Books, 1998.

"Feminists for Animal Rights Newsletter." To subscribe contact Feminists for Animal Rights, P.O. Box 8869, Tucson, Arizona 85738, or <*farinc@hotmail.com*> Website: <*www.envirolink.org/arrs/far*>.

Gaard, Greta, ed. *Ecofeminism: Women, Animals, Nature.* Philadelphia: Temple University Press, 1993.

———"Milking Mother Nature: An Ecofeminist Critique of rBGH." *The Ecologist* 24, no. 6 (November/December 1994), pp. 202–3.

———"Women, Animals, and Ecofeminist Critique." *Environmental Ethics* 18, no. 3 (Winter 1996), pp. 439–41.

———*Ecological Politics: Ecofeminists and the Greens.* Philadelphia: Temple University Press, 1998.

———"Vegetarian Ecofeminism: A Review Essay." Forthcoming. This is a very important review essay. Check my website <*www/triroc.com/sexualpoliticsofmeat/*> for information on its publication when it is available.

Gruen, Lori. "On the Oppression of Women and Animals." *Environmental Ethics* 18, no. 4 (Winter 1996), pp. 441–44.

Greek, C. Ray, M.D., and Jean Swingle Greek, D.V.M. "Sacred Cows and Golden Geese: How Humans Are Harmed by Animal Experimentation." Working title of book scheduled for publication by Continuum International, 2000.

Hawkins, Ronnie Zoe. "Ecofeminism and Nonhumans: Continuity, Difference, Dualism, and Domination." *Hypatia* 13, no. 1 (Winter 1998), pp. 158–97.

Kheel, Marti. "The Killing Game: An Ecofeminist Critique of Hunting." *Journal of the Philosophy of Sport* 23 (1996), pp. 30–44.

Leneman, Leah. "The Awakened Instinct: Vegetarianism and the Women's Suffrage Movement in Britain." *Women's History Review,* 5, no. 2 (1997): 271–87.

Luke, Brian. "A Critical Analysis of Hunters' Ethics." *Environmental Ethics* 19, no. 1 (Spring 1997), pp. 25–44.

———. "Violent Love: Hunting, Heterosexuality, and the Erotics of Men's Predation." *Feminist Studies* 24, no. 3 (Fall 1998), pp. 627–55.

Mason, Jim. *An Unnatural Order: Why We Are Destroying the Planet and Each Other.* New York: Continuum, 1997.

Noske, Barbara. *Beyond Boundaries: Humans and Animals.* Montreal: Black Rose Books, 1997.

Ozeki, Ruth L. *My Year of Meats.* New York: Viking Penguin, 1999.

Rowe, Martin, ed. *The Way of Compassion: Survival Strategies for a World in Crisis.* New York: Stealth Technologies, 1999.

Scholtmeijer, Marian. *Animal Victims in Modern Fiction: From Sanctity to Sacrifice.* Toronto: University of Toronto Press, 1993.

Stepaniak, Joanne. *The Vegan Sourcebook.* Los Angeles: Lowell House. 1998.

Copyright Acknowledgments

The author and publisher gratefully acknowledge permission from the following sources to reprint material in this book:

The University of North Carolina Press for "Feminism, the Great War and Modern Vegetarianism," which appeared in a somewhat different form in *Arms and the Woman,* edited by Helen Cooper, Adrienne Munich, and Susan Squier, copyright 1989 UNC Press. Reprinted by permission.

The *Animals' Agenda* for "Liberate Your Language," by Noreen Mola and the Blacker Family, from the *Animals' Agenda* 6, no. 8 (October 1986). Reprinted by permission of the *Animals' Agenda,* 1301 S. Baylis Street, Suite 325, P.O. Box 25881, Baltimore, MD., 21224.

The Arthur and Elizabeth Schlesinger Library on the History of Women in America, Radcliffe College, Cambridge, Massachusetts, and the late Henry Bailey Stevens for permission to use material in the Agnes Ryan Collection.

University of California Press for "Ritson as His Contemporaries Saw Him," from Bertrand H. Bronson, *Joseph Ritson: Scholar-at-Arms,* University of California Press, 1938, 1966.

Fran Winant for "Eat Rice Have Faith in Women," from *Dyke Jacket: Poems and Songs,* Violet Press, 1980. Reprinted by permission of the author. Violet Press, Post Office Box 398, New York, New York 10009.

The Heresies Collective for "The Sexual Politics of Meat," which appeared in a somewhat different form in *Heresies 21: Food is a Feminist Issue,* (1987). *Heresies,* PO Box 1306, Canal Street Station, New York, New York 10013.

The Program in Women Studies at Princeton University for "The Rape of Animals, the Butchering of Women," which appeared in a somewhat different form in *Violence, Feminism, and the History of Sexuality: Papers from the 4th Annual Graduate Women's Studies Conference: Feminism and its Translations* in *Critical Matrix: Princeton Working Papers in Women's Studies* Special Issue 1 (Spring 1988).

Atheneum Publishers for the text and illustration from page 5 of *Garth Pig and the Ice Cream Lady.* Reprinted with permission of Atheneum Publishers, an imprint of Macmillan Publishing Company from *Garth Pig and the Ice Cream Lady* by Mary Rayner. Copyright © 1977 Mary Rayner.

Alfred A. Knopf, Inc. and Lois Wallace of Wallace Literary Agency, Inc. for permission to quote an excerpt from Marge Piercy's "In the men's room(s)," from *Circles on the Water: Selected Poems of Marge Piercy.* Copyright 1973, 1982 by Marge Piercy.

Macmillan, London and Basingstoke, for permission to use text and illustration from page 5 of *Garth Pig and the Ice Cream Lady* by Mary Rayner.

Illustrations on page 32:

"Crayfish in bikini," a section on a Razoo's mural, photographed by Carol Adams, Dallas, Texas, 1997.

"Deer's Legs," from an ad for "ActionEar Sport," to enable hunters to hear "game." Sent by Delora Wisemoon, Austin, Texas.

"The Happy Hooker," sent by Brian Luke, Ohio.

"Hamtastic" billboard photographed by Lois Davidson, Atlanta, Georgia. 1995.

"I Ate a 'Pig' " photographed by Megan Hagler, Chapel Hill, North Carolina.

"Pig in Bikini," photographed by Cathy Goeggel, at the entrance to the "livestock" tent at the Hawaii State Farm Fair, 1995.

"Makin' Bacon, Hottest Sex Fantasies," match-box cover, New York City. Sent by Jayne Loader.

"Tasty Chick" poster photographed by Marika Holmgren, at a Carl's Jr. outside of Sacramento, California. 1997.

" 'Double D Cup' Breast of Turkey," from Uncommon Ground, a Chicago restaurant, sent by Tai Little.

"I'm not talkin' chicken here," excerpt from Pizza Nova flier, Toronto, Canada, sent by Tim Doucette.

"Turkey" from "turkey hooker" sent by Ingrid Newkirk, People for the Ethical Treatment of Animals.

"Cheep Date," reprinted from *Feminists for Animal Rights* Newsletter "No Comment" department (vol. 6, nos. 3–4 [1991–92]), p. 18. From an advertisement campaign by a department in the Mayor's office, New York City.

Illustrations on page 154: Buttons from Feminists for Animal Rights.

"Ecstatic Vegetarian Farmer" from Cow Cards/Rubber-Stamp Art. © 1981 Marge du Mond. Sent by Mary Hunt and Diann Neu.

"Women and Turkeys against Christmas." By Angela Martin. Leeds Postcards, England. Sent by Susanne Kappeler.

Index